# ASIAN
# REVITALIZATIO

# ASIAN REVITALIZATION

## ADAPTIVE REUSE
### in
### HONG KONG, SHANGHAI, and SINGAPORE

Edited by Katie Cummer and Lynne D. DiStefano

HKU PRESS
香港大學出版社

Hong Kong University Press
The University of Hong Kong
Pokfulam Road
Hong Kong
https://hkupress.hku.hk

ISBN 978-988-8528-55-4 (*Hardback*)
ISBN 978-988-8528-56-1 (*Paperback*)

British Library Cataloguing-in-Publication Data
A catalogue record for this book is available from the British Library.

10 9 8 7 6 5 4 3 2 1

Printed and bound by Hang Tai Printing Co., Ltd. in Hong Kong, China

# Contents

# Acknowledgments

First and foremost, we express our immense appreciation to the individuals who researched and wrote for this publication, contributing case studies, essays, illustrations, and timelines. It has been a lengthy yet worthwhile process, and we thank each of you for your continued dedication to the project. An enormous thank-you to the companies, individuals, institutions, and organizations who have shared their knowledge of and experience with adaptive reuse, including those who have contributed detailed information about the fifteen case studies included in this book. It is our hope that in consolidating and sharing these various journeys and examples of revitalization, we can highlight and promote adaptive reuse as one of the means to meet the sustainability objectives of the 2016 United Nations New Urban Agenda.

Our many thanks to the Faculty of Architecture at The University of Hong Kong for its financial support and the Division of Architectural Conservation Programmes (ACP) for its ongoing assistance and encouragement. With particular appreciation to Lavina Ahuja, who edited the final manuscript, keeping us "on track" with detailed flow charts and ensuring the project came to fruition. And, of course, our appreciation to the editors at Hong Kong University Press.

Last, but not least, a heartfelt thank-you to our families for their patience and support throughout this project. They have inadvertently become advocates and champions of adaptive reuse, a trend that we hope will be similarly followed by our readers.

Katie Cummer and Lynne D. DiStefano
December 2019

# Contributors

**Lavina Ahuja**

*Author and copyeditor*

Lavina Ahuja is an assistant lecturer and senior research assistant in the Division of Architectural Conservation Programmes (ACP) at The University of Hong Kong (HKU). She has been involved with UNESCO Bangkok's initiatives in capacity building for safeguarding cultural heritage resources in the region, particularly with the Asia-Pacific Awards for Cultural Heritage Conservation program. She is an associate editor of *Asia Conserved: Lessons Learned from the UNESCO Asia-Pacific Awards for Cultural Heritage Conservation Volume III (2010–2014)* and *Volume IV (2015– 2019)*. She has a BArch from Mumbai University (India) and an MSc (Conservation) from HKU. She is a registered architect with the Council of Architecture, India, as well as an individual member of the Indian National Committee of the International Council on Monuments and Sites (ICOMOS India). Currently based in Hong Kong, she is a professional member of the Hong Kong Institute of Architectural Conservationists (HKICON).

**Hugo Chan**

*Author*

Dr. Hugo Chan obtained his bachelor's degree in architecture and business administration at Carnegie Mellon University and subsequently his MSc and PhD degrees in urban planning at The University of Hong Kong (HKU). His research interests cover vernacular architecture, historic urban landscapes, heritage management, and urban conservation in Asia, and his PhD dissertation was titled "Urban Conservation of Shanghai's 'Lilong' Space." Prior to his PhD studies at HKU, he worked as an architectural designer and planner in Shanghai and Beijing on a number of architectural conservation and urban revitalization projects of various scales across China. Throughout his studies, he actively participated in a wide array of activities to raise public awareness and advocate actions for cultural heritage conservation efforts in Hong Kong. From 2015 to 2016, he worked with the Yangon Heritage Trust and coauthored *Yangon Heritage Strategy: Combining Conservation and Development to Create Asia's Most Liveable City* (published August 2016). He currently teaches in both the postgraduate and undergraduate programs in HKU's Division of Architectural Conservation Programmes (ACP).

## Fredo Cheung

*Author*

Fredo Cheung is an experienced architect and architectural conservationist. Upon his graduation from The University of Hong Kong in architecture, he first worked at the architectural practice Leigh and Orange and later with Ronald Lu and Partners, specializing in the design of institutional architecture in Hong Kong, mainland China, and the Middle East, winning a number of architectural awards. Upon his graduation from the Division of Architectural Conservation Programmes (ACP) with an MSc (Conservation), he has been involved in conservation projects as a heritage consultant with Purcell and for the Hong Kong SAR government's Architectural Services Department. Currently, he is the lead teacher of courses in ACP's undergraduate program, while pursuing PhD studies in architectural conservation.

## Katie Cummer

*Author and editor*

Dr. Katie Cummer was the founding director of the bachelor of arts in conservation degree (2012–2017) offered by the Division of Architectural Conservation Programmes (ACP) at The University of Hong Kong. She has helped to develop and grow ACP since 2009. After years of living and working in Asia, she has returned to Canada and is now a heritage consultant. Principal of Cummer Heritage Consulting (CHC), her expertise includes conservation education, heritage-focused research, and planning. She is an active researcher and writer, conducting assessments of sites to facilitate informed decision making, including Heritage Assessments and Evaluations, Heritage Conservation Plans and Statements of Significance. She has authored and coauthored a number of academic papers, books, book chapters, and consultancy studies on topics related to heritage conservation, including area conservation planning, the Historic Urban Landscape approach, interpretation, policy studies, and recommendations on best practice for official government use.

She is a professional member of the Canadian Association of Heritage Professionals (CAHP), accredited for the Education, History, and Planning specializations. She is also a professional member of the Canadian National Committee of the International Council on Monuments and Sites (ICOMOS Canada) as well as the Hong Kong Institute of Architectural Conservationists (HKICON). She is the vice president of the BC chapter of the Canadian Association of Heritage Professionals (BCAHP) and a member of the Heritage Advisory Panel (HAP) for the City of Victoria, where she is now based.

## Lynne D. DiStefano

*Author and editor*

Professor Lynne DiStefano, who holds a PhD from the University of Pennsylvania, is a founder and the second director (2003–2005) of the Division of Architectural Conservation Programmes (ACP) at The University of Hong Kong, where she currently serves as an adjunct professor and academic development advisor. She is also a faculty associate at the School of Restoration Arts at Willowbank (Ontario, Canada). She was previously an associate professor at Brescia University College, Western University (Ontario, Canada), as well as chief curator of Museum London (also Ontario, Canada).

She has been extensively involved with UNESCO's efforts in heritage conservation. Since 2006, she has been appointed by ICOMOS as an official technical evaluator for a number of nominated World Heritage Sites in China, Japan, and South Korea, as well as an expert for several reactive monitoring missions in China, Laos, and the Philippines. She has authored and coauthored a number of publications and served as a consultant to local and regional governments, especially in Asia. She is a member of both ICOM and ICOMOS Canada, and currently sits on the board of the Ontario Heritage Trust.

### Ho Yin Lee

*Author*

Dr. Lee Ho Yin is a founder of the postgraduate and undergraduate programs in the Division of Architectural Conservation Programmes (ACP) at The University of Hong Kong (HKU). He was instrumental in amalgamating the conservation programs to establish the division in 2015, and became the founding head of the division. Before joining HKU in 2000, he was an associate director of an architectural practice and has been involved in architectural projects in Hong Kong, Indonesia, mainland China, and Singapore. A well-published academic and an experienced practitioner in built-heritage conservation, he has been appointed by government agencies in Hong Kong, mainland China, and overseas as an expert advisor or a consultant for conservation projects and the designation and monitoring of UNESCO World Heritage Sites. He has been appointed to a number of heritage conservation statutory boards and committees, including the Hong Kong government's Antiquities Advisory Board, Tai Kwun Heritage Working Group (as chair), and Tai Kwun Advisory Committee. In 2017, he was cited in the award certificate for the highest UNESCO conservation award for the Blue House Cluster revitalization project.

### Donovan Rypkema

*Author*

Donovan Rypkema is the president of Heritage Strategies International and principal of PlaceEconomics. Both firms undertake assignments at the nexus of built heritage and economics. Rypkema has worked in forty-nine US states and fifty-two countries. Clients of his have included the World Bank, Inter-American Development Bank, Council of Europe, and UNDP. He teaches a graduate course in heritage economics at the University of Pennsylvania, where he received the G. Holmes Perkins Award for Distinguished Teaching. He also teaches an international course taking Penn students to Shanghai, Belgrade, Galway, Tbilisi, and Yangon.

Rypkema holds a master's degree in historic preservation from Columbia University. He has authored numerous articles, publications, and book chapters on heritage economics. Rypkema's book, *The Economics of Historic Preservation: A Community Leader's Guide*, has been translated into Russian, Georgian, and Korean. He is a member of the UN Economic Commission for Europe Real Estate Market Advisory Group. Rypkema serves on the Board of Directors of Global Urban Development and is a member of the ICOMOS International Scientific Committee on the Economics of Conservation. In 2012, Rypkema received the Louise du Pont Crowninshield Award from the US National Trust, the nation's highest preservation honor, awarded for his lifetime contribution to historic preservation in the United States.

## Ester van Steekelenburg

*Author*

Ester van Steekelenburg (MSc urban planning, University of Amsterdam; PhD urban economics, The University of Hong Kong) is the founder of Urban Discovery, a social enterprise that specializes in urban regeneration and heritage preservation. She studied at Erasmus University's Institute for Housing Studies and worked at Jones Lang LaSalle Hong Kong, and continues to collaborate with different stakeholders in feasibility and impact analysis of adaptive reuse of heritage buildings and regenerating historic districts throughout Asia. Clients include not only multilateral agencies like the World Bank, Asian Development Bank, and the United Nations, but also the Thai Crown Property Bureau, Asia Society, and Royal Institute for Chartered Surveyors. Recent signature projects include an urban regeneration plan for a historic district in Istanbul (Turkey), a heritage management plan for the UNESCO-listed imperial city of Hue (Vietnam), plans for adaptive reuse of historic buildings in Semarang (Indonesia), and an investment program for renovation of historic properties in Yangon (Myanmar). Ester is based in Hong Kong and works across Asia.

## Tiffany Tang

*Researcher and writer*

Tiffany Tang (BSc geography, Chinese University Hong Kong; MA governing the large metropolis, Institut d'études politiques de Paris) is a young graduate with a particular interest in the emerging field of policy makers in Southeast Asia: where cultural development meets urban management. She particularly enjoys community-based research and storytelling projects in her hometown of Hong Kong, but she has also worked in Myanmar and Thailand on cultural mapping and heritage research projects. Tiffany actively participates in community networks and is keen to build bridges with like-minded individuals who want to make Asian cities a better place to live.

## Michael Turner

*Author*

Professor Michael Turner is a practicing architect, the UNESCO chairholder in urban design and conservation studies at the Bezalel Academy of Arts and Design, Jerusalem. His research encompasses urban sustainability, heritage, social inclusion, and urban spaces, contributing many articles and presentations to academic fora and professional meetings over the world. A long-standing member of ICOMOS living in Jerusalem, he has focused on mechanisms for sustainable peace and sites of religious significance, and he has participated in many proceedings, including the Jerusalem-Berlin Forum reviewing the Divided Cities and a Partnership for Peace project with Israeli, Jordanian, and Palestinian academics. Engaged in activities at UNESCO for more than two decades, he has participated in many expert missions and served as a member of the World Heritage Committee between 2005 and 2009. He is special envoy to the World Heritage Centre director reviewing culture for sustainable development and urban heritage, including its recovery and reconstruction, and he has accompanied the UNESCO Recommendation on the Historic Urban Landscape since its inception. He was a contributor to the 2016 *UNESCO Global Report to UNHabitat III* and is an advocate of the UNISDR Resilient Cities Programme.

### Debbie Wong

*Researcher and writer*

Debbie Wong holds a BEnv Design and BArch from the University of Western Australia, an MSc (Conservation) (Distinction) from The University of Hong Kong, and is a professional member of the Hong Kong Institute of Architectural Conservationists (HKICON). She has extensive experience in the arts and heritage education sectors. Specifically, she was responsible for the management and growth of UK art and education programs at the British Council Hong Kong and served as a consultant for arts education programs for Asia Society Hong Kong. As a consultant specializing in conservation and culture, she has also worked in a number of heritage-related research projects and has coauthored a number of academic papers and publications.

In addition to this, she was a part-time assistant professor for the Architectural Conservation Programmes (ACP) at The University of Hong Kong and was instrumental in the research, development, and launch of HKU's Common Core course: World Heritage and Us and its pilot MOOC: The Search for Vernacular Architecture of Asia Part I and II on edX. Currently based in Singapore, she guides regularly at the Peranakan Museum and was the cohead of docent training for the Peranakan Museum (2017–2018).

# Adaptive Reuse: Introduction

Lynne D. DiStefano

## Introduction to the Book

### *Germination of an Idea*

The idea for this publication, examining the adaptive reuse of heritage places in three Asian centers—Hong Kong, Shanghai, and Singapore—has come from two directions. Ester van Steekelenburg (Urban Discovery) and Tiffany Tang (Urban Discovery), both contributors to this publication, mounted an exhibit on adaptive reuse projects in Hong Kong for a Royal Institution of Chartered Surveyors (RICS) conference in Hong Kong in 2015. The exhibit was well received, and the two hoped to extend their work together through a publication. During the same period (and up to the present), the Division of Architectural Conservation Programmes (ACP) in the Faculty of Architecture at The University of Hong Kong was conducting adaptive reuse field studies in Shanghai and Singapore for graduate students—and using examples of adaptive reuse in Hong Kong in its core courses for both undergraduate and graduate students. Not surprisingly, ACP staff and former graduate students are also contributors to the publication.

ACP's focus on adaptive reuse was (and remains) purposeful. Staff have long recognized that one of the best ways to protect heritage buildings and sites is to ensure their appropriate use, especially uses that have a myriad of cultural benefits—economic, environmental, and social. And although ACP is dedicated to the conservation of buildings and sites with recognized heritage values, staff emphasize the importance of considering such sites within a broader urban framework, what is now referred to as the Historic Urban Landscape.

With this approach, the differences between the recognized and the not (yet) recognized fade, and conservationists and planners, among others, can think in a more integrated way about the larger benefits of adaptive reuse—more specifically, about adaptive reuse options that help build livable communities. Encouraging such thinking is the fundamental purpose of this publication.

### *Focus on Three Asian Centers*

There is much to learn from the practice of adaptive reuse in large Asian cities and particularly in such major centers as Hong Kong, Shanghai, and Singapore, where adaptive reuse (or its equivalent) has been considered one of the accepted forms of conservation in the twenty-first century. For example, in Hong Kong, adaptive reuse gained official recognition in 2008 under the government's Revitalising Historic Buildings through Partnership Scheme (Revitalisation Scheme).[1] Through this initiative, selected government-owned heritage buildings are adapted and repurposed for new public uses, such as Lui Seng Chun—a shophouse transformed into a community health center providing affordable Chinese medicine services. A similar situation exists in Shanghai and Singapore, where adaptive reuse is recognized as an appropriate way to adapt and repurpose government-owned heritage properties for economic and social benefit. Examples include Red Town in Shanghai (2007, now partially demolished), which adapted a range of buildings for new uses; and the National Gallery Singapore (2016), which adapts two preexisting institutional buildings and connects them through a dramatic entryway.

Adaptive reuse is not limited to government-owned heritage buildings. As illustrated in this publication, it is increasingly seen as a viable option in the marketplace. Examples abound of businesses, institutions, and private owners undertaking high-profile conversions, especially of distinctive heritage buildings. Private examples include Hong Kong's Asia Society Hong Kong Center, 1933 Shanghai, and Singapore's New Majestic Hotel.

## Relevance

With an increasing number of projects being completed and opened to the public in these three cities, it is timely to examine adaptive reuse within such influential Asian centers—particularly in terms of economic, environmental, and social dimensions.[2] It is also important to examine such adaptive reuse projects in terms of the legal and policy frameworks that control the kind and degree of change, including place-specific constraints and opportunities.[3]

## Objectives

Building on past publications, including government policy documents and extensive fieldwork, the objectives of this publication are to contextualize adaptive reuse in each city and to reveal the impetus behind a wide range of adaptive reuse projects from revitalization in Hong Kong to commercial development in Shanghai and tourism development in Singapore. A further objective is to stimulate discussion by evaluating the economic, environmental, and social benefits of projects, based on a number of generally accepted criteria.

## Format

This introduction defines adaptive reuse within an international and Asian perspective. The first four essays address adaptive reuse and sustainability (the economic,

---

1.  Please note the British spelling of "Revitalisation" is intentional, as this is its proper name as used by the Hong Kong SAR government.
2.  Although four dimensions (cultural, economic, environmental, and social) have recently been put forward, the author prefers to think in terms of three dimensions (economic, environmental, and social) as overlapping components of culture. But, no matter the preference, either approach leads to more holistic thinking.
3.  More than twenty years ago, Florian Steinberg wrote an insightful article, "Conservation and Rehabilitation of Urban Heritage in Developing Countries," *Habitat International* 20 (1996): 463–75. His thinking informs this book, as does the work of the late Ron van Oers, who understood the underlying importance of responsible adaptive reuse in city building. See Ron van Oers, "Managing Cities and the Historic Urban Landscape Initiative—an Introduction," *World Heritage Papers: Managing Historic Cities* (Paris: UNESCO World Heritage Centre, 2010), 7–17.

environmental, and social dimensions) within a broad urban context. Michael Turner addresses adaptive reuse in urban areas, Ester van Steekelenburg looks at adaptive reuse as part of urban sustainability, Donovan Rypkema demonstrates the economic value of retaining older building stock, and Lavina Ahuja outlines the increasing recognition of adaptive reuse projects by the UNESCO Asia-Pacific Awards for Cultural Heritage Conservation. The subsequent three essays and associated timelines for each center (Hong Kong, Shanghai, and Singapore) set out a clear framework for understanding the place-specific case studies that follow the essays. Such pairing of critical essays, timelines, and in-depth case studies provides a detailed understanding of each center's approach to adaptive reuse in the twenty-first century, which the conclusion brings together in a summary of the key salient points.

## *Selection of Case Studies*

Representative projects (five distinctive typologies), publicly or privately funded or both, are presented as in-depth case studies, with each project fully described, contextualized, and evaluated based on three dimensions: economic, environmental, and social. (The number of case studies is fifteen, with an even distribution of five building typologies across all three centers.)

## Introduction to Adaptive Reuse

### *Adaptive Reuse Defined*

"Adaptive reuse" is generally understood to mean adapting or changing a place for a new use. In some jurisdictions the term "repurposing" is used, although this implies that the place itself is not changed, only its use. Other jurisdictions have seized on such terms as "revitalization," which projects a more spirited approach to the adaptive reuse process, or "rehabilitation," which connotes a more material-based approach.[4] The former term suggests that a once-vibrant place has been rejuvenated, but technically, given the meaning of the term, the use could be the same. The latter term covers a wide range of interventions, and the use could be a continuing or new use. Looking at the varying terms used to describe adaptive reuse is an adventure in semantics. And in some instances, even semantics fail us—as there is no standard term for adaptive reuse in Chinese.[5]

The important thing to remember is that all of the terms relate to the use of a particular place. To help in this understanding, the following questions and answers are useful:

1. Is the proposed new use a continuation of—or similar to—the original use or the most recent use? In this case, "revitalization" seems appropriate as a descriptor, although the term has also been used in the context of change of use. "Rehabilitation" is also acceptable.

2. Is the proposed new use markedly different from the original use or most recent use? In this case, either "adaptive reuse" or "repurposing" are the correct

---

4.  In North American conservation standards and guidelines—*Secretary of the Interior's Standards for the Treatment of Historic Properties with Guidelines for Preserving, Rehabilitating, Restoring and Reconstructing Historic Buildings* (2017) and *Standards and Guidelines for the Conservation of Historic Places in Canada* (2nd ed., 2010)—the term "rehabilitation" is used to describe physical change (repair, alterations, additions) within the context of continuing or compatible new use.

5.  The term "adaptive reuse" is not defined in the *Principles for the Conservation of Heritage Sites in China*, rev. ed. (Beijing: ICOMOS China, 2015). However, the term "appropriate use" is defined; its literal meaning in Chinese is "rational + use" (106).

terms, although, as already mentioned, "repurposing" does not necessarily mean physical change, only change of use. "Rehabilitation" is also acceptable.[6]

To summarize, the term "adaptive reuse" generally implies both change of use and change to the fabric of a place. When the place has considerable architectural value, the level of change to the building fabric is usually carefully controlled—or should be. When the place has less architectural value, the level of change to the building fabric can be greater, although this is not always the best approach. Generally, the level of intervention (change) and the level of architectural value should have an inverse relationship. Other cultural heritage values may or may not be affected by higher levels of intervention.

*Literature Review*

Since at least the 1970s, adaptive reuse, as a conservation approach, has been recognized as a beneficial use of redundant properties in the West.[7] The continuing popularity of adaptive reuse as well as revitalization and repurposing is seen in the more recent release of a number of publications intended for practitioners overseas, including *Adaptive Reuse: Preserving Our Past, Building Our Future* (2004) by the Australian government, Department of the Environment and Heritage;[8] *Constructive Conservation in Practice* (2008) and *Constructive Conservation: Sustainable Growth for Historic Places* (2013), both by Historic England. To date, there have been no similar publications for the great urban centers of Asia, with the notable exception of those produced by the Urban Redevelopment Authority (URA) in Singapore.

Asian publications on the topic tend to be more oriented to a general readership or are academic publications focusing on individual buildings or a building cluster. For example, the adaptive reuse of Penang's Cheong Fatt Tze Mansion (now a heritage hotel called the Blue Mansion) has been recorded in a well-written and lavishly illustrated publication intended for wide distribution.[9] The adaptive reuse of Shanghai's The China Merchants Steam Navigation Company Building, one of the celebrated buildings on the Bund, is also well documented in at least one of Chang Qing's publications on mainland China's heritage buildings. As well, there have been articles in professional journals on aspects of adaptive reuse in Asia, including those that look at the conversion of industrial buildings into incubator spaces for the creative industry.

The programs and publications of UNESCO Bangkok are a notable exception. Since 2000, as a way to influence conservation practice in Asia, UNESCO Bangkok holds the yearly Asia-Pacific Awards for Cultural Heritage Conservation. Projects receive Awards of Excellence, Distinction, Merit, or Honourable Mention and are showcased in publications—three to date: *Asia Conserved: Lessons Learned from the UNESCO Asia-Pacific Awards for Cultural Heritage Conservation*, Volumes I (2000–2004), II (2005–2009), and III (2010–2014), with a fourth under preparation. Submissions are judged using eleven criteria, one of which is "appropriate use or

---

6.  William Chapman, "Determining Appropriate Use," in *Asia Conserved: Lessons Learned from the UNESCO Asia-Pacific Awards for Cultural Heritage Conservation (2000–2004)* (Bangkok: UNESCO Bangkok, 2007), 13–20. Chapman distinguishes between continuity of use, return to original use, minimal change of use, and completely new use.

7.  Harold Kalman, *Heritage Planning: Principles and Process* (New York: Routledge, 2014), 240.

8.  It can be argued that this is an Asian publication, but it seems to have had considerable influence worldwide and, hence, is included here. Of course, the same argument can be made for *The Burra Charter*, which is discussed later in the Introduction.

9.  Lin Lee Loh-Lim, *The Blue Mansion: The Story of Mandarin Splendour Reborn* (Penang: Areca Books, 2012).

adaptation of the structure."[10] "The ongoing socio-economic viability and relevance of the project, and provision for its future use and maintenance" are also considered.[11] Both criteria speak to the importance of how places are used, especially within their communities.

In *Streetwise Asia: A Practical Guide for the Conservation and Revitalisation of Heritage Cities and Towns in Asia*, another exception, Elizabeth Vines positions adaptive reuse within the broader framework of revitalization. The book is less about conservation per se and more about helping communities formulate realistic heritage strategies.[12] In talking about adaptive reuse within the framework of the conservation and maintenance of individual buildings, Vines advises:

> Find a new use for your building—Old buildings are best maintained by using them. The active use of an old building with sensitive alterations is more desirable than having a perfectly intact building that is not used. Promote compatible functions within the old building so that its life is restored. This may mean some degree of change, but this can be a better option than creating a non-viable historic building. Such alterations should, if possible, be reversible.[13]

Although intended for a local audience, in 1993, the Singapore Urban Redevelopment Authority (URA) and the Preservation of Monuments Board (PMB) (now National Heritage Board, NHB) published a concise book, *Objectives, Principles and Standards for Preservation and Conservation*.[14] In this early publication, adaptive reuse is defined as "modifying a place to suit it to a compatible use which involves the less [sic] possible loss of national, historical or cultural significance." Significantly, the importance of maintaining the interior is recognized under the category of maintaining the essential character of the building: "If a building is adapted for new uses, the original quality of the interior spaces should be retained."[15] More recently (December 2017), the Singapore URA has produced updated *Conservation Guidelines*[16] for conservation areas and specific typologies, such as the shophouse and bungalow. The guidelines also list incompatible uses for both building typologies and conservation areas.

## Adaptive Reuse in Relevant Conservation Documents

Informing and supporting such publications are a number of regional and international documents that include aspects of adaptive reuse. Internationally, the early *Athens Charter* (1931) and the influential *Venice Charter* (1964) mention appropriate use. The former "recommends the occupation of buildings, which ensures the

---

10. The UNESCO Asia-Pacific Awards for Cultural Heritage Conservation was launched in 2000 by Richard A. Engelhardt, then UNESCO regional advisor for culture in Asia and the Pacific for UNESCO Bangkok. Laurence Loh, one of the continuing judges for the yearly awards, developed the awards criteria, which fall into three categories (Understanding the Place, Technical Achievement, and Social and Policy Impact). Richard A. Engelhardt, ed., *Asia Conserved: Lessons Learned from the UNESCO Asia-Pacific Awards for Cultural Heritage Conservation (2000–2004)* (Bangkok: UNESCO, 2007), 2.

11. Richard A. Engelhardt, ed., *Asia Conserved Volume (2000–2004)*, 3.

12. Elizabeth Vines, *Streetwise Asia: A Practical Guide for the Conservation and Revitalisation of Heritage Cities and Towns in Asia* (Bangkok: UNESCO Bangkok, 2005).

13. Vines, *Streetwise Asia*, 12.

14. Urban Redevelopment Authority and Preservation of Monuments Board, *Objectives, Principles and Standards for Preservation and Conservation* (Singapore: Urban Redevelopment Authority and Preservation of Monuments Board, August 1993), 46.

15. Urban Redevelopment Authority and Preservation of Monuments Board, *Objectives, Principles and Standards*, 24. This is one of the few times where a more general reference to adaptive reuse includes a specific admonition regarding the treatment of the interior.

16. Urban Redevelopment Authority, *Conservation Guidelines* (Singapore: URA Singapore, December 2017), accessed May 19, 2020, https://www.ura.gov.sg/Corporate/Guidelines/Conservation/~/media/3A0DEC0B334141F6967686AD53776C37.ashx.

continuity of their life, . . . but . . . they should be used for a purpose which respects their historic or artistic character,"[17] while the latter asserts that "the conservation of *monuments* is always facilitated by making use of them for some socially useful purpose."[18]

In 1979, the first version of the Australian *Burra Charter* does not include a definition of adaptive reuse per se but uses (there's that word "use") and defines the simpler term "adaptation": "Adaptation means modifying a place to suit new functions without destroying its cultural significance."[19] Three articles are associated with the definition and reveal the recognized complexity of adaptation or adaptive reuse:

> Article 20. Adaptation is acceptable where the conservation of the place cannot otherwise be achieved, and where the adaptation does not substantially detract from its cultural significance.
>
> Article 21. Adaptation must be limited to that which is essential to a use for the place determined in accordance with Articles 6 and 7. . . .[20]
>
> Article 22. Significant material unavoidably removed in the process of adaptation must be securely preserved to enable the future restoration of the place.[21]

In the 1981 edition of the *Burra Charter*, there is an important change in the definition of adaptation: "*Adaptation* means modifying a *place* to suit proposed compatible uses."[22] And "compatible use means a use which involves no change to the culturally significant fabric, changes which are substantially reversible, or changes which require a minimal impact."[23]

There are no relevant changes in the 1988 edition of the *Burra Charter*, but there are significant and telling changes in the 1999 edition. Here, "adaptation" is defined more loosely as "*Adaptation* means modifying a *place* to suit the existing use or a proposed use." "Use" is defined as "the functions of a place, as well as the activities and practices that may occur at the place." And "compatible use" is defined as "a use which respects the *cultural significance* of a *place*. Such a use involves no, or minimal, impact on cultural significance."[24] This is the first time that the *Burra Charter* has mentioned aspects of social value as part of adaptation—or adaptive reuse—considerations.

In the latest edition of the charter (2013), now formally referred to as *The Burra Charter: The Australian ICOMOS Charter for Places of Cultural Significance*, "adaptation" now means "changing a *place*" rather than "modifying a *place*" in the context of suiting "the existing *use* or a proposed *use*." And the definition of use has been expanded to include not only "activities and practices that may occur at the place" but "activities and traditional and customary practices that may occur at the place or are dependent on the place."[25] The use of the word "change" (rather than "modify") is

17. ICOMOS, *The Athens Charter for the Restoration of Historic Monuments (The Athens Charter)* (Athens: First International Congress of Architects and Technicians of Historic Monuments, 1931).

18. ICOMOS, *International Charter for the Conservation and Restoration of Monuments and Sites (The Venice Charter)* (Venice: Second International Congress of Architects and Technicians of Historic Monuments, 1964), emphasis original.

19. Australia ICOMOS, *Burra Charter* (Burra: Australia ICOMOS, August 1979).

20. Article 6: "The conservation options appropriate to a place or a part of a place must first be determined by an understanding of its cultural significance and its physical condition." Article 7: "The conservation options chosen will determine which uses are compatible. Compatible uses are those involving no change, changes which are substantially reversible, or changes which have a minimal impact on the cultural significant fabric." Australia ICOMOS, *Burra Charter*, 1979.

21. Australia ICOMOS, *Burra Charter*, 1979.

22. Australia ICOMOS, *Burra Charter* (Burra: Australia ICOMOS, 1981), emphasis original.

23. Australia ICOMOS, *Burra Charter*, 1981.

24. Australia ICOMOS, *Burra Charter: The Australian ICOMOS Charter for Places of Cultural Significance* (Burra: Australia ICOMOS, 1999), emphasis original.

25. Australia ICOMOS, *The Burra Charter: The Australia ICOMOS Charter for Places of Cultural Significance* (Burra: Australia ICOMOS, 2013).

more dramatic in its meaning and leads us to the challenge of how to maintain the integrity of a heritage place—in all of its tangible and intangible complexity—within the developing or redeveloping urban environment, in particular.

To return to charters and documents as indicators of current thinking on adaptive reuse, it is important to consider two Asian documents: the second edition of the *China Principles* (2015),[26] which guides the mainland Chinese approach to conservation, including adaptive reuse; and the *Hoi An Protocols* (2009),[27] created to guide conservation in Asia, including adaptive reuse, within the specific context of authenticity. In the recent version of the *China Principles*, Tong Mingkang, as the president of ICOMOS China and deputy director-general of the State Administration of Cultural Heritage, China, contributes a foreword, in which he acknowledges that one of the major challenges facing China's cultural heritage is improving the appropriate use of sites:

> There is a section (Chapter 5) dedicated to appropriate use which looks at this issue from the perspective of maintaining existing use through to adaptive re-use. This section also spells out the principles and methodology for appropriate use. It emphasizes that retaining the original function of a site or adapting it for modern use must take into consideration its values, attributes, state of conservation, and setting, as well as research and presentation, with emphasis on public benefits and sustainability.... This is in itself an important advance in the conservation of China's cultural heritage.[28]

Several articles (6, 40, 44, and 45) are devoted to appropriate use. Article 44, Retaining Historic Function, has particular relevance to current adaptive reuse challenges in Asia:

> Sites that retain their historic function, particularly those where the traditional way of life has become an integral part of the site's values should be encouraged to continue that function.[29]

Part of the accompanying commentary includes a cautionary note:

> Ensuring continuing historic function is a means of conserving the values of this heritage. When managing such a site, special effort should be made to protect the original function. Changes to the use should only be considered after careful consideration. Special attention should be given to avoid the transformation of a residential precinct into a commercial district, as this seriously diminishes its values and authenticity.[30]

The cautionary note leads us directly to the other Asian document of particular importance, the *Hoi An Protocols*, which focuses on "assuring and preserving" the authenticity of heritage places. Use is one of the eight aspects of authenticity, and adaptive reuse has the potential to undermine this aspect.[31]

> Wherever possible, existing historic building stock should be conserved, upgraded and reused in sympathetic ways. The focus should be on assisting residents of properties to continue residential use. Continued residential use may not always be feasible or desirable, and former housing stock may need to be adapted for

---

26. ICOMOS China, *Principles for the Conservation of Heritage Sites in China*, rev. ed. (Beijing: ICOMOS China, 2015).

27. UNESCO, *The Hoi An Protocols for Best Conservation Practice in Asia: Professional Guidelines for Assuring and Preserving the Authenticity of Heritage Sites in the Context of the Cultures of Asia* (Bangkok: UNESCO Bangkok, 2009).

28. ICOMOS China, *China Principles*, 57.

29. ICOMOS China, *China Principles*,103.

30. ICOMOS China, *China Principles*, 103.

31. UNESCO, *Hoi An Protocols*.

commercial or community use. This must not be done at the cost of displacement of populations and homogenization or commercialization of originally diverse precincts.[32]

## Adaptive Reuse Debate

In most cases involving heritage places, adaptive reuse is seen as a way to conserve buildings or structures while allowing for respectful change. Sometimes the change is within the context of continuing use, but frequently the use is a new or different use. Some conservation professionals have long argued that the best new use is one closest to the original use. Penang's Cheong Fatt Tze Mansion (the Blue Mansion) is an example of this approach, as the current use (a heritage hotel) continues the residential function of the traditional multigenerational Chinese mansion (Fig. 1.1).[33] More liberal practitioners argued with considerable "ammunition" that the best new use is quite simply a viable use that needs a home.[34] Examples abound for this approach and can be found throughout the case studies provided in this book.

**Figure 1.1:** Cheong Fatt Tze Mansion (the Blue Mansion) in Penang, Malaysia, built in 1904 and revitalized in 1995. It is an award-winning adaptive reuse project, which revitalized a Chinese mansion into a boutique hotel. (Source: Ian Babbitt.)

Both arguments have their merit. A use similar to the original use suggests social continuity and understanding of Spirit of Place. However, rather than lose a building that has architectural, historic, or contextual value, a dramatically different new use may not only save the building but activate economic and social values in new and supportive ways. Clearly, there is no one option for ensuring the success of adaptive reuse projects. However, as demonstrated in this publication, understanding a city in all its dimensions (economic, environmental, and social), helps governments, institutions, and private developers choose the best options for the continuing use or adaptive reuse of a wide range of built heritage assets.

---

32. UNESCO, *Hoi An Protocols*, 33.

33. The Blue Mansion, a UNESCO award-winning project, was carried out by Laurence Loh, one of Asia's most experienced conservation architects, and its insightful interpretation reflects the input of both Laurence Loh and Lin Lee Loh-Lim.

34. Hal Kalman, a Canadian conservationist (previously cited), has argued that adaptive reuse is a "happy marriage" between an available site and a use needing a home.

## Adaptive Reuse in the Greater Context of Adaptation

Michael Turner, one of the contributors to this book, notes that adaptive reuse is part of the larger conversation about "survival of the fittest," the phrase used by Herbert Spencer and adopted by Charles Darwin to better describe natural selection. The phrase remains relevant, although its exact meaning has evolved since the late nineteenth century.[35] Expanding on this theme, Atul Gawande, an American surgeon and regular contributor to the *New Yorker* has observed in a recent article:

> Medicine is a complex adaptive system: it is made up of many interconnected, multilayered parts, and it is meant to evolve with time and changing conditions. . . . Adaptation requires two things: mutation and selection. Mutation produces variety and deviation; selection kills off the least functional mutations.[36]

If we substitute "medicine" with "buildings," the relevance and importance of appropriate or compatible adaptive reuse becomes clearer. And to take the analogy further, buildings can be designed in anticipation of probable change. Sheila Conejos, in an award-winning PhD thesis, "Designing for Future Building Adaptive Reuse," has proposed seven design criteria for new buildings that could facilitate future adaptive reuse: long life (physical), location (economic), loose fit (functional), low energy (technological), sense of place (social), quality standard (legal), and context (political).[37]

Widening our understanding of adaptive reuse allows us to make more informed decisions about what to keep (and why) and, in anticipation of the future, what to build (and why). This publication offers an instructive way forward for decision makers and the myriad of people who care about the places in which they live and work. Perhaps it can be viewed as a "call to responsible action."

## Bibliography

Australia ICOMOS. *Burra Charter*. Burra: Australia ICOMOS, August 1979.

Australia ICOMOS. *Burra Charter*. Burra: Australia ICOMOS, 1981.

Australia ICOMOS. *Burra Charter: The Australian ICOMOS Charter for Places of Cultural Significance*. Burra: Australia ICOMOS, 1999.

Australia ICOMOS. *The Burra Charter: The Australia ICOMOS Charter for Places of Cultural Significance*. Burra: Australia ICOMOS, 2013.

Conejos, Sheila. "Designing for Future Building Adaptive Reuse." PhD thesis, Bond University, Gold Coast, Australia, 2013.

Engelhardt, Richard A., ed. *Asia Conserved: Lessons Learned from the UNESCO Asia-Pacific Awards for Cultural Heritage Conservation (2000–2004)*. Bangkok: UNESCO, 2007.

Gawande, Atul. "The Upgrade—Why Doctors Hate Their Computers." *New Yorker*, November 18, 2018, 62–63.

ICOMOS. *The Athens Charter for the Restoration of Historic Monuments (The Athens Charter)*. Athens: First International Congress of Architects and Technicians of Historic Monuments, 1931.

ICOMOS. *International Charter for the Conservation and Restoration of Monuments and Sites (The Venice Charter)*. Venice: Second International Congress of Architects and Technicians of Historic Monuments, 1964.

---

35. Michael Turner, "Essay for Proposed Book on Adaptive Reuse," e-mail to editor (Katie Cummer), January 17, 2019.
36. Atul Gawande, "The Upgrade—Why Doctors Hate Their Computers," *New Yorker*, November 18, 2018, 67.
37. Sheila Conejos, "Designing for Future Building Adaptive Reuse" (PhD thesis, Bond University, Gold Coast, Australia, 2013). I am grateful to Rowenna Wood, an associate at Purcell (UK), for this reference and to Michael Morrison, a partner at Purcell (UK), for putting us in touch.

ICOMOS China. *Principles for the Conservation of Heritage Sites in China*. Beijing: ICOMOS China, revised 2015.

Kalman, Harold. *Heritage Planning: Principles and Process*. New York: Routledge, 2014.

Loh-Lim, Lin Lee. *The Blue Mansion: The Story of Mandarin Splendour Reborn*. Penang: Areca Books, 2012.

UNESCO. *The Hoi An Protocols for Best Conservation Practice in Asia: Professional Guidelines for Assuring and Preserving the Authenticity of Heritage Sites in the Context of the Cultures of Asia*. Bangkok: UNESCO, 2009.

Urban Redevelopment Authority. *Conservation Guidelines*. Singapore: URA Singapore, December 2017. Accessed May 19, 2020. https://www.ura.gov.sg/Corporate/Guidelines/Conservation/~/media/3A0DEC0B334141F6967686AD53776C37.ashx.

Urban Redevelopment Authority and Preservation of Monuments Board. *Objectives, Principles and Standards for Preservation and Conservation*. Singapore: Urban Redevelopment Authority and Preservation of Monuments Board, August 1993.

Vines, Elizabeth. *Streetwise Asia: A Practical Guide for the Conservation and Revitalisation of Heritage Cities and Towns in Asia*. Bangkok: UNESCO Bangkok, 2005.

# Essays

# Adaptive Reuse within Urban Areas

Michael Turner

Adaptive reuse is an essential component of a living city. The Pantheon in Rome is the emblematic global example providing the ultimate proof of the adage "survival of the adaptive," survival being conditional to the one that is able to adapt best and adjust to the changing moral, physical, political, social, and spiritual environment in which it finds itself, referencing the Darwinian natural selection hypothesis of descent with modification.[1]

For an architectural monument or an individual building, adaptive reuse is considered an integral part of a diary of events, becoming, in the words of the Venice Charter, "inseparable from the history to which it bears witness and from the setting in which it occurs," underscoring that "the valid contributions of all periods . . . must be respected, since unity of style is not the aim of a restoration."[2] Thirty years on, *The Nara Document on Authenticity* extended these values beyond the original 1977 attributes developed in *The Operational Guidelines for the Implementation of the World Heritage Convention* of "design, materials, workmanship and setting," to include "form and design, materials and substance, use and function, traditions and techniques, location and setting, and spirit and feeling, and other internal and external factors."[3] The application of these sources permits the elaboration of all possible urban transformations through assessing the degree to which authenticity is present in, or expressed by, each of these significant attributes.[4]

## Challenges

The dissonance of life spans between a building's fabric, furnishings, use, and the contextual changes surrounding its setting is frequently accommodated through adaptive reuse whereby the physical attribute of the material fabric is retained. This becomes all the more relevant when we address the concerns of sustainability and the importance for the conservation of our physical resources by extending the life of a building.

1. L. C. Megginson, "Lessons from Europe for American Business," *Southwestern Social Science Quarterly* 44, no. 1 (1963): 3–13.
2. ICOMOS, *International Charter for the Conservation and Restoration of Monuments and Sites (The Venice Charter)* (Venice: Second International Congress of Architects and Technicians of Historic Monuments, 1964).
3. ICCROM, ICOMOS and UNESCO, *The Nara Document on Authenticity (1994)* (Nara: Nara Conference, 1994), article 13.
4. UNESCO, Operational Guidelines for the Implementation of the World Heritage Convention, WHC.16/01 (Paris: UNESCO, 2016), para. 85.

However, the adaptive reuse of the urban fabric is more complex, as the socio-economic aspects of surrounding neighborhoods change at dramatically different speeds, providing a challenge for both historic buildings and ensembles. The 2011 UNESCO *Recommendation on the Historic Urban Landscape* addresses these very issues with an approach going "beyond the notion of the historic ensemble to include the wider setting and context,"[5] which can also be identified in the retrofitting of the diverse components that make up our urban heritage.

This approach must be supplemented by the continuity of urban memory and intangible community values, which may be understood through the adaptive reuse of ideas, images, and texts. These resemble buildings in that over time they may become unsuitable by persisting in their original purposes. "While adaptive reuse is an alternative to demolition, the adaptive reuse of ideas, texts and images saves them from vanishing. As a result, the intellectual environment, like a city, preserves at least in part its traditional outlook, although serving new programmatic requirements."[6]

## Setting and Context

Although the 2005 ICOMOS *Xi'an Declaration* sets out the definitions of context and setting,[7] these terms are too often applied interchangeably. In adopting the dictionary meanings relating to play scripts, setting is the text describing *where* and *when* an event takes place, and context is the *situation* or *circumstances* in which the event occurs. It is the context, encircling a historic ensemble, that provides meaning and can be used to characterize the circumstances within which the city evolved and that can help in its interpretation. The authentication and integrity of the urban context needs to be extended beyond the physical fabric to include economic, environmental, and social processes, or any combination of them, surrounding the events or place. Applying policies of adaptive reuse will challenge contextual continuity, requiring the establishment of close analogies with the structure and morphology of the preexisting fabric and the appropriateness of a design vocabulary.[8]

### Urban Layers

The Historic Urban Landscape (HUL) approach considers and identifies layers extending beyond physical boundaries, not simply as possible buffer zones but as liminal spaces in their own right. This allows for an interaction of activities and a range of interventions that may provide mutual benefits, including "an added layer protection"[9] for a building or ensemble and the potential growth that this may provide for adjoining areas. In this way, urban sustainability is better realized.

The question is not so much one of the values and attributes of a place as of the urban narratives and texts and their interpretations. Adaptive reuse moves the focus of value from use to other attributes, such as materials and substance and spirit and feeling, in determining urban continuity and renewed identities over time. Specifically, it is related to understanding the differences between synchronic and diachronic heritage. Synchrony and diachrony are two different and complementary viewpoints

5.  UNESCO, *Recommendation on the Historic Urban Landscape* (Paris: UNESCO, 2011).
6.  E. Freschi and P. A. Maas, "Conceptual Reflections on Adaptive Reuse," in *Adaptive Reuse: Aspects of Creativity in South Asian Cultural History*, ed. E. Freschi and P. A. Maas (Wiesbaden: Harrassowitz Verlag, 2017), 11–28.
7.  ICOMOS, *Xi'an Declaration on the Conservation of the Setting of Heritage Structures, Sites and Areas* (Xi'an: ICOMOS, 2005).
8.  J. Cody and F. Siravo, "The Search for Contextual Continuities," in *Historic Cities: Issues in Urban Conservation*, ed. J. Cody and F. Siravo (Los Angeles: Getty Conservation Institute, 2019), 285–93.
9.  UNESCO, Operational Guidelines, para. 104.

in linguistic analysis that may be applied in reading the urban scene. Simply stated, the synchronic approach considers the moment in time without taking history into account, while the diachronic approach considers development and evolution over time.[10]

While this composite environment may enrich the urban experience, it can also provide a basis for new meanings of the "historic block" that are emerging in East Asia, where the dynamics of change are so great. Adding to this urban complexity, each layer or component part might be alternatively synchronic or diachronic.[11] The adaptive reuse of Hong Kong's Tai Kwun—Centre for Heritage and Arts complex is an exceptional example of the new synchronic adaptive reuses being tempered with the diachronic memory evoked by the physical fabric. While the current discourse favors the diachronic approach, interpretations in the digital age benefit from augmented and virtual realities that may provide innovative perceptions in the comprehension and interpretation of our environment and its layered history. This will render unnecessary physical reconstructions of the past in setting and context and provide new dimensions for spirit and feeling by authenticating the new values.

## Sustainability

The 2015 United Nations Sustainable Development Goals and the 2016 UN-Habitat New Urban Agenda afford new roles for addressing urbanism.[12] Target 11.4 is to "strengthen efforts to protect and safeguard the world's cultural and natural heritage," to achieve Sustainable Development Goal 11, in making "our cities and human settlements inclusive, safe, resilient and sustainable."[13]

With the mantra of *culture as an enabler/driver for sustainable development*, the UNESCO Division for Creativity provides a framework for measurable cultural indicators, including such added values as economic growth, employment, and livelihoods, enhanced by cohesion, culture, and social inclusion.[14] These goals and measurable targets are valuable in considering and evaluating a "heritage block" surrounded by urban discord. Should urban blocks be relegated to a museum role by architectural periods? Engaging with the urban mechanisms of the Recommendation on the Historic Urban Landscape, the Sustainable Development Goals, and the New Urban Agenda allows for a more integrated approach for urban conservation to include added socio-economic values and environmental sustainability. Moreover, the consequences of local community participation and governance will often affect housing, infrastructure, public spaces, and spatial design, and they need to be added to the balance of benefits that should be evaluated through results-based management.[15]

Indeed, physical confrontations are often shocking, especially with high-rise towers surrounding three-story buildings of the past, demonstrating a new form of

---

10. Ferdinand de Saussure, *Course in General Linguistics*, 3rd ed. (New York: Philosophical Library, 1959).

11. Michael Turner, *Landscapes of Modernism in World Heritage* (Kaunas: Lithuanian National Commission for UNESCO and Kaunas City Municipality, 2019), 111–17.

12. United Nations Habitat, New Urban Agenda, A/RES/71/256 (October, 2016), http://habitat3.org/the-new-urban-agenda/.

13. United Nations General Assembly, Transforming Our World: The 2030 Agenda for Sustainable Development, A/RES/70/1 (October 21, 2015), https://www.un.org/ga/search/view_doc.asp?symbol=A/RES/70/1&Lang=E.

14. UNESCO Director-General, *Culture for the 2030 Agenda* (Paris: UNESCO, 2018).

15. The Review of Results-Based Management at the United Nations—A/63/268/Office of Internal Oversight Services defines RBM as a *"management strategy by which processes, outputs and services contribute to the achievement of clearly stated expected accomplishments and objectives. It is focused on achieving results, improving performance, integrating lessons learned into management decisions and monitoring and reporting on performance."*

urban fabric conceived as an urban heritage bathtub (Fig. 2.1),[16] as an innovative alternative for sustainable urban management. If these factors are consciously extended, social inclusion and urban resilience may be provided to surrounding communities beyond the boundaries of the urban heritage block. However, it is the unseen and intangible component that sustains the DNA of a city, its spirit and soul embedded in its characteristics, and that may provide a stronger sense of identity through adaptive reuse rather than anachronistic museum uses or the deletion of urban memory through redevelopment.

**Figure 2.1:** Schematic section and plan explaining the concept of an urban bathtub. (Source: Michael Turner.)

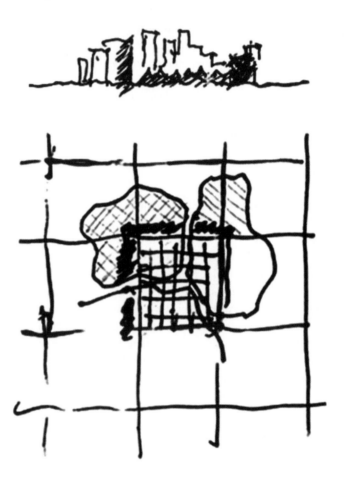

## Concluding Observation

The reality of the increased pressures of development, resulting in large-scale demolitions, leaves a new legacy that needs to be redefined. This includes identifying the values of the remaining physical attributes from past decades or possibly creating new values through contemporary interventions. Urban adaptive reuse is *process* oriented as opposed to the architectural refit that is *project* oriented. Regardless of its challenges, this new approach brings together many disciplines with multiple communities and a rewarding experience for future generations by engaging with the continuity of the intangible spirit and feeling.

---

16. An urban bathtub can be understood as an urban area where a low-rise city block designated as heritage is surrounded by taller structures. A cross section through the block and the surrounding buildings is reminiscent of a traditional bathtub. Symbiotic relationships between the heritage block and the surrounding urban fabric generate an urban ecosystem mutually sustaining their economic and social development.

# Bibliography

Cody, J., and F. Siravo. "The Search for Contextual Continuities." In *Historic Cities: Issues in Urban Conservation*, edited by J. Cody and F. Siravo, 285–293. Los Angeles: Getty Conservation Institute, 2019.

Freschi, E. and P. A. Maas. "Conceptual Reflections on Adaptive Reuse." In *Adaptive Reuse: Aspects of Creativity in South Asian Cultural History*, edited by E. Freschi and P. A. Maas, 11–28. Wiesbaden: Harrassowitz Verlag, 2017.

Giacalone Ramat, Anna, Caterina Mauri, and Piera Molinelli, eds. *Synchrony and Diachrony: A Dynamic Interface*. Philadelphia, PA: John Benjamins North America, 2013.

ICCROM, ICOMOS, and UNESCO. *The Nara Document on Authenticity (1994)*. Nara: Nara Conference, 1994.

ICOMOS. *International Charter for the Conservation and Restoration of Monuments and Sites (The Venice Charter)*. Venice: Second International Congress of Architects and Technicians of Historic Monuments, 1964.

ICOMOS. *Xi'an Declaration on the Conservation of the Setting of Heritage Structures, Sites and Areas*. Xi'an: ICOMOS, 2005.

Megginson, L. C. "Lessons from Europe for American Business." *Southwestern Social Science Quarterly* 44, no. 1 (1963): 3–13.

Saussure Ferdinand de. *Course in General Linguistics*. 3rd ed. New York: Philosophical Library, 1959.

Turner, M. *Landscapes of Modernism in World Heritage*, 111–17. Kaunas: Lithuanian National Commission for UNESCO and Kaunas City Municipality, 2019.

UNESCO. Operational Guidelines for the Implementation of the World Heritage Convention. WHC.16/01. Paris, 2016.

UNESCO. *Recommendation on the Historic Urban Landscape*. Paris: UNESCO, 2011.

UNESCO Director General. *Culture for the 2030 Agenda*. Paris: UNESCO, 2018.

United Nations General Assembly. Transforming Our World: The 2030 Agenda for Sustainable Development. A/RES/70/1. October 21, 2015. https://www.un.org/ga/search/view_doc.asp?symbol=A/RES/70/1&Lang=E.

United Nations Habitat. New Urban Agenda, A/RES/71/256. October, 2016. http://habitat3.org/the-new-urban-agenda/.

# Cultural Heritage as a Driver for Sustainable Cities

Ester van Steekelenburg

When the United Nations (UN) announced its worldwide fifteen-year Sustainable Development Goals (SDGs) in 2015, UNESCO lauded the inclusion of culture for its "unparalleled recognition."[1] It was the first time that culture featured so prominently on the international development agenda. Culture, cultural heritage, and cultural landscape have now been recognized on the international stage as playing an important role in defining and achieving sustainable urban growth.

This is rightly so, considering that tangible and intangible cultural heritage bring a variety of benefits to urban areas and are vital aspects of livable and sustainable cities. These benefits range from the value of compact and dense urban forms to the availability of accessible public spaces in recognizing diversity, enhancing social cohesion, and maintaining human scale. Across the world, from Australia to North America, governments and developers have started recognizing the importance of historic towns, historic districts, and the historic parts of cities for their distinctive qualities and unique sense of place. Such places attract tourism, encourage employment and local investment, and foster sustainable development.

Yet, in Asia, the awareness of the role of culture and heritage as contributors to sustainable urban growth is still in its infancy. Often, in Asia's highly competitive urban economy, financial feasibility is the key deciding factor, which makes it difficult to put together a viable business case for regeneration in place of demolition. To have a more fundamental debate on the long-term societal value of heritage for creating livable and lovable cities, there is a need for city makers and developers to appreciate, understand, and quantify the wider economic, environmental, and social costs and benefits. This essay briefly examines the relationship between heritage revitalization and sustainable urban development, with reference to the state of affairs in the case study cities of Hong Kong, Shanghai, and Singapore.

## Culture in the Sustainable Development Goals and the New Urban Agenda

In 2015, world leaders agreed on global goals to make the world a better place by 2030.[2] They formulated seventeen Sustainable Development Goals (SDGs) and cor-

---

1. United Nations General Assembly, *Transforming Our World: The 2030 Agenda for Sustainable Development*, A/RES/70/1 (October 21, 2015), https://www.un.org/ga/search/view_doc.asp?symbol=A/RES/70/1&Lang=E.
2. United Nations General Assembly, *Transforming Our World*.

responding targets, 169 in all. These global goals are groundbreaking for two reasons: (1) for the first time, cities are seen as places where a large part of the world now lives, and, therefore, there is a need for extra attention when it comes to policy, planning, and investment (indeed, Goal 11 is completely dedicated to cities); and (2) never before has the role of heritage and culture in human development been so explicitly recognized and articulated. Culture is no longer a "luxury"; it has become mainstream. Global Goal 11—Sustainable Cities and Communities—has eleven targets with matching indicators, and the fourth one is "to strengthen efforts to protect and safeguard the world's cultural and natural heritage."[3]

In addition, there is the 2016 New Urban Agenda (NUA),[4] another key United Nations (UN) document that will drive urban policy making in the coming decades. The NUA comprises a series of approximately 170 commitments that 190 nations have endorsed. Six specifically mention built heritage.[5] The interesting thing about the NUA is that this is the first time a UN agency has explicitly used its mandate to solicit, support, and drive change not on the national level but on the city level. With this, the UN increasingly recognizes that with the rapid development of the twenty-first century, it will largely be cities rather than nations that define policy and practice in urban development, responding to the "need for alignment between cities and towns and national planning objectives in their role as drivers of national economic and social development."[6] National policy frameworks will continue to lead, but it is at the local level where the biggest change will take place, in terms of creating governance and implementation competencies. Increasingly, it will be local authorities, local citizens, and local developers who are tasked with the management of the urban cultural landscape.

Furthermore, it is not just the recognition of an explicit heritage target in the NUA; culture, cultural heritage, and historic urban areas are recognized for their role in bettering urban life. Protection and restoration of old buildings are no longer standalone projects but parts of larger contexts that promote reuse and rehabilitation as solutions for affordable housing, better public spaces, energy-efficient buildings, and sustainable urbanization. With the increased prominence of culture on the agendas of policy makers, it is time to better articulate and quantify the cultural, economic, environmental, and social values of heritage for communities, government officials, property owners, and real estate developers.

## Measurable Impact of Culture and Heritage on Sustainable Urban Development

In recent years, the positive impact of culture and heritage on sustainable urban development has become a measurable value. The relevance of heritage to each of the three

---

3. United Nations, *Tracking Progress towards Inclusive, Safe, Resilient and Sustainable Cities and Human Settlements: SDG 11 Synthesis Report—High Level Political Forum 2018* (July 2018), https://unhabitat.org/sdg-11-synthesis-report/.

4. United Nations Habitat, New Urban Agenda, A/RES/71/256 (October, 2016), http://habitat3.org/the-new-urban-agenda/.

5. NUA #38: leverage natural and cultural heritage in cities to safeguard and promote cultural infrastructures; #45: develop urban economies, building on cultural heritage and local resources; #60: support sustainable tourism and heritage conservation activities; #124: include culture as a priority component of urban plans; #125: support leveraging cultural heritage for sustainable urban development.

6. UN General Assembly, *New Urban Agenda*.

prongs of sustainable development—economic, environmental, and social—has been extensively discussed and well documented by institutions[7] and scholars[8] alike.

## Economic

The positive economic outcomes related to the adaptive reuse of heritage buildings are multiple. The following section highlights its significant aspects in an Asian context.

### Capital Works Investment and Job Creation

Rehabilitation is more labor intensive than new construction. Greater labor intensity means more jobs and more local payrolls. While materials are often imported from around the globe, labor is usually purchased from across the street. Since workers spend their paychecks, there is a significantly greater multiplier effect with rehabilitation than with new construction, as evidenced by a study in heritage districts across the United States.[9] Furthermore, in most countries throughout the world, and certainly in Asia, there is a skills shortage of craftspeople trained to work on heritage buildings. Therefore, a strategy that encourages the rehabilitation of heritage buildings combined with job training for the required skill set has both short- and long-term economic impacts: in the short term with more jobs and in the long-term with a larger workforce of trained craftspeople.

### Fostering Creative Industries and Local Business Development

A 2012 UNESCO report underlines the proven impact and relevance of heritage and cultural creative industries and cultural infrastructure as strategic tools for revenue generation and job creation.[10] Its program evaluations from across the world found a positive return on investment in culture, specifically in the "the cultural sector's contribution to the economy and poverty alleviation."[11] Worth noting here is the link between cultural heritage and creative industries. Studies in the United States and Europe[12] show that, "in places where the historic fabric is nurtured, creative economies flourish. Concurrently, the growth of a creative class that consistently

7.  For example: Getty Conservation Institute, *Economics and Heritage Conservation* (Los Angeles: Getty Conservation Institute, 1998); Guido Licciardi and Rana Amirtahmasebi, *The Economics of Uniqueness: Investing in Historic City Cores and Cultural Assets for Sustainable Development* (Washington, DC: World Bank, 2012); UNESCO Director-General, *Culture Urban Future: Global Report on Culture for Sustainable Urban Development*, CLT-2016/WS/18, 2016.

8.  Scholars who have explicitly focused on the economics of heritage include E. C. Avrami, "Cultural Heritage Conservation and Sustainable Building: Converging Agendas." *Industrial Ecology* (December 2004): 1–15; Walter Jamieson, "Cultural Heritage Tourism Planning and Development: Defining the Field and Its Challenges." *APT Bulletin* 29, no. 3/4, Thirtieth Anniversary Issue (1998): 65–67; N. Lichfield, *Economics in Urban Conservation* (Cambridge: Cambridge University Press, 1988); R. Mason, "Assessing Values in Conservation Planning: Methodological Issues and Choices." In *Assessing the Values of Cultural Heritage: Research Report*, edited by M. De La Torre. Los Angeles: Getty Conservation Institute, 2002; Donovan D. Rypkema, *The Economics of Historic Preservation: A Community Leader's Guide* (United States: National Trust for Historic Preservation in the United States, 2005); and D. Throsby, "Conceptualising Heritage as Cultural Capital." In *Heritage Economics*, edited by P. King, 7–14 (Canberra: Australian Heritage Commission, 2001).

9.  Rypkema, *The Economics of Historic Preservation*.

10. UNESCO, *Culture: A Driver and an Enabler of Sustainable Development*, thematic think piece (2012), http://www.unesco.org/new/fileadmin/MULTIMEDIA/HQ/post2015/pdf/Think_Piece_Culture.pdf.

11. By January 2012, culture was included in 70 percent of the United Nations' Development Assistance Frameworks, compared to 30 percent in 2005.

12. Donovan D. Rypkema and Hristina Mikić, *Cultural Heritage and Creative Industries* (Serbia: Creative Economy Group Foundation and Penn Design Studio, 2016).

engages with structures from the past maintains use-value, and prevents such fabric from growing obsolete and disappearing."[13] These observations are important as the growing creative economy is increasingly in the spotlight as an urban job creator. A worldwide study in 2008 found that creative industries in Asia represent one of the most rapidly expanding sectors in the economy, with an annual growth rate of nearly 10 percent.[14]

## Economic Security and Increase in Property Values

Another contribution, which has been identified in multiple countries around the world, is the positive impact on property values when heritage is protected. For residents and developers, heritage properties provide long-term investment value that holds up in fluctuating markets because of the uniqueness of place. In Europe, "enthusiasm for historic urban cores and heritage assets can translate into higher values – not just financial value, but economic and social value as well."[15] Many argue that this may be true only for urban areas with strict planning guidelines and height restrictions and will not hold up in Asia's booming urban economies with their inflated land and property prices.

Yet recent research suggests that, even in Singapore and Hong Kong, renovation of heritage properties makes economic sense: "Shophouses are attractive to investors for their heritage value, as well as the potential for capital appreciation, which is supported by their limited and static supply. Over the last decade, historic shophouses have increased in value 50 percent more compared to condominiums."[16] In Hong Kong, a recent conversion of a historic family home near the city center into an apartment building boosted the building's value. "The flats at Kennedy Terrace could fetch 50 per cent more than adjacent buildings in the area."[17] Interestingly, as distinctive heritage properties are increasingly hard to come by in these two cities, a trend has been observed of Singapore-based boutique developers venturing out to nearby emerging markets, such as Malaysia, Myanmar, and Vietnam, to buy and repurpose historic properties.[18] Sustainable cities need sustainable tax revenues and the value premium that heritage districts are able to generate can provide some of that revenue.

## Heritage-Based Recreation and Cultural Tourism

While a golf course, a casino, or an amusement park can be built anywhere, the distinctive historic architecture of a city simply cannot be replaced. It is that distinctiveness that can be a magnet for tourism. Cultural tourism ideally should bring benefits

13. Anmaar Javed Habib and Joshua D. Bevan, "GIS Mapping of Relationships between Cultural Heritage and Creative Industries," in *A Geospatial Analysis of the Intersection between Historic Fabric and the Creative Economy*, ed. Donovan D. Rypkema and Hristina Mikić (Serbia: Creative Economy Group Foundation and Penn Design Studio, 2016), 66.

14. United Nations, *The Challenge of Assessing the Creative Economy; Towards Informed Policy-Making*, UNCTAD/DITC/2008/2 (2008), https://unctad.org/en/pages/PublicationArchive.aspx?publicationid=945.

15. BPF Deloitte Real Estate, Historic England, and RICS, *Heritage Works: A Toolkit of Best Practice in Heritage Regeneration* (Historic England: Colourhouse, 2017), https://www.bpf.org.uk/sites/default/files/resources/Heritage-Works-14July2017-for-web.pdf.

16. Brad Kelly, "Singapore's Shophouses Spark Investment Boom," *JLL Real Views*, December 22, 2016, https://www.jll.com.au/en/trends-and-insights/workplace/singapore-shophouses-spark-investment-boom.

17. Ka-sing Lam, "Preserving Heritage Boosts Value of Li Family Home in Mid-levels," *South China Morning Post*, November 21, 2018, https://www.scmp.com/property/hong-kong-china/article/2174187/preserving-heritage-boosts-value-li-family-home-hong-kong.

18. Cities Development Initiative for Asia, *Heritage Works: A Pilot Urban Regeneration Study in Yangon Final Report*, 2016.

to host communities and provide important means for them to care for and maintain their heritage.[19] The World Tourism Organization estimates that cultural tourism now accounts for 40 percent of the world's tourism revenue. A recent report affirms that "cultural tourism is important in terms of tourist numbers, but it is perhaps even more significant in terms of expenditure. Cultural tourists tend to be relatively high spending, and are important in generating income and employment. The combination of culture and tourism can be a powerful driver of economic activity."[20]

The growth in the industry shows no signs of slowing. A 2017 global study shows "that worldwide tourism is one of the fastest growing economic segments and heritage tourism is one of the fastest growing components of this industry."[21] In fact, the economic connection between cultural tourism and local economic development is so well established that, increasingly, the debate revolves around the wider economic and societal benefits. A 2016 UNESCO report exploring the benefits of cultural tourism beyond economic returns notes, "Travelling to experience the culture of others also means gaining a direct appreciation of cultural diversity, establishing new cultural ties, and helping to keep our cultural heritage alive and promote general economic development."[22]

## Environmental

The link between heritage buildings and the environmental component of sustainable development is perhaps less well documented. Yet, as with the economic prong, there is a strong environmental case for maintaining heritage buildings.

### Reduction of Construction Waste

In Hong Kong, the construction industry generates over 10 million tons of construction waste each year; taking up nearly 30 percent of landfill space.[23] While most countries, including Singapore, report declining trends in construction waste generation,[24] Hong Kong's continues to rise every year.[25] As the city is running out of landfills, this poses an increasingly challenging situation.

### Green Building

Discarding a building is discarding the energy used to construct it in the first place. Globally, as governments have simultaneously pushed for energy conservation as well as heritage conservation, the private sector has responded with ways to make existing buildings more energy efficient, while still conserving the character and physical fabric that are important in maintaining the building's significance. International research shows that rehabilitated historic buildings are almost always less consumptive of

---

19. ICOMOS, "Managing Tourism at Places of Heritage Significance, 1999," (October 1999), https://www.icomos.org/en/newsletters-archives/179-articles-en-francais/ressources/charters-and-standards/162-international-cultural-tourism-charter.

20. World Tourism Organization, *Tourism and Culture Synergies* (Madrid: UNWTO, 2018).

21. World Travel & Tourism Council, *Travel & Tourism Economic Impact 2017* (2017).

22. UNESCO Director-General, *Culture Urban Future*.

23. "Waste Data & Statistics," Environmental Protection Department, Government of Hong Kong SAR, last modified April 27, 2018, https://www.wastereduction.gov.hk/en/assistancewizard/waste_red_sat.htm.

24. Vivian Wing-Yan Tam and Weisheng Lu, "Construction Waste Management Profiles, Practices, and Performance: A Cross-Jurisdictional Analysis in Four Countries," *Sustainability* 8, no. 2 (2016): article no. 190.

25. Environmental Protection Department, *Reuse, Reduction and Recycle of Construction and Demolition Waste* (Hong Kong: Environment Bureau, 2011).

energy than new "green" buildings.[26] Especially in Asia's tropical climates, buildings that predate air conditioning demonstrate ways to achieve greater modern energy efficiency. With shaded façades, thick walls, high ceilings, and ingenious cross ventilation, they were built to keep air circulating and heat out. Hong Kong's revitalized police station in Tai Po won the city's Green Building Award in 2016, for conserving such traditional approaches to air flow and energy efficiency, as well as for serving as a model for other buildings throughout Hong Kong and the region.[27]

## The Three Prongs of Sustainable Urban Development Now Have a Fourth Sibling—Culture

With the New Urban Agenda (NUA) and Sustainable Development Goals (SDGs), culture is now increasingly recognized by international bodies as the fourth pillar of sustainable development (Fig. 3.1).[28] This is a relatively new field; it is only in recent years that scholars have started to explore the link between culture and the quality of the built environment.[29] One of the pioneers in this area, Alex Opoku of the University College London, says, "The cultural dimension of sustainability creates solid bridges with the other three dimensions of sustainable development. Culture is a key element in the concept of sustainable development as it frames people's relationships and attitudes towards the built and the natural environment."[30] A 2016 UNESCO report zooms in on the role of culture for sustainable urban development: "Culture is key to what makes cities attractive, creative and sustainable. History shows that culture is at the heart of urban development, evidenced through cultural landmarks, heritage and traditions."[31]

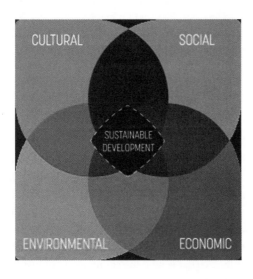

**Figure 3.1:** Culture as the fourth pillar of sustainable development. (Source: US ICOMOS.)

26. Mariela Alfonzo, *Older, Smaller, Better: Measuring How the Character of Buildings and Blocks Influences Urban Vitality* (Washington, DC: Preservation Green Lab in association with the National Trust for Historic Preservation, 2014).

27. "Green Building Award 2016 Award Presentation cum HKGBC 7th Anniversary," Hong Kong Green Building Council, last modified November 23, 2016, https://www2.hkgbc.org.hk/eng/gba_20161122.aspx.

28. Policy Statement on Culture as the Fourth Pillar of Sustainable Development was introduced in UNESCO's Universal Declaration on Cultural Diversity (2001) included in the Synthesis Report of the UN Secretary-General on the Post-2015 Agenda, and subsequently adopted by the Executive Bureau of United Cities and Local Governments (UCLG) in 2010 as part of the Local Agenda 21.

29. Alfonzo, *Older, Smaller, Better.*

30. Alex Opoku, "The Role of Culture in a Sustainable Built Environment," in *Marketing Strategy, Strategic Planning and Corporate Social Responsibility: An Exploratory Research* (Unites States: Springer International, 2015).

31. UNESCO, *Culture Urban Future.*

Yet cities across Asia are starting to look more and more alike. Old neighborhoods are razed to make way for more shopping malls and skyscrapers, often with very little cultural or architectural reference to what once was. Buildings are disappearing, and with them collective memories, personal stories, and urban identities. In this time of rapid urban change and globalization, redefining urban identity will be a major challenge, and preserving Asia's urban traditions and streetscapes may very well be the answer.

When cities lose their individuality, they become indistinguishable from one another. The damage is permanent, not short term. When one's city could as well be in Canada as in China, in Venezuela as in Vietnam, the citizens' sense of "this is my city" is dissipated. Regardless of the economic or political system, the rapid urbanization of Asia combined with the worldwide push for localization, as represented particularly in the NUA, reinforces the importance of place attachment. However, when a city's architecture, street patterns, public spaces, and urban character are indistinguishable from elsewhere, attachment becomes nearly impossible. The destruction of character-defining built heritage moves a city from being "somewhere" to being "anywhere." And the distance from anywhere to nowhere is short.

In economics it is the differentiated product that commands a monetary premium. The demolition of a city's heritage buildings is stealing from future generations not just their rightful legacy of earlier generations but also the opportunity to live in a differentiated and competitive city.

## Social

As global thinking about cultural heritage preservation progressively shifts away from built monuments toward intangible living heritage, the debate is increasingly about the value of preserving urban culture and heritage for people, urban communities, and society at large. The social facet of sustainable urban regeneration is further explored in the following section.

### Collective Memory and Sense of Belonging

From London to Mumbai to Sydney, most people value historic houses and consider a historic streetscape an important part of an area's character and identity.[32] Aesthetics, history, memory, and nostalgia all contribute to a sense of place. In the 1980s, when Singapore struggled to give its multicultural population a sense of belonging, it radically changed its urban renewal policy. As stated by the city's minister of education in an interview, "Singapore cannot just bulldoze and build as it embarks on its next 50 years. Instead it has to infuse the old with the new, to instill a strong sense of belonging in its people. . . . That is why the country cannot just focus on economics, but must also build history, memory, and identity. To foster that sense of belonging, it is important to preserve memories and heritage."[33]

Article 38 of the New Urban Agenda (NUA) specifically mentions "the leverage of natural and cultural heritage in cities and human settlements as a way to strengthen social participation and the exercise of citizenship."[34] Indeed, international

32. English Heritage, Gareth Maeer, Amelia Robinson, and Marie Hobson, eds., *Values and Benefits of Heritage: A Research Review* (London: Heritage Lottery Fund, April 2016); Michael Loveday, "Economic and Social Benefits of Heritage Preservation," (BBL presentation, World Bank, Washington, DC, March 18, 2010).
33. Minister of Education Ong Ye Kung quoted in Melissa Lin, "Important to Foster Sense of Belonging, Says Minister," *The Straits Times*, April 24, 2016.
34. United Nations General Assembly, *New Urban Agenda*.

evidence suggests that culture and heritage could be tools for policy makers as Asia's megacities struggle to find answers to issues of common identity and a sense of belonging among the millennial generation. For example, a selection of Hong Kong's newspaper headlines from 2018 shows growing social unrest: "Why Hong Kong Youth Struggle with Chinese Identity"; "Hong Kong's Identity Crisis: Hongkongers Confront Questions of Belonging"; and "Three in Ten HK Students Have an Issue with Identity."[35] The city's identity is a much-debated topic, and for Hong Kong's chief executive, Carrie Lam Cheng Yuet-ngor, a prime policy concern. In her acceptance speech in 2017, she said, "Hong Kong, our home, is suffering from quite a serious divisiveness, it is my top priority to heal it." Worldwide, heritage preservation and revitalization of old neighborhoods are increasingly used as tools for community building and linking a new generation with an older one: "The buildings and the landscape ensure that our quality of life is improved and that community cohesion is maintained."[36] Moreover, these initiatives "often provide social benefits through community involvement and raising the community's awareness of its heritage, which are especially valuable in understanding contemporary multicultural urban societies and celebrating exclusive collective identities."[37]

## Urban Livability and Community Resilience

Cultural heritage buildings in cities are often local landmarks that people identify with, such as churches and temples, commercial and government buildings, and schools and universities. However, residential buildings, small shops, or even streetscapes can be defining elements for the character of a place. Old neighborhoods hold values that are perhaps not directly measurable in monetary terms but do enhance the long-term well-being of residents.[38] Place-making researchers consistently mention four factors when it comes to defining what "makes a great place": human scale that people can relate to, a healthy mix of culture and commerce, easy access by different modes of transport, and sociable places where people can meet each other.[39] Historical neighborhoods often contain all these elements—street pavements made for walking, easily accessible communal spaces, a comfortable coexistence of residential and commercial functions, and a vibrancy that is difficult to replicate and often lost in skyscraper cities. In this way, cultural heritage assets contribute to urban livability.

As the famous American philosopher Wallace Stegner once said, "If you don't know where you are, you don't know who you are."[40] Research in the United States and Europe shows that a strong sense of place makes people relate to their surroundings more easily and, as a result, care more and even invest more in maintaining it.[41] It therefore comes as no surprise that after natural disasters the first place people gather, the first set of buildings that get renovated are those that matter to the local community—the libraries, temples, and town halls. In fact, recent research explores the explicit role of cultural heritage as a tool for building urban resilience.[42]

35. *South China Morning Post*, November 12, 2016, and April 19, 2018; *EJ Insight*, April 2018, respectively.
36. Thompson M. Mayes, *Why Old Places Matter: How Historic Places Affect Our Identity and Well-being* (Lanham, MD: Rowman & Littlefield, 2018).
37. UNESCO Museum International, *The Social Benefits of Heritage, Museum International*, LXIII (63), 1–2/249–250 (2011), https://unesdoc.unesco.org/ark:/48223/pf0000216604.
38. Patricia Montemurri, "Using Tactical Preservation to Revive Neighbourhoods," *Urban Land*, August 10, 2018, https://urbanland.uli.org/economy-markets-trends/using-tactical-preservation-to-revive-neighborhoods-outside-downtown-detroit/.
39. Project for Public Spaces, "What Makes a Successful Place?," accessed January 25, 2019, https://www.pps.org/article/grplacefeat.
40. Wallace Stegner, *The Sense of Place* (Madison: Wisconsin Humanities Committee, 1986).
41. Ed MacMahon, "The Power of Uniqueness," *Forum Journal* 29, no. 3 (2015): 63.
42. ICOMOS and International Scientific Committee for Risk Preparedness, *Heritage and Resilience: Issues*

## Heritage—A Shared Responsibility

In many Asian cities, heritage policies are outdated, as they were put in place at a time when economic growth and expansion were the priorities, including building more infrastructure, more housing, more offices, and bigger shopping centers. As a result, heritage-related legislation is typically limited to a narrow definition of built heritage of architectural or historic significance, revealing a lack of understanding of what constitutes heritage. Such protective and reactive legislation offers few carrots among the sticks. For example, the Hong Kong Antiquities and Monuments Ordinance, much like its name, is an "antique." It was enacted in 1976, and there have been only minor amendments since that time.

In addition, the public bodies associated with heritage often have limited executive powers and are confined to the cultural area. The Antiquities and Monuments Office (AMO) in Hong Kong is a case in point. First, it is a relatively low-level government body and, therefore, lacks the power to lead and influence other departments in the government bureaucracy. This is particularly challenging for its Antiquities Advisory Board, as it provides advice to other bodies under statutory provision, but there is no obligation to take that advice. Even worse, the grading system is inadequate; unlike Declared Monuments, Graded Historic Buildings are not subject to statutory protection. Therefore, any privately-owned building of historic value can be demolished.

Heritage is no longer the domain of architects, archaeologists, and historians. For example, Shanghai's Excellent Historical Building Protection Committee of Experts, which was established in 2004, includes people from various fields, such as architecture, branding, cultural relics, economics, history, marketing, planning, and real estate. Among the twenty members, only six are government officials.[43]

Heritage is much more than just publicly listed monuments. It is big office buildings, bridges, industrial warehouses, military barracks, open squares, residential buildings, small shops, streetscapes, and tunnels, very little of it publicly owned. For example, Singapore has given conservation status to more than 7,000 buildings in more than one hundred areas.[44] Shanghai, meanwhile, after decades of "constructive destruction," has gone full circle and started to appreciate its heritage once more. The city now has 4,500 historic alleys, areas, buildings, districts, monuments, and sites—of which more than 1,000 are listed—and all the listed buildings must be strictly protected and cannot be demolished.[45] This includes former industrial buildings, garden villas, and lane dwellings. The list is regularly updated, with the last additions made as recently as 2017. By comparison, Hong Kong has only 120 Declared Monuments and 1,444 Graded Historic Buildings,[46] of which more than a third (479) are Grade 3, "buildings of some merit," which in the urban reality often means a green flag for redevelopment.[47]

In the coming decades, urban heritage will need to become a shared responsibility beyond the domain of archaeologists, cultural officers, and historians. It will need to become an integral part of the job of city planners, place makers, and urban

---

*and Opportunities for Reducing Disaster Risks* (Switzerland: UN Office for Disaster Risk Reduction, 2013).

43. Xiaohua Zhong and Xiangming Chen, "Demolition, Rehabilitation, and Conservation: Heritage in Shanghai's Urban Regeneration 1990–2015," *Journal of Architecture and Urbanism* 41 (2017): 82–91.

44. Architectural Conservation Programmes, HKU and Centre for Architectural Heritage Research, CUHK, *Consultancy Study on the Heritage Conservation Regimes in Other Jurisdictions* (Hong Kong: Development Bureau, Government of Hong Kong SAR, 2014).

45. Zhong and Chen, "Demolition, Rehabilitation, and Conservation," 82–91.

46. These figures are cited as of June 2019.

47. Cecilia Chu and Kylie Uebergang, *Saving Hong Kong's Cultural Heritage* (Hong Kong: Civic Exchange, 2002).

designers. They will need to understand and articulate the values and relevance of heritage in today's urban context and will need to include culture as a priority component in building codes, coastal management policies, strategic development policies, urban plans and strategies, and zoning guidelines.

This means that Asia's urban heritage policies need a refocus. As already stated, more carrots are required among the sticks and a more proactive approach is the need of the hour. Singapore and Macau are examples of governments that provide fiscal incentives not only to owners of historic buildings but also to the companies that set up businesses within those buildings.[48] These two cities have also built in a mechanism for the government to claim preferential right to acquire monuments or even expropriate historic properties when the situation calls for it.

## Short-Term Financial Viability versus Long-Term Economic Impact of Urban Regeneration

In Asia's competitive land and real estate markets, meaningful discussions about culture and heritage must include a discussion of economic value. Demolition and new built are the norm, and one cannot fault property owners for considering redevelopment as the most viable option. To renovate an old building without being able to increase plot ratio is simply not an attractive development proposition in a context of soaring land and property prices.

That is the case if one looks at financial return from an investment in the short term; however, if one looks at the cultural, economic, environmental, and social returns on an investment in the long term, the value proposition is undeniable. Feasibility studies convincingly show that historic towns, historic districts, and the historic parts of cities are valued for their uniqueness and sense of place.[49] They attract employment, local investment, and tourism. They create a distinctive place that people can relate to and that makes them feel comfortable, places where people want to live, play, work, and spend their money.

A 2014 World Heritage Institute Study in Shanghai, based on the latest UNESCO Historic Urban Landscape approach, assessed the feasibility of revitalizing, preserving, and protecting eight Shanghai *lilong* (low-rise alley housing complexes built in the late nineteenth and early twentieth centuries). Even though the old buildings were not necessarily of outstanding architectural value, the benefits were found to include long-term cultural, environmental, and social factors.[50] The short-term financial cost-benefit analysis justified tearing down the buildings and replacing them with forty-story condominiums, but when the long-term economic impact was factored in, the entire equation changed, and protection of the *lilong* could be justified.

It may be hard to find owners and developers of individual properties with such a long-term vision, and this is where the government needs to step in. In recent years, there have been examples of boutique developers who sought a specific demographic or family firms with a historic interest in a building; however, this is not the norm. It is the government's responsibility (ideally, with community input) to create a vision to revive a city's older neighborhoods using a value proposition that works both ways—a positive return on investment for owners and developers and a livable community for residents, while being respectful of the historic streetscape.

---

48. Carine Lai, *Treating the Symptoms: A Critical Review of the URA in Hong Kong* (Hong Kong: Civic Exchange, 2013).
49. Mayes, *Why Old Places Matter*.
50. World Heritage Institute for Training and Research in Asia and the Pacific, based at Tongji University in Shanghai in collaboration with Heritage Strategies International.

Shanghai has a designated Urban Regeneration Implementation Unit under the Shanghai municipal government. In Singapore, heritage conservation is an integral part of the Urban Redevelopment Authority (URA), the city's planning agency. Yet, in Hong Kong, the Urban Renewal Authority (URA) is often perceived as "just another developer" operating on a for-profit basis.[51] Hong Kong's URA has even been referred to as "a cosmetic attempt to patch up the physical manifestations of market failure."[52]

## Area-Based Regeneration: A Tool for the Future

Looking at the adaptive reuse of individual properties, it is sometimes difficult to make the financial feasibility work. In addition, individual projects may keep the story of one building alive, but if they are not connected to a larger context, they do not create value for the city as a whole. This is a problem. For example, in Hong Kong, the Cattle Depot Artist Village (further elaborated in the Industrial case study section), a former slaughterhouse and now a creative center in To Kwa Wan, is not connected to the neighborhood and the local community. Worse yet, Murray House, which once stood in Central Hong Kong as part of the cantonment, was dismantled and supposedly rebuilt stone by stone in Stanley, a village on the southern end of the island. No longer a quarters for officers, it currently offers visitors a selection of restaurants, among other things. Its "fit" within Stanley is debatable.[53]

There is an old cliché that the three most important things in real estate are "location, location, location." But the economic value of property does not emerge just from the location of the building's four walls; it comes from the broader context (economic, physical, political, and social) within which that building exists. That is why most sustained success stories in heritage-based revitalization are not about the restoration of a single building but an area-wide strategy that benefits all building owners.[54]

Experience shows that area-based schemes with a clear vision and fair rules, free of unnecessary restrictions, can create attractive value propositions whereby developers, public or private, are keen to participate. In Singapore, establishing conservation areas has been successful in preserving historic districts and areas of special character, such as Chinatown, Kampong Glam, and Little India.[55] Another Asian success story in area-based revitalization is Xintiandi in Shanghai's French Concession, a quarter with a high concentration of old houses in distinctive *shikumen*-style—two- or three-story brick townhouses typical for Shanghai in the early twentieth century. The run-down houses were perhaps not of significant heritage value individually, but because the approach was both to adaptively reuse some structures and to protect a large area, the neighborhood became attractive for significant investment by both the public and private sectors.[56] Critics will argue it has gentrified the area, yet its significance in protecting aspects of urban heritage is undeniable. Since its completion in 2002, it

51. A statement acknowledged by then-secretary for development Carrie Lam at a July 2009 presentation to the Royal Institute of Chartered Surveyors.
52. Hong Kong Legislator Christine Loh on the URA bill in 2007 quoted in Lai, *Treating the Symptoms.*
53. Debate on Murray House featured on HK Institute of Architects, *Liberal Studies Teaching Kit fir Senior Secondary Cirruculum: Hong Kong Today: Conservation & Revitalization of Historic Buildings [Teacher's Notes]* (Hong Kong: Commissioner for Heritage's Office, 2012), accessed April 3, 2020, http://minisite.proj.hkedcity.net/hkiakit/getResources.html?id=3629; Chu and Uebergang, *Saving Hong Kong's Cultural Heritage.*
54. Rypkema, *The Economics of Historic Preservation.*
55. Architectural Conservation Programmes, HKU and Centre for Architectural Heritage Research, CUHK, *Consultancy Study.*
56. Zhong and Chen, "Demolition, Rehabilitation, and Conservation," 82–91.

has triggered revitalization projects in other areas—projects with the primary aim of developing vibrant districts that are attractive to tourists and foreign investment.

## A Holistic Approach to Unlock the Full Value of Cultural Heritage

In Shanghai and Singapore, conservation has become an integral part of the planning process, tailored to the cities' unique characteristics. Yet, in Hong Kong, among many government departments and construction industry players, conservation is still largely seen as an obstacle to development, not part of it.[57] A number of studies have been done, both solicited and unsolicited, on how Hong Kong can press for more comprehensive and transparent conservation legislation and a holistic approach to the discipline.[58]

Following the New Urban Agenda (NUA) principles, the essential ingredients to make heritage a true driver of sustainable development are (1) a dedicated multidisciplinary unit with a long-term social mandate that sits within in an urban development agency, (2) broadened protective measures not just for buildings but also streetscapes, and (3) an area-based approach to heritage conservation. One can only hope that some of these recommendations will be taken on board as the topic resurfaces as a priority area for the current administration in Hong Kong and to help build the business case for heritage-led urban regeneration in other cities throughout Asia.

## Bibliography

Alfonzo, Mariela. *Older, Smaller, Better: Measuring How the Character of Buildings and Blocks Influences Urban Vitality*. Washington, DC: Preservation Green Lab in association with the National Trust for Historic Preservation, 2014.

Architectural Conservation Programmes, HKU, and Centre for Architectural Heritage Research, CUHK. *Consultancy Study on the Heritage Conservation Regimes in Other Jurisdictions*. Hong Kong: Development Bureau, Government of Hong Kong SAR, 2014.

Avrami, E. C. "Cultural Heritage Conservation and Sustainable Building: Converging Agendas." *Industrial Ecology* (December 2004): 1–15.

BPF, Deloitte Real Estate, Historic England, and RICS. *Heritage Works: A Toolkit of Best Practice in Heritage Regeneration*. Swindon, Historic England: Colourhouse, 2017. https://www.bpf.org.uk/sites/default/files/resources/Heritage-Works-14July2017-for-web.pdf.

Cities Development Initiative for Asia. *Heritage Works: A Pilot Urban Regeneration Study in Yangon Final Report*. 2016.

Chu, Cecilia, and Kylie Uebergang. *Saving Hong Kong's Cultural Heritage*. Hong Kong: Civic Exchange, 2002.

English Heritage, Gareth Maeer, Amelia Robinson, and Marie Hobson, eds. *Values and Benefits of Heritage: A Research Review*. London: Heritage Lottery Fund, April 2016.

Environmental Protection Department. *Reuse, Reduction and Recycle of Construction and Demolition Waste*. Hong Kong: Environment Bureau, 2011.

Environmental Protection Department. "Waste Data & Statistics." Last modified April 27, 2018. https://www.wastereduction.gov.hk/en/assistancewizard/waste_red_sat.htm.

---

57. Lai, *Treating the Symptoms*.
58. Some examples include Chu and Uebergang, *Saving Hong Kong's Cultural Heritage*; Michael Yu, *Built Heritage Conservation Policy in Selected Places* (Hong Kong: Research and Library Services Division Legislative Council Secretariat, 2008); Lai, *Treating the Symptoms*; GHK (Hong Kong) Ltd., *Study on the Feasibility, Framework and Implementation Plan for Setting up a Statutory Heritage Trust in Hong Kong* (Hong Kong: Development Bureau, Government of Hong Kong SAR, 2013); Architectural Conservation Programmes, HKU and Centre for Architectural Heritage Research, CUHK, *Consultancy Study*.

Getty Conservation Institute. *Economics and Heritage Conservation*. Los Angeles: Getty Conservation Institute, 1998.

GHK (Hong Kong) Ltd. *Study on the Feasibility, Framework and Implementation Plan for Setting Up a Statutory Heritage Trust in Hong Kong*. Hong Kong: Development Bureau, Government of Hong Kong SAR, 2013.

Habib, Anmaar Javed, and Joshua D. Bevan. "GIS Mapping of Relationships between Cultural Heritage and Creative Industries." In *A Geospatial Analysis of the Intersection between Historic Fabric and the Creative Economy*, edited by Donovan D. Rypkema and Hristina Mikić, 65. Belgrade, Serbia: Creative Economy Group Foundation and Penn Design Studio, 2016.

Hong Kong Green Building Council. "Green Building Award 2016 Award Presentation cum HKGBC 7th Anniversary." Last modified November 23, 2016. https://www.hkgbc.org.hk/eng/news/press_201601123.aspx.

Hong Kong Institute of Architects. *Conservation & Revitalization of Historic Buildings: A Liberal Studies Teaching Kit*. Hong Kong: Commissioner of Heritage's Office, 2012. Accessed April 3, 2020. http://minisite.proj.hkedcity.net/hkiakit/getResources.html?id=3629.

ICOMOS and International Scientific Committee for Risk Preparedness. *Heritage and Resilience: Issues and Opportunities for Reducing Disaster Risks*. Geneva, Switzerland: United Nations Office for Disaster Reduction (UNISDR), 2013.

Jamieson, Walter. "Cultural Heritage Tourism Planning and Development: Defining the Field and Its Challenges." *APT Bulletin* 29, no. 3/4, Thirtieth Anniversary Issue (1998): 65–67.

Lai, Carine. *Treating the Symptoms: A Critical Review of the URA in Hong Kong*. Hong Kong: Civic Exchange, 2013.

Licciardi, Guido, and Rana Amirtahmasebi. *The Economics of Uniqueness: Investing in Historic City Cores and Cultural Assets for Sustainable Development*. Washington, DC: World Bank, 2012.

Lichfield, N. *Economics in Urban Conservation*. Cambridge: Cambridge University Press, 1988.

Loveday, Michael. "Economic and Social Benefits of Heritage Preservation." BBL presentation, World Bank, Washington, DC, March 18, 2010.

MacMahon, Ed. "The Power of Uniqueness." *Forum Journal* 29, no. 3 (2015): 63.

Mason, R. "Assessing Values in Conservation Planning: Methodological Issues and Choices." In *Assessing the Values of Cultural Heritage: Research Report*, edited by M. De La Torre. Los Angeles: Getty Conservation Institute, 2002.

Mayes, Thompson M. *Why Old Places Matter: How Historic Places Affect Our Identity and Well-Being*. Lanham, MD: Rowman & Littlefield, 2018.

Montemurri, Patricia. "Using Tactical Preservation to Revive Neighbourhoods." *Urban Land*, August 10, 2018. https://urbanland.uli.org/economy-markets-trends/using-tactical-preservation-to-revive-neighborhoods-outside-downtown-detroit/.

Opoku, Alex. "The Role of Culture in a Sustainable Built Environment." In *Marketing Strategy, Strategic Planning and Corporate Social Responsibility: An Exploratory Research*, edited by Andrea Chiarini. Cham, Switzerland: Springer International, 2015.

Project for Public Spaces. "What Makes a Successful Place?" Accessed January 25, 2019. https://www.pps.org/article/grplacefeat.

Rypkema, Donovan D. *The Economics of Historic Preservation: A Community Leader's Guide*. Washington DC, United States: National Trust for Historic Preservation in the United States, 2005.

Rypkema, Donovan D., and Hristina Mikić. *Cultural Heritage and Creative Industries*. Belgrade, Serbia: Creative Economy Group Foundation and Penn Design Studio, 2016.

Stegner, Wallace. *The Sense of Place*. Madison: Wisconsin Humanities Committee, 1986.

Tam, Vivian Wing-Yan, and Weisheng Lu. "Construction Waste Management Profiles, Practices, and Performance: A Cross-Jurisdictional Analysis in Four Countries." *Sustainability* 8, no. 2 (2016): article no. 190.

Throsby, D. "Conceptualising Heritage as Cultural Capital." In *Heritage Economics*, edited by P. King, 7–14. Canberra: Australian Heritage Commission, 2001.

United Nations. The Creative Economy Report 2008: *The Challenge of Assessing the Creative Economy; Towards Informed Policy-Making*. UNCTAD/DITC/2008/2 (2008). https://unctad.org/en/Docs/ditc20082cer_en.pdf.

United Nations. *Tracking Progress towards Inclusive, Safe, Resilient and Sustainable Cities and Human Settlements: SDG 11 Synthesis Report—High Level Political Forum 2018*. July 2018. https://unhabitat.org/sdg-11-synthesis-report/.

United Nations General Assembly. *The Road to Dignity by 2030: Ending Poverty, Transforming All Lives and Protecting the Planet*. Synthesis report of the Secretary-General on the post-2015 agenda. A/69/700. December 2014. https://www.un.org/en/development/desa/publications/files/2015/01/SynthesisReportENG.pdf.

United Nations General Assembly. *Transforming Our World: The 2030 Agenda for Sustainable Development*. A/RES/70/1. October 21, 2015. https://www.un.org/ga/search/view_doc.asp?symbol=A/RES/70/1&Lang=E.

United Nations Habitat. New Urban Agenda. A/RES/71/256. October, 2016. http://habitat3.org/the-new-urban-agenda/.

UNESCO. *Culture: A Driver and an Enabler of Sustainable Development*. Thematic think piece. 2012. http://www.unesco.org/new/fileadmin/MULTIMEDIA/HQ/post2015/pdf/Think_Piece_Culture.pdf.

UNESCO Director-General. *Culture Urban Future: Global Report on Culture for Sustainable Urban Development*. CLT-2016/WS/18. 2016.

UNESCO Museum International. *The Social Benefits of Heritage, Museum International*. LXIII (63), 1–2/249–250. 2011. https://unesdoc.unesco.org/ark:/48223/pf0000216604.

World Travel & Tourism Council. *Travel & Tourism Economic Impact 2017*. 2017.

World Tourism Organization. *Tourism and Culture Synergies*. Madrid: UNWTO 2018.

Yu, Michael. *Built Heritage Conservation Policy in Selected Places*. Hong Kong: Research and Library Services Division Legislative Council Secretariat, 2008.

Zhong, Xiaohua, and Xiangming Chen. "Demolition, Rehabilitation, and Conservation: Heritage in Shanghai's Urban Regeneration 1990–2015." *Journal of Architecture and Urbanism* 41 (2017): 82–91.

# Measuring the Impacts: Making a Case for the Adaptive Reuse of Heritage Buildings

Donovan Rypkema

## Introduction

In an ideal world, perhaps it would not be necessary to make a case for the adaptive reuse of heritage buildings. Decision makers in both the public and private sectors, including building owners, would simply recognize the importance and logic of reusing existing assets. But today, with public policy decisions often requiring quantitative justification and building owners rightfully expecting reasonable returns on their investments, the "do it because it's a heritage building" plea is often insufficient to spur appropriate action. It is frequently necessary to "prove" that adaptive reuse is a preferable course of action and that it can be done through the application of metrics—usually (although not always) quantitative measures demonstrating the positive impacts of adaptive reuse.

## Critical Variables for Metrics

These measurements are most useful when there are multiple metrics, some measuring the impacts within the building itself and others for the immediate surroundings. Also, some metrics apply to the private sector and others to the public sector. Which metrics are used depend on three variables: (1) what data are meaningful, (2) what data are reliable, and (3) what data are accessible. For data to be meaningful, they must bear a relationship—directly or indirectly—to the adaptive reuse project. For data to be reliable, it is necessary that there is a high degree of confidence that the numbers being used are objective and the method for collecting the data defensible. For the data to be accessible, an entity needs to collect the data and make them available for use in the analysis. Ideally, data are collected by a transparent government agency and kept consistently over time. However, sometimes data collected by universities, local business groups, foundations, institutions, or even private-sector corporations can meet the three tests of meaningful, reliable, and accessible. For most metrics, it is also necessary to collect the data over time. If the argument is being made that the adaptive reuse of a building resulted in positive change, then data before and after the project is completed need to be compared.

## *Internal Metrics*

Impacts that affect the adaptive reuse of the property itself are *internal metrics*. These will certainly affect the property owner but may impact the public sector as well. While the impacts to the owner will be primarily economic, the public-sector measurable impacts might be cultural, environmental, and social as well as economic.

### Private Internal Metrics

There are at least four ways that the impact of an adaptive reuse project may be measured to determine the impact on the property owner. First, regardless of what the owner has on his or her financial statement, a building that is empty or underutilized (as un-rehabilitated heritage buildings often are) can be a liability rather than an asset. While little or no revenue may be generated, there are still expenses in owning the building, including property taxes, insurance, security, and at least a minimum amount of maintenance. Adaptive reuse moves the building back into the asset column. Further, in real estate practice there is the concept of a building having two "lives," the remaining physical life of the structure and its remaining economic life. Remaining physical life is how much longer the building will last until it literally falls down. Remaining economic life is the number of future years that the building can produce a positive economic return. Often, unused heritage buildings are near the end of both lives. Adaptive reuse extends both the physical and economic lives of a building. This means building owners (and their bankers and investors) can look forward to long-term revenues from the asset.

The second measurement of internal return to the owner can be calculated through the change in the amount of cash flow. *Cash flow* is the amount of money remaining after (1) rents are collected (2) expenses of the building are paid, and (3) expenses of the financing (i.e., mortgage payments) are made. Any residual money is what flows to the owner and is a key measurement of return. Cash flow can be measured in the change of total cash-flow receipts, but it can also be measured as the rate of increased cash flow as a percentage of additional investment.

For example, consider an underutilized heritage building that is currently generating a cash flow of HK$100,000 per year. After revitalization, the building generates HK$500,000 per year. So, the impact to the owner is +HK$400,000 per year. However, assume that to revitalize the building an investment of HK$10,000,000 was required. This means the increased cash flow is providing a 4 percent return on the owner's multimillion-dollar investment (HK$400,000 ÷ HK$10,000,000).

Often, the end of economic life comes because of the functional obsolescence of the property. *Functional obsolescence* is a reduction in the utility or desirability of a building because (1) it was designed for a use that no longer exists; (2) the building layout is inefficient; or (3) the systems, such as electrical, heating, or plumbing, are outdated. Heritage buildings are frequently demolished because they are (or are claimed to be) "functionally obsolete." But adaptive reuse is the environmental and rational alternative response to functional obsolescence. At its most basic, adaptive reuse is the reinsertion of a new utility into a building that has lost its old utility. This is why many adaptive reuse projects are the conversion of, say, an antiquated industrial building into market-rate housing. Adaptive reuse is a possible cure for functional obsolescence.

Finally, an internal metric for the owner can be the overall *return on investment*. This can be approached in a manner similar to the metrics discussed above for measuring cash flow. The major differences are (1) a return on investment calculation is done on the entire investment, not just the new investment in rehabilitation; and (2) the return is measured on net operating income rather than cash flow. The difference between these two concepts is that cash flow is what remains after the expenses of the building *and* the mortgage payments are included; *net operating income* is the amount of receipts after the expenses of the building but *before* deducting mortgage payments. Technical distinctions aside, the questions are the same—is the *amount* of net operating income greater after the adaptive reuse investment, and is the *rate* of return greater after the adaptive reuse?

In many cases, these measurements are made before and after the adaptive reuse project has taken place. However, as a useful tool for heritage advocates, it is helpful to make these calculations based on reasonable assumptions and reliable numbers *before* the project happens. Indeed, it is usually necessary to make the case in advance for the owner or developer to proceed with adaptive reuse rather than demolition. The process of making these assumptions is called *pro forma analysis*.

### Public Internal Metrics

Frequently, there are metrics that demonstrate positive impacts to the public sector generated by the building project itself. Usually, these are tax-based benefits measured by tax generation during the adaptive reuse process and after the project is completed. Measurable public sector returns can include increases in the value added tax (VAT) collection, personal and corporate income taxes, and ad valorem taxes from the property in its post-rehabilitation condition. In many cities there are also enterprise funds—usually from public or quasi-public utility providers, such as electricity, water and sewer, and perhaps others. Vacant and underutilized buildings do not generate much in enterprise-fund receipt; adaptive reuse building projects generally do.

### Environmental Internal Metrics

In recent years, more and more research has been conducted on the environmental benefits of the adaptive reuse of heritage buildings. One of two such measurements is called *embodied energy*. The Australian government defines "embodied energy" as "the energy consumed by all of the processes associated with the production of a building, from the mining and processing of natural resources to manufacturing, transport and product delivery."[1] Thus, a building standing represents all of the embodied energy that was incorporated into its construction. To throw the building away is equivalent to throwing away that much energy. Calculations in the United States indicate that a 50,000–square foot (4,645–square meter) warehouse building represents 55,000 MBTU in embodied energy.

The other internal environmental metric is the impact on solid-waste landfills from demolition debris. In most parts of the world, between 25 percent and 40 percent of everything in a landfill is from construction debris, and much of that is generated by buildings that have been torn down.[2] Landfills are increasingly expensive, both financially and environmentally. Environmental economists in the United States have estimated that a 50,000–square foot warehouse, if demolished, would add 2,500 tons in construction debris to the local landfill.

1. Australian Government, "Embodied Energy," accessed May 11, 2018, http://www.yourhome.gov.au/materials/embodied-energy.
2. Joseph Cronyn and Evans Paull, "Heritage Tax Credits: Maryland's Own Stimulus to Renovate Buildings for Productive Use and Create Jobs, an $8.53 Return on Every State Dollar Invested," *Abell Report* 22, no. 1 (March 2009): 1.

## Social Internal Metrics

A building sitting vacant or underutilized also has the potential of having negative social impacts. On the public safety side, this means a greater risk of fire and building collapse. Vacant buildings are also often the location of illegal occupancy as well as nefarious activities, such as drug dealing, prostitution, and the sale of stolen and illegal goods. In addition, there is the cultural loss—current and future—of a heritage building in a deteriorating condition. The adaptive reuse and subsequent occupancy of a deteriorating heritage building significantly reduces or eliminates most of these negative social consequences.

## *External Metrics*

While many of the internal metrics of an adaptive reuse project impact the owner of the property, nearly all of the external metrics affect others—nearby property and business owners, local taxing authorities, and the public at large. There are ways to measure the impact of an adaptive reuse project beyond the boundaries of the property itself. The economic term for these impacts is *externalities*. Listed below are six examples of possible metrics for ascertaining the external impacts of an adaptive reuse project, along with possible data sources:

+ Adjacent property values. There are few variables that have a larger negative impact on the value of nearby properties than proximity to an empty and deteriorating building. Even a vacant heritage building can depress the values of neighboring buildings. Conversely, adaptive reuse projects can often increase the value of properties in the immediate area. If the local jurisdiction levies property taxes, the properties upon which the taxes are paid are probably assigned some value. As value goes up, so do property taxes. This is known as *ad valorem* taxation. Because there needs to be some basis of taxation, local authorities should have a permanent record of the valuation assigned to each property in a given area over time. These records can demonstrate the change in value of adjacent property values before and after an adaptive reuse project. Alternatively, local real estate brokers may be able to provide data on sales in the area over a period of time through which a rate of value change before and after an adaptive reuse project can be calculated.
+ Business licenses. One of the common results of an adaptive reuse project, particularly within a commercial district, is an increase in business activity in the area. Many municipalities require obtaining a business license to operate in the formal economy. Historical records of the number of outstanding business licenses before and after an adaptive reuse project can be an excellent impact metric.
+ Occupancy rates. Most businesses want to be near other active businesses. When one storefront or an entire building is vacant, there is a greater risk there will be more vacancies in the area. Conversely, when an empty building becomes redeveloped, vacancy rates in nearby buildings often fall. Some cities systematically track vacancies, and this data is an excellent indicator of whether an adaptive reuse project positively affected occupancy rates in its immediate vicinity. Some commercial districts have a business association or merchants' group that tracks vacancies, which can be a useful data source as well.
+ Rents. There are, of course, some potentially negative impacts of rising rents. But rents are also an indicator of the desirability of an area and the underlying demand for space in a neighborhood. All things being equal, rising

rents are both an indicator of increasing demand for space in an area and an expression of confidence in the future of the location. Real estate brokers, real estate appraisers, and property managers may have data on rent levels in the neighborhood over a number of years. A change in the rate at which rents are increasing before and after an adaptive reuse project can be a good indicator that the project has increased business confidence in the future of the area.

+ Building permits. Adaptive reuse projects often spur additional nearby activity in both new construction and additional adaptive reuse projects. This is because the demonstrated success of one project reduces the risk level for subsequent projects. It might be possible to look at the number of building permits issued two or three years before an adaptive reuse project was completed and two or three years afterward, to see whether an adaptive reuse project was a catalyst for additional investment.

+ Crime. It is not unusual to see the level of criminal activity higher in areas with large numbers of vacant buildings. Local police departments nearly always keep track of the number and nature of crimes and their locations. They may be willing to provide this data. When it is available, crime data can be a very useful metric demonstrating an important additional public benefit achieved in part because of an adaptive reuse project.

## Metrics without Numbers

The metrics listed above—both internal and external—can be helpful in making the case for adaptive reuse. Most are dependent, however, on data that is meaningful, reliable, and accessible. In much of the world, however, this data is not available. Are there alternatives to demonstrate the positive impacts of an adaptive reuse project? There are two that might serve as a more qualitative substitute when the data for quantitative measures does not exist or is not accessible.

The first is survey based. While they can be time consuming and labor intensive, surveys of those affected by a project could give some indication of the project's impact. Among those that might be surveyed are residents of the area; businesses both in and near the project, owners of other properties in the area, and customers and visitors to the area, among others. However, care must be given to the wording of the surveys so that the results will be seen as credible.

The second is a periodic visual survey of the area. This can indicate a positive (or negative) change in the area over time based on photographs. Ideally, the survey should include 100 percent of the buildings in the immediate area (perhaps three or four square blocks) of an adaptive reuse project and start one or two years before the project begins and continue for one or two years after its completion. Even if no quantitative data is available, such a photographic survey would indicate changes in occupancy levels, buildings' conditions, quality and quantity of businesses, and other potential factors.

## Conclusion

It is insufficient to claim "adaptive reuse makes sense." Advocates for adaptive reuse need to demonstrate that this is indeed the case. Two or three metrics based on reliable data and collected for a reasonable amount of time before and after the project can provide the basis for effectively advocating for adaptive reuse and the policies that would support it. This can be helpful in garnering support from property owners, government officials, and other institutions in the community.

# Bibliography

Australian Government. "Embodied Energy." Accessed May 11, 2018. http://www.
      yourhome.gov.au/materials/embodied-energy.

Cronyn, Joseph, and Evans Paull. "Heritage Tax Credits: Maryland's Own Stimulus to Ren-
      ovate Buildings for Productive Use and Create Jobs, an $8.53 Return on Every State
      Dollar Invested." *Abell Report* 22, no. 1 (March 2009): 1.

# Adaptive Reuse and Regional Best Practice

Lavina Ahuja

## Introduction

While examining the adaptive reuse of heritage places in the three urban centers, Hong Kong, Shanghai, and Singapore, it is also worthwhile to scale down and reposition them within a larger regional context. With an increasing number of adaptive reuse projects being completed in these Asian metropolises, a heightened emphasis is laid on quality instead of quantity. Regional best practices in built heritage conservation and adaptive reuse can be identified and showcased through the UNESCO Asia-Pacific Awards for Cultural Heritage Conservation (Heritage Awards, for short). Established in 2000 by the Culture Unit of UNESCO Bangkok, Asia-Pacific Regional Bureau for Education, the Heritage Awards program is the only initiative of its kind in the region, in terms of recognition and outreach.

This chapter briefly outlines the UNESCO Heritage Awards program as well as its categories and criteria. The awards program is examined as an indicator of conservation best practice. Award-winning projects from the three centers are discussed as examples to articulate the evolution of adaptive reuse in the region, with brief concluding notes on the impact of the awards in Asia and beyond.

## Structure of the Heritage Awards

As the only United Nations agency with a mandate in culture, UNESCO's efforts toward encouraging sustainable cultural heritage management are evident through its various programs and initiatives at international, regional, and national levels. As the organization's flagship strategy in built heritage conservation, the annual Heritage Awards program demonstrates how to sustain and enhance cultural heritage sites through good conservation practice.

Across the Asia-Pacific region, cultural heritage sites are under threat, and a number of these sites are in the hands of private or civic owners. The Heritage Awards program is an initiative to recognize private-sector achievements and public-private partnerships in conserving such sites. It is also a means to inspire and mobilize the private sector to prioritize conservation by disseminating a higher recognition of the value of heritage.

The Heritage Awards have two categories, Award for Cultural Heritage Conservation and Award for New Design in Heritage Contexts (renamed from Jury Commendation for Innovation in 2011). The winning projects of the Award for Cultural Heritage Conservation are selected on the basis of eleven criteria, which can be broadly understood under the three umbrellas of (1) understanding the place, (2) technical achievement, and (3) social and policy impact.[1] Winning projects receive Awards of Excellence, Distinction, Merit, or Honourable Mention (Award of Excellence being the highest category) based on the extent to which they exemplify the various criteria.

Established in 2005, the Award for New Design in Heritage Contexts recognizes newly built structures that demonstrate outstanding design well integrated into historic contexts that enhance the historic character of the place and contribute to its cultural continuum.[2] Winning projects are selected based on the understanding and articulation of the category's eight criteria that are expressed through design interventions.

The year 2019 marks twenty years of the Heritage Awards. Over this period, the program has acknowledged a diverse range of approaches to conservation practice and the adaptive reuse of heritage places. During these two decades, the awards program has received 777 entries from twenty-seven countries and recognized 247 winning projects (228 recipients in the Award for Cultural Heritage Conservation category and nineteen recipients in the New Design in Heritage Contexts category).[3] These annual awards are selected by a panel of international jury members chaired by UNESCO. The jury panel is comprised of conservation experts representing various nationalities across the region with in-depth knowledge in specialized fields, such as intangible cultural heritage, materials and techniques of conservation, modern architecture, and traditional craftsmanship, among others. The sheer number of award-winning projects represents the influence of the awards in the evolving trend of conservation and adaptive reuse in the Asia-Pacific region. Winning projects have become models for best practice, predicated on the framework of the Heritage Awards and validated by professional practice in the region and beyond.

## Adaptive Reuse and Conservation Best Practice

The validity of UNESCO's Heritage Awards as a standard for conservation best practice can be traced by the number of entries received each year and the nature of award-winning projects. Although the first five years of the awards saw a noteworthy number of museum adaptive reuse projects,[4] there were also outstanding examples that deviated from this conventional approach. In the inaugural cycle of the Heritage Awards, the Award for Most Excellent project (now known as the Award of Excellence) was given to Cheong Fatt Tze Mansion (in Penang, Malaysia), a boutique hotel adapted from a Chinese-style mansion. The project was celebrated for the high-quality restoration of the historic building while infusing it with a new purpose that upholds the spirit of the place. The restoration and adaptive reuse of Cheong Fatt Tze Mansion pioneered a conservation movement in Penang and over time the project has become a model for conservation best practice.

The three urban centers forming the focus of this book (Hong Kong, Shanghai, and Singapore) have been recognized by UNESCO's Heritage Awards through various award-winning projects over the last twenty years, as also mentioned in their individual chapters in this book. The award-winning projects in each of the three centers are summarized in the Table 5.1 with a brief description of their conservation interventions.

1. UNESCO Bangkok, "About the Awards," Asia-Pacific Heritage Awards, accessed November 22, 2019, https://bangkok.unesco.org/content/about-awards.
2. UNESCO Bangkok, "About the Awards."
3. UNESCO Bangkok, "Winning Projects," Asia-Pacific Heritage Awards, accessed November 22, 2019, https://bangkok.unesco.org/content/winning-projects.
4. William Chapman, "Determining Appropriate Use," in *Asia Conserved: Lessons Learned from the UNESCO Asia-Pacific Awards for Cultural Heritage Conservation (2000–2004)*, ed. Richard A. Engelhardt (Bangkok: UNESCO, 2007), 13–20.

**Table 5.1:** List of projects recognized by the UNESCO Heritage Awards in Hong Kong, Shanghai, and Singapore.

| | | Hong Kong | |
|---|---|---|---|
| Year | Heritage Award | Project | Conservation intervention |
| 2000 | Outstanding Project | Hung Shing Old Temple | Restoration of a Chinese temple |
| 2000 | Outstanding Project | Ohel Leah Synagogue | Restoration of a synagogue |
| 2001 | Award of Merit | King Law Ka Shuk Temple | Restoration of a Chinese temple |
| 2003 | Award of Merit | Catholic Cathedral of the Immaculate Conception | Restoration of a cathedral |
| 2005 | Award of Merit | St. Joseph's Chapel | Restoration of a chapel |
| 2005 | Award of Merit | Tung Wah Coffin Home | Restoration of a cultural institution |
| 2006 | Award of Merit | St. Andrew's Church | Restoration of a church |
| 2006 | Honourable Mention | Liu Ying Lung Study Hall | Restoration of a Chinese-style study hall |
| 2007 | Award of Merit | Little Hong Kong | Adaptive reuse of a military facility as a wine cellar |
| 2007 | Jury Commendation for Innovation | Whitfield Barracks | Adaptive reuse of two barrack blocks as a heritage center |
| 2008 | Honourable Mention | Béthanie | Adaptive reuse of a religious building as an educational institute |
| 2009 | Honourable Mention | Academy of Visual Arts (Former Royal Air Force Officers' Mess) | Adaptive reuse of an officers' mess as a university facility |
| 2011 | Honourable Mention | SCAD Hong Kong* | Adaptive reuse of a magistracy building as an educational institute |
| 2013 | Award of Merit | Tai O Heritage Hotel* | Adaptive reuse of a police station as a boutique hotel |
| 2015 | Award of Distinction | Saltpans of Yim Tin Tsai | Restoration of traditional saltpans |
| 2015 | Honourable Mention | YHA Mei Ho House Youth Hostel* | Adaptive reuse of a public housing building as a youth hostel |
| 2016 | Honourable Mention | Old Tai Po Police Station* | Adaptive reuse of a police station as a center for sustainable living |
| 2017 | Award of Excellence | Blue House Cluster* | Adaptive reuse of shophouses as a residential and multifunctional service complex |
| 2019 | Award of Excellence | Tai Kwun—Centre for Heritage and Arts | Adaptive reuse of a police station and prison complex as a cultural center |
| 2019 | New Design in Heritage Contexts | The Mills | Adaptive reuse of industrial buildings as a creative design hub |

*projects under the Revitalisation Scheme

| | | Shanghai | |
|---|---|---|---|
| | Heritage Award | Project | Conservation intervention |
| 2004 | Honourable Merit | Suzhou Warehouse | Adaptive reuse of a warehouse as a design studio |
| 2006 | Award of Distinction | Bund 18 | Adaptive reuse of a bank building as a high-end commercial building |
| 2009 | Award of Merit | Huai Hai Lu 796 | Adaptive reuse of residential villas as a high-end commercial building |
| 2016 | Award of Distinction | Holy Trinity Cathedral | Restoration of a cathedral |

**Table 5.1** (cont'd)

| | Heritage Award | Project | Conservation intervention |
|---|---|---|---|
| | | **Singapore** | |
| 2001 | Honourable Mention | Thian Hock Temple | Restoration of a Chinese temple |
| 2002 | Award of Merit | Convent of the Holy Infant Jesus (CHIJMES) | Adaptive reuse of a historic convent as a lifestyle and recreational complex |
| 2007 | Honourable Mention | Old St. Andrew's School | Restoration of a missionary school |
| 2008 | Jury Commendation for Innovation | 733 Mountbatten Road | Restoration and new works for a bungalow |
| 2010 | Award of Excellence | Hong San See Temple | Restoration of a Chinese temple |
| 2014 | Award of Merit | Wak Hai Cheng Bio Temple | Restoration of a Chinese temple |
| 2014 | Jury Commendation for Innovation | Lucky Shophouse | Adaptive reuse of a shophouse as a residential unit |
| 2016 | Honourable Mention | Cathedral of the Good Shepherd and Rectory Building | Restoration of a cathedral |

In all three centers, adaptive reuse projects have been recognized in the formative years of the Heritage Awards program. The Convent of the Holy Infant Jesus (CHIJMES) (Fig. 5.1) was Singapore's first adaptive reuse project to receive a Heritage Award (2002 Award of Merit). The success of the adaptive reuse of the historic convent as a lifestyle and recreational complex was illustrated by its use as "a lively urban hub (that) underscores the valuable potential from both a commercial and heritage point of view in revitalizing, rather than abandoning or replacing, historic buildings."[5]

**Figure 5.1:** The Convent of the Holy Infant Jesus (CHIJMES), Singapore's first adaptive reuse project to receive a Heritage Award (2002 Award of Merit). (Source: Ho Yin Lee.)

Shanghai's first project to be acknowledged with a Heritage Award was the Suzhou River Warehouse (2004 Honourable Mention) at 1305 South Suzhou Road (Fig. 5.2). The jury commended the adaptive reuse project for the "innovative adaptation of the warehouse for reuse as a design studio (that) has demonstrated

---

5. UNESCO Bangkok, "Project profiles for 2002 UNESCO Heritage Award winners," press release (2002), https://bangkok.unesco.org/sites/default/files/assets/article/Asia-Pacific%20Heritage%20 Awards/files/2002-winners.pdf.

the feasibility of innovative and modern uses of industrial buildings."[6] The project championed the development of the area as an enclave for artists giving a new lease of life to warehouses and buildings along the Suzhou River that were abandoned in the late 1980s.

**Figure 5.2:** Suzhou River Warehouse, Shanghai's first project to receive a Heritage Award (2004 Honourable Mention), with university students visiting to learn about the site's conservation. (Source: Ian Babbitt.)

In the case of Hong Kong, the early examples of adaptive reuse projects to win Heritage Awards are Little Hong Kong (2007 Honourable Mention, further elaborated as the case study on Crown Wine Cellars of this book) and the Whitfield Barracks (2007 Jury Commendation for Innovation). Whitfield Barracks (Fig. 5.3) were adapted as the Heritage Discovery Centre by introducing a lightweight structure that "provides a fitting counterpoint to the 90-year old barracks and integrates seamlessly into the surrounding park context."[7] The number of award-winning projects in Hong Kong began to steadily increase in the second decade of the Heritage Awards with a notable number of projects under the Hong Kong SAR government's Revitalising Historic Buildings through Partnership Scheme (Revitalisation Scheme).[8] Initiated in 2008, this scheme became an arbiter for public-private partnerships where selected government-owned heritage buildings were revitalized in collaboration with nongovernmental, nonprofit organizations for social enterprise operations. Hong Kong's Blue House Cluster (further elaborated in the case study section of this book), included in Batch II of the Revitalisation Scheme, received the Award of Excellence in the 2017 Heritage Awards for its "unprecedented civic effort to protect marginalized local heritage in one of the world's most high-pressure real estate markets."[9]

6.    UNESCO Bangkok, "Baltit Fort (Karimabad, Hunza, Pakistan) Awarded Top Prize in the UNESCO 2004 Asia-Pacific Heritage Awards," press release (September 1, 2004), https://bangkok.unesco.org/sites/default/files/assets/article/Asia-Pacific%20Heritage%20Awards/files/2004-winners.pdf.

7.    UNESCO Bangkok, "Maitreya Temples (Ladakh, India) Win Award of Excellence in the 2007 UNESCO Asia-Pacific Heritage Awards, Whitfield Barracks (Hong Kong SAR, China) Win Jury Commendation for Innovation in the 2007 UNESCO Asia-Pacific Heritage Awards," press release (August 16, 2007), https://bangkok.unesco.org/sites/default/files/assets/article/Asia-Pacific%20Heritage%20Awards/files/2007-winners.pdf.

8.    Please note the British spelling of "Revitalisation" is intentional, as this is its proper name as used by the Hong Kong SAR government.

9.    UNESCO Bangkok, "2017 Heritage Awards: Conservation of Working Class Housing in Hong Kong Receives Top Honor," press release (November 1, 2017), https://bangkok.unesco.org/content/2017-heritage-awards-conservation-working-class-housing-hong-kong-receives-top-honor.

**Figure 5.3:** Whitfield Barracks, one of Hong Kong's early projects to receive a Heritage Award (2007 Jury Commendation for Innovation). (Source: Ho Yin Lee.)

As in any awards program, it is essentially the criteria that set the precedent for winning entries. For the Heritage Awards, these criteria are also indicators for conservation best practice in the region and beyond. Focusing on adaptive reuse projects, the criteria on conveying the spirit of the place, compatibility of added elements, appropriate use, and contributing to the local community's socio-economic wellbeing define the benchmarks of a project's long-term viability and technical achievements.[10]

Meeting these criteria often entails a series of decisions. Determining the "appropriate use" of a place depends on the "intensity of use" and the "level of intervention."[11] While the condition of the place also is an influencing factor, projects that can deliver a subtle balance between the selected new use and the degree of intervention set the standard for good conservation practice. Singapore's Lucky Shophouse (2014 Jury Commendation for Innovation) converted a former shophouse in a historic district into a residential unit. The project not only retained the building's 1920s structure and footprint but also used passive design interventions to create an up-to-date and energy-efficient structure.[12]

Inserting an appropriate new use in a historic building also necessitates technical innovation and skill. While international conservation charters advocate that "new work should be readily identifiable as such," it is the award-winning projects that demonstrate technical solutions to the "problems" of inserting new additions within historic contexts.[13] The ease of this decision-making may vary for different building typologies. For example, the scale of an industrial building, such as the Suzhou River Warehouse in Shanghai, can readily accommodate the requirement for modern building amenities and services, whereas, in a high-density residential typology, like Hong Kong's Blue House Cluster, these requirements can only be introduced externally. From the trend of award-winning projects, it can be concluded that "best

---

10. All the criteria for the Heritage Awards can be found at UNESCO Bangkok, "About the Awards."
11. William Chapman, "Determining Appropriate Use."
12. UNESCO Bangkok, "Awarded Projects," March 17, 2020, https://bangkok.unesco.org/sites/default/files/assets/article/Asia-Pacific%20Heritage%20Awards/files/2014-winners.pdf.
13. Australia ICOMOS, *Burra Charter* (Burra: Australia ICOMOS, August 1979); Susan Balderstone, "Adding New Elements," in *Asia Conserved: Lessons Learned from the UNESCO Asia-Pacific Awards for Cultural Heritage Conservation (2000–2004)*, ed. Richard A. Engelhardt (Bangkok: UNESCO, 2007), 40–45

projects have often been those where the interventions were least visible . . . and where the new uses minimally alter the historic character and 'feeling' of the place."[14]

Observations from examining the development of the Heritage Awards program suggest that while there are several deciding factors that determine a project's performance and sustainability, the most lasting examples of conservation and adaptive reuse surface from partnerships between various stakeholders. As explained by Richard Engelhardt, UNESCO Regional Advisor for Culture in Asia and the Pacific (1994–2008) and currently on the Heritage Awards' jury panel, "during the first decade of the awards programme, the majority of projects were driven by a single, determined champion of conservation, not necessarily a professional, but nonetheless someone experienced in the field. . . . During the second decade of the awards programme, there was a shift, with fewer projects driven by a single champion and more projects with their origin in a community consensus that the conservation of the property in question represents a public good."[15] Adaptive reuse projects that emerge from community dialogue and stakeholder partnerships not only extend the tangible life of the heritage place but also contribute to the continuity of its associated intangible values.

## Conclusion

The UNESCO Heritage Awards program has been firmly established as a standard-setting benchmark for conservation in the region.[16] The nature of award-winning projects points to the evolving trends in conservation and adaptive reuse, where previously under–appreciated typologies are revitalized with new uses. This shift strengthens the argument that heritage should be accessible to all swathes of society and not concentrated in the hands of a few.

The Heritage Awards are a recognition of excellence in built heritage conservation and winning projects serve as drivers for best practice in safeguarding cultural heritage at local, national, and regional levels. The growing acceptance of adaptive reuse as a conservation strategy for heritage places is validated through award-winning projects, which demonstrate public-private partnerships, improved capacity of technical works, and the impact of appropriate new uses on social and community cohesion.

## Bibliography

Australia ICOMOS. *Burra Charter*. Burra: Australia ICOMOS, August 1979.

Chapman, William, ed. *Asia Conserved Volume III: Lessons Learned from the UNESCO Asia-Pacific Awards for Cultural Heritage Conservation (2010–2014)*. China: UNESCO and Southeast University Press, 2019.

Engelhardt, Richard A., ed. *Asia Conserved: Lessons Learned from the UNESCO Asia-Pacific Awards for Cultural Heritage Conservation (2000–2004)*. Bangkok: UNESCO, 2007.

Unakul, Montira Horayangura, ed. *Asia Conserved Volume II: Lessons Learned from the UNESCO Asia-Pacific Awards for Cultural Heritage Conservation (2005–2009)*. Bangkok: iGroup Press, 2013.

UNESCO Bangkok. "UNESCO Asia-Pacific Heritage Awards." Accessed November 22, 2019. https://bangkok.unesco.org/theme/asia-pacific-heritage-awards.

---

14. William Chapman, "Determining Appropriate Use."
15. Richard A. Engelhardt, "Cultural Heritage Conservation and Partnership," in *Asia Conserved Volume III: Lessons Learned from the UNESCO Asia-Pacific Awards for Cultural Heritage Conservation (2010–2014)*, ed. William Chapman (China: UNESCO, Southeast University Press, 2019), 38–47.
16. Engelhardt, "Cultural Heritage Conservation and Partnership."

# New Lease of Life: The Evolution of Adaptive Reuse in Hong Kong

Katie Cummer, Ho Yin Lee, and Lynne D. DiStefano

## Introduction

This chapter explores the development and evolution of adaptive reuse in Hong Kong. To effectively understand the approach locally, a quick overview of the city's conservation field is given, followed by a discussion of early adaptive reuse examples and how the practice has developed and evolved since then. Challenges of the local approach are addressed, with concluding remarks on the future of adaptive reuse in Hong Kong.

## Overview: Hong Kong's Approach to Conservation

Hong Kong's first, and thus far only, conservation-related legislation was passed following the economic boom that took place during the 1960s and 1970s, which resulted in an increased consideration of Hong Kong's identity and heritage resources.[1] As was the international trend at the time, this was in relation to "Antiquities" and "Monuments."[2] Indeed, UNESCO's 1972 World Heritage Convention provided the basis for Hong Kong's 1976 Antiquities and Monuments Ordinance (Cap. 53), and the enforcing agency of the law was the Antiquities and Monuments Office (AMO), established in the same year as the ordinance, which was tasked with the responsibility of protecting and preserving Hong Kong's "antiquities," namely, archaeological sites and historic monuments. Referencing the methodology of archaeology and artifact restoration, built heritage sites were either preserved in their current state or, when necessary, restored to their original.

Given the restrictions associated with this conservation approach, only sixty-five Declared Monuments were designated between 1976 and the last day of colonial rule on June 30, 1997. Those declared consisted mostly of government and institutional buildings in the urban areas as well as communally owned village buildings in the rural areas.[3] During this twenty-one-year period, numerous private and public buildings of considerable merit were demolished with minimal public outcry, as there

---

1. Tracey L. D. Lu, "Heritage Conservation in Post-colonial Hong Kong," *International Journal of Heritage Studies* 15, nos. 2–3 (March–May 2009): 259.
2. Esther H. K. Yung and Edwin H. W. Chan, "Problem Issues of Public Participation in Built-Heritage Conservation: Two Controversial Cases in Hong Kong," *Habitat International* 35 (2011): 459.
3. Antiquities and Monuments Office (AMO), "Declared Monuments in Hong Kong," accessed July 9, 2016, http://www.amo.gov.hk/en/monuments.php.

was a greater emphasis, citywide, placed on new development.[4] Poignant examples of such lost architectural heritage are the Victorian-period Hong Kong Club Building (completed in 1897, demolished in 1981), the Edwardian-period General Post Office (completed in 1911, demolished in 1976), and the Art Deco–period Chinese Methodist Church (completed in 1936, demolished in 1994), among many others.

A lack of focus on heritage conservation persisted in the city following the handover in July 1997 and was exacerbated by a problematic governmental department framework. During this period, there was minimal integration of conservation initiatives within the government.[5] "An organizational chart of the time shows that at least fifteen departments across five bureaus were charged with specific tasks related to the conservation of heritage resources. Coordination and especially "ownership" of a project were frequently problematic."[6]

A major problem was that, from July 1997 to July 2007, the AMO was the only government agency with statutory authority to carry out heritage conservation, and it was a very small office. It ranked lowest in the government hierarchy, and it was organized under the Home Affairs Bureau, which had no technical expertise in building-related work. At the time, the AMO was staffed by museum curators trained in archaeology, history, and the fine arts, and for them to carry out built heritage conservation work, they had to borrow building-work professionals from the Architectural Services Department (ArchSD) under a different bureau (the Environment, Transport and Works Bureau) that had expertise in carrying out building works. One can easily imagine the red tape involved for an office-level bureaucracy to solicit the cooperation of a more senior department-level bureaucracy, both of which answered to different bureau secretaries.

Adding to the problem was the establishment of an independent quasi-governmental agency, known as the Urban Renewal Authority (URA), in 2000. As part of its mandate to carry out the "4 Rs" (Redevelopment, Rehabilitation, Revitalization and pReservation) under its urban renewal agenda, the URA had (and still has) independent authority over conservation projects within areas designated for urban renewal. A constant struggle for the URA was (and continues to be) balancing its heritage conservation mandate with the land-use issues and developmental pressures facing Hong Kong.

All in all, there were too many varied branches handling aspects of conservation-related work, resulting in inefficiency and fragmented project ownership. The problem was only partially alleviated in July 2007 when a new bureau, the Development Bureau (DevB), was formed. This brought together under one roof the government departments responsible for architectural services, buildings, civil engineering, lands, planning, and other related services. The AMO and URA were then required to answer to the new secretary for development as well.

The impetus for the formation of this new bureau was a series of crises that catapulted the case for conservation forward. These included the protests over the demolition of the Central Star Ferry Pier in 2006 (Fig. 6.1) and the adjacent Queen's Pier in 2007.[7] Despite the immense and drawn-out public protest to save the Star Ferry Pier, it was still demolished in 2006; and the Queen's Pier was dismantled and

4.  Lu, "Heritage Conservation in Post-colonial Hong Kong," 260.
5.  Elizabeth Kenworthy Teather and Chun Shing Chow, "Identity and Place: The Testament of Designated Heritage in Hong Kong," *International Journal of Heritage Studies* 9, no. 2 (2003): 113.
6.  Lynne D. DiStefano, Ho Yin Lee, and Katie Cummer, "Hong Kong Style Urban Conservation" (paper presented at the 17th ICOMOS General Assembly and Scientific Symposium, UNESCO Headquarters, Paris, November 27 to December 2, 2011): 30.
7.  Yung and Chan, "Problem Issues of Public Participation in Built-Heritage Conservation."

put in storage in 2007.[8] It was with the loss of these two piers that Hong Kong's heritage conservation became a more prominent issue for both the public and the government.[9] The result, in particular, was a greater focus and clearer articulation of the Hong Kong Special Administrative Region government's policy toward conservation.

**Figure 6.1:** The former Central Star Ferry Pier and the protest display against its proposed demolition, 2006. (Source: Howard Cummer.)

This development and greater dedication to the conservation cause is distinctly visible in the 2007 policy address by the second chief executive of the Hong Kong SAR, Donald Tsang Yam-kuen. It had eight paragraphs covering a range of issues in relation to heritage conservation and laid down the framework for how conservation would be carried out in Hong Kong. As set out in Paragraph 51:

> In my view, revitalisation, rather than preservation alone, should be pursued to maximise the economic and social benefits of historic buildings. This is in line with the concept of sustainable conservation.[10]

This better-articulated conservation policy aimed at rectifying a number of the previous shortcomings of Hong Kong's heritage conservation approach. For example, one of the major advancements made as a result of this address was the establishment of a government bureau specifically intended to address conservation issues—The Commissioner for Heritage's Office (CHO) within the new Development Bureau (DevB). This more centralized approach to conservation saw the introduction of schemes, such as the Revitalising Historic Buildings through Partnership Scheme (Revitalisation Scheme),[11] under which numerous historic buildings have been saved from demolition and given a new lease of life.

8.  Agnes Shuk-mei Ku, "Remaking Places and Fashioning an Opposition Discourse: Struggle over the Star Ferry Pier and the Queen's Pier in Hong Kong," *Environment and Planning D: Society and Space* 30 (2012): 12–13 and 17; and Joan C. Henderson, "Conserving Hong Kong's Heritage: The Case of Queen's Pier," *International Journal of Heritage Studies* 14, no. 6 (November 2008): 541–43.

9.  Yung and Chan, "Problem Issues of Public Participation in Built-Heritage Conservation," 457.

10. Office of the Chief Executive, *2007–08 Policy Address* (Hong Kong: Hong Kong SAR Government, October 10, 2007), http://www.policyaddress.gov.hk/07-08/eng/policy.html.

11. Please note the British spelling of "Revitalisation" is intentional, as this is its proper name as used by the Hong Kong SAR government.

It was only with the introduction of the Revitalisation Scheme in 2008 that the government formally adopted adaptive reuse as the preferred approach to the conservation of its own heritage buildings, which were not Declared Monuments. Buildings chosen for the scheme are those listed as Grade 1, 2, or 3 Historic Buildings, which are not statutorily protected.[12] Under this scheme, such government-owned heritage buildings are revitalized, or in other words adapted for new uses. Critically, the Revitalisation Scheme is part of a larger sustainability agenda. To understand the importance of this policy shift, it is helpful to recall Hong Kong's early approaches to adaptive reuse.

## Early Approach to Adaptive Reuse in Hong Kong

Although conservation was not as prominent or dominant an issue in the mid-twentieth century, there was still a tradition of adaptive reuse in the city, even if it was not formally named as such. In particular, numerous government-owned buildings changed use over time. Two notable examples are the Old Tsan Yuk Maternity Hospital (Fig. 6.2), opened in 1922, which first became the Tsan Yuk Social Service Centre in 1955 and later the Western District Community Centre in 1973; and the Old Pathological Institute, opened in 1906, which became a medical store in the 1970s and was converted into the Museum of Medical Sciences in 1996.

**Figure 6.2:** The Old Tsan Yuk Maternity Hospital on Western Street, built in 1922; an early adaptive reuse example in Hong Kong. Once a new maternity hospital was opened nearby on Hospital Road, this red brick building became the Social Service Centre in 1955 and the Western District Community Centre in 1973, which it continues to be today. (Source: Ho Yin Lee.)

Indeed, this pattern of converting former government buildings into cultural facilities, in particular museums with commercial components, such as restaurants and shops, was a popular approach in Hong Kong, especially before the 2008 introduction of the Revitalisation Scheme. It saw a bilinear top-down approach to adaptive reuse reflected in the funding sources for construction and operation, with cultural facilities as the prerogative of government agencies and commercial facilities

12. The Historic Building grading system is explained on the AMO website: http://www.amo.gov.hk/en/built2.php.

outsourced to business operators. Unfortunately, the results were sometimes, if not frequently, disappointing. Even the government-appointed commissioner for heritage, José Yam Ho-san, has admitted:

> The government's old way of preserving buildings was "too passive". By turning Kom Tong Hall . . . and Flagstaff House into the Sun Yat-sen Museum and Museum of Tea Ware respectively, the buildings are simply museums displaying artefacts . . . rather than being reused actively by the community.[13]

Using heritage buildings as museums has turned out to be a costly initiative. Not only was the capital outlay sizeable, but the operating costs have far outstripped any revenue generated by these institutions. There is also the question of whether such museums can draw sufficient visitors to justify the capital investment and operating costs. In the case of the Dr. Sun Yat-sen Museum, the museum was adapted from a 1914 mansion known as Kom Tong Hall (Fig. 6.3). The project cost the government HK$53 million to acquire the property, HK$91.3 million for the building works, and about HK$6.7 million to operate annually when first completed in 2005.[14] The published operating cost in 2017–2018 was approximately HK$10.7 million.[15] This was set against a projected annual revenue, based largely on admission tickets, of HK$0.636 million (this is the 2005 projected figure, while the published revenue for 2017–2018 was HK$0.106 million).[16] This would cover less than 1 percent of the museum's annual recurrent expenditure.[17]

**Figure 6.3:** Kom Tong Hall, a 1914 mansion that was first adapted from its residential use in 1960 by the Church of Jesus Christ of Latter-day Saints for worship services and other church-related activities. After four decades, it was purchased by the Hong Kong SAR government and converted into the Dr. Sun Yat-sen Museum in 2006. (Source: Ho Yin Lee.)

---

13. Enid Tsui and Elaine Yau, "More Hong Kong Heritage Being Saved, but Critics Question Uses It's Being Put To," *South China Morning Post* (January 10, 2016; updated May 31, 2016), accessed July 9, 2016, http://www.scmp.com/lifestyle/article/1899479/more-hong-kong-heritage-being-saved-critics-question-uses-its-being-put.

14. Home Affairs Bureau, "Conversion of Kom Tong Hall for use as the Dr Sun Yat-sen Museum," Legislative Council Paper No. CB(2)777/04-05(03) (January 31, 2005), accessed August 13, 2016, http://www.legco.gov.hk/yr04-05/english/panels/ha/papers/ha0204cb2-777-3e.pdf.

15. Leisure and Cultural Services Department (LCSD), *Dr. Sun Yat-sen Museum Financial Figures for 2017/2018* (Hong Kong: Hong Kong SAR Government, August 23, 2018), https://www.lcsd.gov.hk/CE/Museum/sysm/en_US/web/sysm/aboutus/financial.html.

16. Leisure and Cultural Services Department (LCSD), *Dr. Sun Yat-sen Museum Financial Figures for 2017/2018*.

17. Home Affairs Bureau, "Conversion of Kom Tong Hall for use as the Dr Sun Yat-sen Museum."

Given the cost of adapting and operating a heritage building or site as a cultural facility, the government has outsourced such projects to nongovernmental organizations (NGOs) that have independent financial resources. Two such examples are the Old Dairy Farm Depot (Fig. 6.4), built in 1892, which became the Fringe Club in 1983, a nonprofit arts organization that has successfully operated in that space for more than thirty years; and the Former Explosives Magazine Compound, built in stages starting in the mid-nineteenth into the early twentieth century, which is today the Asia Society Hong Kong Center.

**Figure 6.4:** The Old Dairy Farm Depot, built in 1892 and expanded in 1913, was abandoned in the 1970s. It became the Fringe Club in 1983 and has successfully continued with this new use for more than thirty years. (Source: Ka Sing Yu.)

The Former Explosives Magazine Compound is the remnant of one of the colony's oldest military barracks, Victoria Barracks, containing a cluster of four revitalized heritage buildings: specifically, one mid-nineteenth-century explosive magazine and an early twentieth-century one, Magazine A and Magazine B, which are both Grade 1 Historic Buildings converted into an exhibition hall and a hundred-seat multipurpose theater respectively; a mid-nineteenth-century laboratory building, the Old Laboratory, which is also a Grade 1 Historic Building converted into meeting rooms and offices; and a 1930s army block, GG Block, which is a Grade 2 Historic Building converted into the center's administrative offices.[18] The additions of a new building for large functions and needed services, as well as a modern bridge linking the buildings together, creates a functional site that meets the programmatic needs of the new center.

Opened in 2012, the adaptive reuse of the Former Explosive Magazine Compound into the Asia Society Hong Kong Center is seen, for the most part, positively. Since its opening, the center has been able to host close to one hundred arts and culture programs for the public annually.[19] Financially, it is sustainable, as the HK$400 million project was funded entirely by the private sector, with donations and financial contributions from local and international individuals and organizations, including HK$102.5 million from a local charity organization, the Hong Kong

18. For visuals of this revitalized site, please see "Our Site," Asia Society Hong Kong Center, https://asia society.org/hong-kong/visit/rebirth-former-explosives-magazine.

19. Asia Society Hong Kong Center, "About the Hong Kong Center," accessed February 1, 2019, https:// asiasociety.org/hong-kong/about-hong-kong-center.

Jockey Club.[20] However, the perceived preferential treatment given to Asia Society (it was given a twenty-one-year lease of the site for a nominal HK$1,000) and the lavish funding from wealthy donors have led to the public perception that the project is "elitist" and a "private club."[21] The center has since worked hard to dispel these labels through free guided tours and increased public programing.

The Hong Kong Jockey Club has in fact been a major driving force behind the private push for adaptive reuse in the city with its support of a number of key projects. Through its Charities Trust, the Hong Kong Jockey Club has borne the financial burden of undertaking enormously expensive adaptive reuse projects, such as the conversion of the Former Central Police Station Compound (Fig. 6.5) (consisting of a cluster of buildings dating from the nineteenth century to mid-twentieth century) into a center for public programs in heritage and contemporary art and of a disused flatted factory building (a 1950s design that was completed in 1977) into a multidisciplinary artists' center. The former project, named Tai Kwun (the local colloquial name for the police station)—Centre for Heritage and Arts, is arguably the biggest and most ambitious adaptive reuse project in the history of Hong Kong, with an upfront capital cost of HK$1.8 billion.[22] The Jockey Club Creative Arts Centre, while lesser in scale and scope, still cost close to HK$100 million.[23] A pattern that began to emerge with Hong Kong's early adaptive reuse was that every project was unique, costing different amounts of money and facing different challenges, with some results seen more favorably than others. Of course, for every "successful" adaptive reuse project in Hong Kong, there is a range of problematic examples as well.

**Figure 6.5:** The Former Central Police Station Compound pre-revitalization in 2014. The revitalized site, comprising sixteen revitalized historic buildings with two new contemporary structures, officially opened in 2018 as Tai Kwun—Centre for Heritage and Arts. (Source: Ian Babbitt.)

20. Hong Kong Jockey Club (HKJC), "Jockey Club Helps Revitalize Former Explosives Magazine into Dynamic Arts and Cultural Hub" (Hong Kong: The Hong Kong Jockey Club, February 9, 2012), http://corporate.hkjc.com/corporate/corporate-news/english/2012-02/news_2012020902006.aspx.

21. Fionnuala McHugh, "Let There Be Light: Will Caravaggio Bring the Asia Society out of the Shadows?" *Post Magazine*, March 8, 2014, http://www.scmp.com/magazines/post-magazine/article/1440883/let-there-be-light-will-caravaggio-bring-asia-society-out.

22. Tai Kwun, "Club Announces HK$1.8 Billion 'Gift for Hong Kong' That Will Conserve Central Police Station Site as New Cultural Icon," press release (October 11, 2007), http://www.taikwun.hk/en/press-release/club-announces-hk1-8-billion-gift-for-hong-kong-that-will-conserve-central-police-station-site-as-new-cultural-icon/.

23. General Administrative Office (GAO), "Jockey Club Creative Arts Centre," *Hong Kong Baptist University*, accessed July 25, 2017, https://gao.hkbu.edu.hk/en/spu/jccac.html.

## Early Problematic Cases of Adaptive Reuse in Hong Kong

There have been a number of issues with the adaptive reuse of government-owned heritage properties for tourist-oriented commercial usage. Such projects have been met with skepticism, given the limited benefit to local communities. Three well-known cases vividly illustrate the problem: Western Market, the Former Stanley Police Station, and the Former Marine Police Headquarters, all of which are Declared Monuments (respectively declared in 1990, 1984, and 1994).

The Western Market (Fig. 6.6) was originally a complex of two blocks, North and South Blocks, but the former block, completed in 1844, was demolished in 1980. The remaining South Block, completed in 1906, ceased operation in 1989 when the market was relocated to a new nearby complex. After temporary use as a "centre of traditional traders, arts and crafts,"[24] the building was transformed into "a place of lifestyle shopping and leisure activities,"[25] as described by the project proponent, the Urban Renewal Authority (URA). However, the net result, summed up in a *South China Morning Post* article, was "disappointing," as "the lack of an overall development concept means it now looks like a small shopping mall."[26] A CNN article put it even more bluntly: "The tragedy of the Western Market is that it's billed by tourism promoters as a piece of 'living heritage.' The truth is, all of the life has been sucked out of it."[27]

**Figure 6.6:** The North Block of Western Market, built in 1906. Originally a food market, it is today a mixed-use market selling a range of goods, largely targeting tourists rather than its local community. (Source: Ho Yin Lee.)

24. Urban Renewal Authority, "Western Market," last modified September 10, 2011, accessed August 13, 2016, http://www.ura.org.hk/en/projects/heritage-preservation-and-revitalisation/central/western-market.aspx.

25. Urban Renewal Authority, "Western Market."

26. Yvonne Liu, "Hong Kong's Historic Districts, Buildings at Risk as Profit Maximized," *South China Morning Post*, October 17, 2013, accessed August 13, 2016, http://www.scmp.com/property/hong-kong-china/article/1333306/hong-kongs-historical-districts-buildings-risk-profit.

27. Christopher DeWolf, "9 Hong Kong Tourist Traps—for Better or Worse," *CNN Travel*, last modified October 27, 2010, accessed August 13, 2016, http://travel.cnn.com/hong-kong/play/9-hong-kongs-best-and-worst-tourist-traps-535602/.

In the case of the Former Stanley Police Station (Fig. 6.7), the problem was similar. It was a building completed in 1859 and recognized as the oldest surviving police station building in Hong Kong. After it ceased to function as a station in 1974, it was first used as a government office and subsequently placed under the care of the Government Property Agency (GPA), which leased it out as a government property despite its status as a Declared Monument. In the 1990s, it was adapted as an upmarket restaurant, but the business attracted neither sufficient tourists nor local customers to be sustainable. In 2003, the property became a supermarket; however, this was also controversial, generating questions from the public about appropriate uses for Declared Monuments.[28] Despite the outcry, the place continues to operate as a supermarket to this day (as of 2019).

**Figure 6.7:** The Former Stanley Police Station, built in 1859. It ceased being used for police operations in 1974 and has since then been used as office space and most recently as a supermarket. (Source: Ho Yin Lee.)

In the case of the Former Marine Police Headquarters (Fig. 6.8), built in 1884 and in use until 1996, the adaptive reuse of this large site was led by the Tourism Commission under the Economic Development and Labour Bureau. Under the commission's agenda to "engage private sector resources in suitable projects with commercial potential,"[29] the site, endowed with a fifty-year lease, was transformed into a boutique hotel, high-end restaurants, and luxury-brand shops. Despite commercial success since its 2009 opening, the renamed site, Heritage 1881, has drawn ongoing public criticism for the upmarket commercialization of a Declared Monument that excludes a large sector of local people.

28. Chloe Lai and Fox Yi Hu, "Wellcome Keen to Keep Heritage Store," *South China Morning Post* (January 31, 2007), accessed August 13, 2016, http://www.scmp.com/article/580186/wellcome-keen-keep-heritage-store; and Chloe Lai, "Retailers Not Ruled Out for Historic Police Station," *South China Morning Post*, March 25, 2007, accessed August 13, 2016, http://www.scmp.com/article/586372/retailers-not-ruled-out-historic-police-station.

29. Tourism Commission, Economic Development and Labour Bureau, "Former Marine Police Headquarters," Legislative Council Brief, file ref. ESB CR 22/24/17 (July 3, 2002), accessed August 13, 2016, http://www.tourism.gov.hk/resources/english/paperreport_doc/legco/2002-07-03/MPHQ-LegCo_Paper_(Eng).pdf.

**Figure 6.8:** The Former Marine Police Headquarters, built in 1884, is today a mixed-use boutique hotel and high-end shopping destination known as Heritage 1881. (Source: Ho Yin Lee.)

In retrospect, the two main issues for these early attempts at adaptive reuse of heritage buildings in Hong Kong relied on top-down decision-making and prioritized financial considerations over social ones. This, in particular, upset an increasingly vocal public who saw such decision making as lacking connection with and relevance to the local communities. Given the social context of Hong Kong, the valuable lessons learned from these early projects is that the adaptive reuse of government-owned properties has to be based on a public-private partnership model and not be out-sourced to nongovernmental entities. It is this understanding that has been applied to the projects under the Revitalisation Scheme, discussed in greater detail below. Fortunately, the government has recognized these problems and set about to change them. The change came in the form of the 2007 conservation policy, which placed greater emphasis on more careful and considered adaptive reuse of heritage buildings citywide.

## Adaptive Reuse in Hong Kong after the 2007 Conservation Policy

The new conservation policy attempted to meet public demand for conservation using a two-pronged approach that tackles the government's role from within and the community's expectations from without. For the government, the new built heritage policy entailed a reorganization of the government's administrative structure to form the new Development Bureau (DevB). Led by the secretary for development, the new bureau would become the primary agency responsible for built heritage conservation in the city. As stated in the policy address:

> In the next five years, the Government will step up our work on heritage conservation. A Commissioner for Heritage's Office, to be set up in the Development Bureau, will provide a focal point for public participation and the Government's heritage conservation work. This shows that heritage conservation will be a long-term commitment of the Government.[30]

The second part of the two-pronged approach targeted the community. As Chief Executive Tsang also announced in his policy address:

---

30. Office of the Chief Executive, "2007–08 Policy Address," para. 55.

At present, quite a number of historic buildings are owned by the Government. I will seek to revitalise them by introducing a new scheme which will allow non-governmental organisations to apply for adaptive re-use of these historic buildings. As a start, six to eight buildings will be offered under the scheme. We hope they can be transformed creatively into unique cultural landmarks. The *modus operandi* of social enterprise under commercial management will be adopted to achieve a win-win situation.[31]

This is the policy statement that ushered in the Revitalising Historic Buildings through Partnership Scheme (Revitalisation Scheme). Under this scheme, government-owned non–statutorily protected (but graded) heritage buildings are open to application by nongovernmental, nonprofit organizations for social enterprise operations. One of the criteria for assessing the applicants' proposals is "how the community would be benefited" at both the district and local community level.[32] This socially oriented approach to the implementation of Hong Kong's built heritage conservation policy is explained more clearly in the Legislative Council paper (2009), "Background Brief on Revitalising Historic Buildings through Partnership Scheme":

> The Administration has adopted the social enterprise (SE) approach whereby non-profit-making non-governmental organizations (NGOs) were invited to submit proposals on a competitive basis to revitalise the historic buildings and the proposed usage should take the form of a SE. Non-profit-making organizations (NPOs) that have acquired charitable status under Section 88 of the Inland Revenue Ordinance are eligible to submit proposals.[33]

The inclusion of NGOs and NPOs operating in a public-private partnership in the Revitalisation Scheme is a revision of the previous policy of exclusive government involvement in conservation projects. However, the government's partnership involvement is crucial to this socially oriented conservation approach, as the high capital cost of these projects has to be borne by the government to make the scheme feasible. In this regard, it is notable that the scheme is funded by the government's well-endowed Capital Works Reserve Fund, where all land premiums have been deposited since the early 1980s.[34] The scheme received HK$1 billion of initial funding in 2007 for the first batch of buildings,[35] and it was expanded to five batches of buildings in 2016, with a cumulative fund of almost three times the initial investment.[36]

As a pilot scheme to demonstrate the viability of adaptive reuse, the Revitalisation Scheme is expansive in scope, involving government-owned buildings that had functioned for educational, health-care, law, market, military, police, religious, residential, and social welfare purposes, amounting to five batches of twenty-one buildings.[37] The new uses focusing on "how the community would be benefited"[38] provides compel-

---

31. Office of the Chief Executive, "2007–08 Policy Address," para. 53.
32. Legislative Council, HKSAR, "Background Brief on Revitalising Historic Buildings through Partnership Scheme," Legislative Council Paper No. CB(1)816/08-09(04) (February 24, 2009): item 6(c), accessed July 9, 2016, http://www.legco.gov.hk/yr08-09/english/panels/dev/papers/dev0224cb1-816-4-e.pdf.
33. Legislative Council, HKSAR, "Background Brief on Revitalising Historic Buildings through Partnership Scheme," item 4.
34. Stan Hok-wui Wong, "Real Estate Elite, Economic Development and Political Conflicts in Postcolonial Hong Kong," *China Review* 15, no. 1 (Spring 2015): 8, accessed July 9, 2016, http://www.researchgate.net/publication/275856601_Real_Estate_Elite_Economic_Development_and_Political_Conflicts_in_Postcolonial_Hong_Kong.
35. Office of the Chief Executive, "2007–08 Policy Address," para 53.
36. Commissioner for Heritage's Office, private communication with the authors, November 2018.
37. Although a total of twenty-seven buildings are listed in five batches, some have been withdrawn from the scheme or relisted in other batches. For details, see individual batches under "Revitalisation Scheme" at https://www.heritage.gov.hk/en/rhbtp/about.htm.
38. Legislative Council, HKSAR, "Background Brief on Revitalising Historic Buildings through Partnership Scheme," item 6(c).

ling demonstration to the public of the social benefits derived from such projects. It appears that adaptive reuse in Hong Kong has progressed from the pre-2008 focus on museums and cultural facilities to the post-2008 community-oriented new uses that serve a social agenda. This has resulted in a growing public acceptance and appreciation of such projects.

## Growing Public Acceptance of Revitalization Projects Citywide

While some remain critical and skeptical of the approach and projects, overall, there has been a growing acceptance of adaptive reuse as an appropriate conservation approach for Hong Kong. As stated in an article in the property section of the *South China Morning Post*, entitled "Preserving the Past in New Buildings Is Back in Fashion," the reporter writes:

> Using architectural innovation to make an existing structure viable again seems preferable on many levels: it retains some linkage to the past, saves construction waste and, sometimes, can even be more cost-effective than starting from scratch. Architects call this "adaptive reuse." And if it has not yet come to a neighbourhood near you, chances are it is not far away.[39]

The Hong Kong public has become more accepting of adaptive reuse as a way of conserving Hong Kong's heritage buildings, largely because of increased exposure. Greater awareness of this approach has come from numerous projects earning local and international recognition. For example, five of the projects to date (as of 2019) under the Revitalisation Scheme have earned international recognition by winning the prestigious UNESCO Asia-Pacific Awards for Cultural Heritage Conservation. These include the Savannah College of Art and Design (SCAD) Hong Kong, adapted from a district courthouse (completed in 2010); the Tai O Heritage Hotel (Fig. 6.9), adapted from a police station (completed in 2012); the YHA Mei Ho

**Figure 6.9:** The Old Tai O Police Station, built in 1902, was revitalized as the Tai O Heritage Hotel in 2012. (Source: Hong Kong Heritage Conservation Foundation Limited.)

39.  Peta Tomlinson, "Preserving the past in new buildings is back in fashion," *South China Morning Post* (July 9, 2014), accessed July 9, 2016, http://www.scmp.com/property/hong-kong-china/article/1549176/preserving-past-new-buildings-back-fashion.

House Youth Hostel (Fig. 6.10), adapted from a public housing block (completed in 2013); The Green Hub, adapted from the Old Tai Po Police Station into a center for sustainable living (completed in 2015); and, more recently (2017), the grassroots social housing project of the Blue House Cluster, adapted from a collection of early twentieth-century working-class shophouses into mixed residential and social enterprise use (completed in stages through the early 2010s). Both SCAD and the Blue House Cluster are addressed in greater detail as two of the Hong Kong case studies of this book.

**Figure 6.10:** Mei Ho House, formerly part of the Shek Kip Mei Housing Estate, pre-revitalization in 2009. The revitalized site, the Mei Ho House Youth Hostel, was opened in 2013. (Source: Ho Yin Lee.)

Other projects, although they have not necessarily won awards (at least not yet), have gained public acceptance through socially oriented new uses that have benefitted their immediate communities. A case in point is Lui Seng Chun, a 1931 shophouse that was among the first batch of buildings listed under the Revitalisation Scheme. Since 2012, the building has been transformed into a community health-care center operated by the Hong Kong Baptist University's School of Chinese Medicine. In its new role, the building serves the needs of the aging population of the Sham Shui Po District, which has a preference for traditional Chinese medicine. During his 2013 visit to Hong Kong, Director of the State Administration of Cultural Heritage (SACH) Li Xiaojie singled out Lui Seng Chun as an exemplary adaptive reuse project "for all of the public to enjoy, not for the benefit of a select few."[40]

Beyond the government, the Revitalisation Scheme has opened new grounds for built heritage conservation in Hong Kong by demonstrating not only the social benefit of adaptive reuse but also new possibilities in financing such projects. The scheme has attracted the interest of property developers in considering the option of financing adaptive reuse projects that would serve both conservation and commercial interests. A project known as The Camphora has demonstrated this viability. Formerly known as Parmanand House, this is a HK$30 million adaptive reuse project entirely funded by a local developer, who converted the 1963 composite building (mixed commercial

---

40. Adrian Wan, "Hong Kong's Architectural Heritage Conservation Is Praised," *South China Morning Post*, July 24, 2013, accessed July 9, 2016, http://www.scmp.com/news/hong-kong/article/1289433/hong-kongs-heritage-methods-praised.

and residential uses) into a high-end serviced apartment. It won the 2015 Special Architectural Award for Heritage and Adaptive Reuse, conferred by the Hong Kong Institute of Architects.[41]

Another developer-funded project is the HK$700 million adaptive reuse of a 1950s textile factory as a creative center for fashion to be an incubator for young designers. Completed in 2018, The Mills (Fig. 6.11) joins a steadily increasing number of developer-funded adaptive reuse projects in Hong Kong and was in fact recognized with an award for New Design in Heritage Contexts in the 2019 UNESCO Asia-Pacific Awards for Cultural Heritage Conservation (along with Tai Kwun–Centre for Heritage and Arts). Such projects include those funded by the Urban Renewal Authority (URA), whose budget is derived from property redevelopment in partnership with private developers under the urban renewal agenda, receiving no public money. Two examples of URA projects are the rehabilitation of a row of 1930 shophouses on Prince Edward Road West (Fig. 6.12) with some of the units adapted for an art-based community and nongovernmental organization (NGO) usage, and the adaptive reuse of a row of shophouses on Shanghai Street as art-based retailing and community facilities. From such projects, there is steady progress in recognizing the future of adaptive reuse by "integrating heritage conservation with the business and creative-industry sectors to develop financing and creative adaptive-reuse strategies."[42]

**Figure 6.11:** The former Nan Fung cotton-spinning factories, built in the 1950s and 1960s, have been revitalized into a design hub known as The Mills. (Source: Ashish Ahuja.)

41. Hong Kong Institute of Architects (HKIA), "HKIA Annual Awards 2015," accessed July 25, 2016, http://www.building.hk/forum/2015hkia.pdf.

42. Ho-Yin Lee, "Welcome Embrace of a Living City," *South China Morning Post* (October 11, 2007), accessed July 9, 2016, https://www.scmp.com/article/611086/welcome-embrace-living-city.

**Figure 6.12:** Rehabilitated row of 1930s shophouses along Prince Edward Road West. (Source: Ian Babbitt.)

## Concluding Remarks: The Future of Adaptive Reuse in Hong Kong

Understandably, adaptive reuse projects in Hong Kong have faced a range of challenges; however, as the number of completed projects has grown, so, too, has the number of "successful" and inspirational projects. With each passing year, subsequent adaptive reuse projects build off of and learn from the process and results of those that came before it. That being said, the government's hallmark program, the Revitalisation Scheme, is not beyond criticism. For a metropolis the size of Hong Kong, its scale and scope are relatively small, although one could argue that it is a step in the right direction as more and more projects, both public and private, are embarked upon citywide. Concerns have been raised by the professional community over the scheme, in particular, the lack of public and professional involvement in the selection of buildings and the high application costs for the applying non-profit-making organizations (NPOs). The application costs for unsuccessful applicants are especially problematic. Unfortunately, while the complaints are justified, there can be only one successful applicant, and the work that goes into the proposals helps to produce the best possible results for these historic places.

Despite the criticisms, the 2008 Revitalisation Scheme is one of the most significant initiatives for implementing Hong Kong's conservation policy and for encouraging the growth of adaptive reuse projects throughout the city. Under this scheme, government-owned heritage buildings that are not Declared Monuments have been successfully "revitalized" and adapted for new uses. Echoing English Heritage's statement on constructive conservation, the Commissioner for Heritage's Office, the government agency overseeing the execution of the scheme, states, "We are committed to put our historic buildings to good adaptive re-use."[43] Whether it be adaptive reuse, constructive conservation, or revitalization, the definitions amount to the same emphasis on permitting alterations and changes for the purpose of giving heritage buildings "a new lease of life for the enjoyment of the public" (the slogan for the government's Revitalisation Scheme) through culturally and socially relevant new uses.[44]

---

43. Commissioner for Heritage's Office (CHO), "About the Scheme: Revitalising Historic Buildings through Partnership Scheme," *Development Bureau, Government of the Hong Kong Special Administrative Region*, last modified July 13, 2017, http://www.heritage.gov.hk/en/rhbtp/about.htm.
44. Commissioner for Heritage's Office (CHO), "About the Scheme."

Through the diversity and growing number of both government and private adaptive reuse ventures, a critical mass of completed revitalized projects demonstrates the validity and value of adaptive reuse in Hong Kong and beyond. With new projects recognized and awarded regularly, the case for conservation and revitalization is being made on an impressive scale, particularly for a single city. In fact, of the near-twenty years' worth of UNESCO Asia-Pacific Awards for Cultural Heritage Conservation, Hong Kong has received 8 percent of the awards (as of 2019).[45] Considering the fact that it is in competition with entire countries, such as Australia, China, India, Japan, and Malaysia, among many others, Hong Kong should be proud of what it has accomplished and inspired to continue. With the results to date in mind, it is hoped that such practice can be further encouraged and promoted both locally and in the region, to better protect valuable heritage resources with creative new uses for future generations to enjoy.

## Bibliography

Antiquities and Monuments Office (AMO). "Declared Monuments in Hong Kong." Accessed July 9, 2016. http://www.amo.gov.hk/en/monuments.php.

Asia Society Hong Kong Center. "About the Hong Kong Center," 2018. Accessed February 1, 2019. https://asiasociety.org/hong-kong/about-hong-kong-center.

Australia ICOMOS. *The Burra Charter: The Australia ICOMOS Charter for Places of Cultural Significance.* Australia ICOMOS, 2013. Accessed July 9, 2016. http://australia. icomos.org/wp-content/uploads/The-Burra-Charter-2013-Adopted-31.10.2013. pdf.

Commissioner for Heritage's Office (CHO). "About the Scheme: Revitalising Historic Buildings through Partnership Scheme." *Development Bureau, Government of the Hong Kong Special Administrative Region, 2008.* Last modified July 13, 2017. http://www. heritage.gov.hk/en/rhbtp/about.htm.

DeWolf, Christopher. "9 Hong Kong Tourist Traps—for Better or Worse." *CNN Travel,* October 27, 2010. Accessed August 13, 2016. http://travel.cnn.com/hong-kong/ play/9-hong-kongs-best-and-worst-tourist-traps-535602/.

DiStefano, Lynne D., Ho Yin Lee, and Katie Cummer. "Hong Kong Style Urban Conservation." Paper presented at the 17th ICOMOS General Assembly and Scientific Symposium, UNESCO Headquarters, Paris, November 27 to December 2, 2011.

English Heritage. "Constructive Conservation: Sustainable Growth for Historic Places." Accessed July 9, 2016. https://historicengland.org.uk/images-books/publications/ constructive-conservation-sustainable-growth-historic-places/.

Financial Secretary. "Capital Works Reserve Fund (Payments)." In *The 2015–16 Budget.* Hong Kong: Financial Secretary of the Government of the Hong Kong Special Administrative Region, February 25, 2015. http://www.budget.gov.hk/2015/eng/ pdf/cwrf-08.pdf.

General Administrative Office (GAO). "Jockey Club Creative Arts Centre." *Hong Kong Baptist University.* Accessed on July 25, 2017. https://gao.hkbu.edu.hk/en/spu/jccac. html.

Henderson, Joan C. "Conserving Hong Kong's Heritage: The Case of Queen's Pier." *International Journal of Heritage Studies* 14, no. 6 (November 2008): 540–54.

Heritage BC. "Definitions and Heritage." Heritage BC, n.d. https://heritagebc.ca/ resources/definitions-heritage-faqs/.

Home Affairs Bureau. "Conversion of Kom Tong Hall for Use as the Dr Sun Yat-sen Museum." Legislative Council Paper No. CB(2)777/04-05(03), January 31, 2005. Accessed August 13, 2016. http://www.legco.gov.hk/yr04-05/english/panels/ha/ papers/ha0204cb2-777-3e.pdf.

---

45. UNESCO Bangkok, "Asia-Pacific Heritage Awards: Winning Projects," last modified October 14, 2019, https://bangkok.unesco.org/content/winning-projects.

Hong Kong Institute of Architects (HKIA). "HKIA Annual Awards 2015." Accessed July 25, 2017. http://www.building.hk/forum/2015hkia.pdf.

Hong Kong Jockey Club (HKJC). "Club Announces HK$1.8 billion 'Gift for Hong Kong' That Will Conserve Central Police Station Site as New Cultural Icon." Press release, October 11, 2007. Accessed July 25, 2017. https://www.hkjc.com/english/news/news_2007101116973.htm.

Hong Kong Jockey Club (HKJC). "Jockey Club Helps Revitalize Former Explosives Magazine into Dynamic Arts and Cultural Hub." Last modified February 9, 2012. Accessed on July 25, 2017. http://corporate.hkjc.com/corporate/corporate-news/english/2012 02/news_2012020902006.aspx.

Ku, Agnes Shuk-mei. "Remaking Places and Fashioning an Opposition Discourse: Struggle over the Star Ferry Pier and the Queen's Pier in Hong Kong." *Environment and Planning D: Society and Space* 30 (2012): 5–22.

Lee, Ho Yin, and Lynne D. DiStefano. "Purposeful Repurposing: Adaptive Reuse of Hong Kong's Heritage Buildings." In *Hong Kong: Our Smart City in the Next 30 Years*. Proceedings of The Hong Kong Institute of Surveyors Annual Conference 2014, organized by the Hong Kong Institute of Surveyors, held in Hong Kong, September 13, 2014, 22–25. Hong Kong: Hong Kong Institute of Surveyors, 2014.

Legislative Council, HKSAR. "Background Brief on Revitalising Historic Buildings through Partnership Scheme." Legislative Council Paper No. CB(1)816/08-09(04), February 24, 2009. Accessed July 9, 2016. http://www.legco.gov.hk/yr08-09/english/panels/dev/papers/dev0224cb1-816-4-e.pdf.

Leisure and Cultural Services Department (LCSD). *Dr. Sun Yat-sen Museum Financial Figures for 2017/2018*. Hong Kong: Hong Kong SAR Government, August 23, 2018. https://www.lcsd.gov.hk/CE/Museum/sysm/en_US/web/sysm/aboutus/financial.html.

Lu, Tracey L. D. "Heritage Conservation in Post-colonial Hong Kong." *International Journal of Heritage Studies* 15, nos. 2–3 (March–May 2009): 258–72.

McHugh, Fionnuala. "Let There Be Light: Will Caravaggio Bring the Asia Society Out of the Shadows?" *Post Magazine*, March 8, 2014. Accessed August 13, 2016. http://www.scmp.com/magazines/post-magazine/article/1440883/let-there-be-light-will-caravaggio-bring-asia-society-out.

O'Donnell, Patricia M., and Michael Turner. *The Historic Urban Landscape Recommendation: A New UNESCO Tool for a Sustainable Future*. Paris: UNESCO, July 28, 2012.

Office of the Chief Executive. *Chief Executive's Policy Address 1999*. Hong Kong: Hong Kong SAR Government, June 26, 2000. http://www.policyaddress.gov.hk/pa99/english/speech.htm.

Office of the Chief Executive. *2007–08 Policy Address*. Hong Kong: Hong Kong SAR Government, October 10, 2007. http://www.policyaddress.gov.hk/07-08/eng/policy.html.

Prott, Lyndel V. "The Impact of Policy on Cultural Heritage Protection." In *Cultural Heritage in Asia and the Pacific: Conservation and Policy: Proceedings of a Symposium held in Honolulu, Hawaii, September 8–13, 1991*, edited by Margaret G. H. Mac Lean, 1–14. Los Angeles: The Getty Conservation Institute, 1993.

Teather, Elizabeth Kenworthy, and Chun Shing Chow. "Identity and Place: The Testament of Designated Heritage in Hong Kong." *International Journal of Heritage Studies* 9, no. 2 (2003): 93–115.

Tourism Commission, Economic Development and Labour Bureau. "Former Marine Police Headquarters." Legislative Council Brief, file ref. ESB CR 22/24/17, July 3, 2002. Accessed August 13, 2016. http://www.tourism.gov.hk/resources/english/paperreport_doc/legco/2002-07-03/MPHQ-LegCo_Paper_(Eng).pdf.

Urban Renewal Authority. "Western Market." Last modified September 10, 2011. Accessed August 13, 2016. http://www.ura.org.hk/en/projects/heritage-preservation-and-revitalisation/central/western-market.aspx.

UNESCO Bangkok. "Asia-Pacific Heritage Awards: Winning Projects." Last modified October 14, 2019. Accessed October 18, 2019. https://bangkok.unesco.org/content/winning-projects.

Wong, Stan Hok-wui. "Real Estate Elite, Economic Development and Political Conflicts in Postcolonial Hong Kong." *China Review* 15, no. 1 (Spring 2015): 1–38. Accessed July 9, 2016. http://www.researchgate.net/publication/275856601_Real_Estate_Elite_Economic_Development_and_Political_Conflicts_in_Postcolonial_Hong_Kong.

Yung, Esther H. K., and Edwin H. W. Chan. "Problem Issues of Public Participation in Built-Heritage Conservation: Two Controversial Cases in Hong Kong." *Habitat International* 35 (2011): 457–66.

# Hong Kong Timeline

Fredo Cheung and Ho Yin Lee

This timeline sets out Hong Kong's major conservation-related entities, initiatives, legislation, and milestones from 1976 to 2019, including entries for the five Hong Kong case studies outlined in this publication.

| | |
|---|---|
| 1976 (January) | Antiquities and Monuments Ordinance is enacted. Its enforcing government agency, the Antiquities and Monuments Office (AMO), is established along with a government-appointed advisory body, the Antiquities Advisory Board (AAB). |
| 1978 (October) | Rock Carving at Big Wave Bay is designated as the first Declared Monument in Hong Kong. |
| 1983 | Hong Kong Museum of History, the adaptive reuse of two barrack blocks (built in the 1890s) of the former Whitfield Barracks in Tsim Sha Tsui (the current site of Kowloon Park), opens, making it among Hong Kong's earliest adaptive reuse projects.[1] |
| 1983 (December) | Fringe Club, the adaptive reuse of the old Dairy Farm Depot (built in 1892) at Lower Albert Road, Central, opens as a non-profit-making arts organization. |
| 1984 | Flagstaff House Museum of Tea Ware, the adaptive reuse of Flagstaff House (built in 1846) in Central, former residence of the Commander of British Forces in Hong Kong, opens.[2] |
| 1988 (November) | Hong Kong Police Museum, adaptive reuse of the Wan Chai Gap Police Station (built in 1938) at Coombe Road on the Peak, opens. |
| 1997 (July) | The Handover of Hong Kong (the return of Hong Kong's sovereignty from Britain to China). |
| 2000 (January) | Urban Renewal Authority (URA) is formed as an independent quasi-governmental agency. |
| 2000 (August) | China's first specialized built heritage conservation postgraduate programme, MSc (Conservation), is launched at The University of Hong Kong. |

---

1. In 1991, the Hong Kong Museum of History was relocated from the two barrack blocks of the former Whitfield Barracks to a purpose-built museum complex. The two barrack blocks were used for the museum's storage until 1998, when plans were in place for its adaptive reuse as the Hong Kong Heritage Discovery Centre.
2. One of the oldest surviving colonial buildings in Hong Kong, Flagstaff House was originally built in 1846 as the official residence of the Commander of the British Forces in Hong Kong and was known as Headquarters House until 1932. In 1981, the building was handed over to the Hong Kong government, and in 1984, it was adapted as the Flagstaff House Museum of Tea Ware.

| | |
|---|---|
| 2001 | Cattle Depot Artist Village, the adaptive reuse of the front portion of the former quarantine depot and slaughterhouse (built in 1908) in To Kwa Wan, opens as a cultural arts center. (This is one of the five Hong Kong case studies.) |
| 2004 (February) | Hong Kong SAR government's public consultation document, *Review of Built Heritage Conservation Policy*, is released. However, findings from this study are not followed up due to the SARS (severe acute respiratory syndrome) epidemic in Hong Kong. |
| 2004 (March) | Crown Wine Cellars (Little Hong Kong), the adaptive reuse of the former Central Ordnance (Munitions) Depot (built in 1937) in Shouson Hill, opens as a private members' club and wine cellar. (This is one of the five Hong Kong case studies.) |
| 2005 | Hong Kong Heritage Discovery Centre, the adaptive reuse of the two barrack blocks of the former Whitfield Barracks, opens as a heritage center after its initial adaptive reuse in 1983 as a museum of history. |
| 2006 (November) | Massive public protest is initiated against the demolition of the Star Ferry Pier and Queen's Pier at Edinburgh Place, Central (part of the Central Reclamation Phase III project). |
| 2006 (December) | Star Ferry Pier at Edinburgh Place, Central, is demolished despite widespread public protests. |
| 2006 (December) | Dr. Sun Yat-sen Museum, the adaptive reuse of Kom Tong Hall (built in 1914) in Central, a former private residence, opens. |
| 2007 (July) | Development Bureau (DevB) is formed as part of the re-organization of the Hong Kong SAR Government Secretariat. |
| 2007 (August) | Queen's Pier, adjacent to the demolished Star Ferry Pier, is closed for dismantling. |
| 2007 (August) | Crown Wine Cellars (Little Hong Kong) is recognized with an Award of Merit and Whitfield Barracks is recognized with a Jury Commendation for Innovation in the 2007 UNESCO Asia-Pacific Awards for Cultural Heritage Conservation. These are Hong Kong's first two adaptive reuse projects to be recognized by the awards program.[3] |
| 2007 (October) | "Revitalisation" becomes the government's official terminology for adaptive reuse, as announced by the Chief Executive of the Hong Kong SAR in his annual policy address (in which he also announced the Built Heritage Conservation Policy), "revitalisation, rather than preservation alone, should be pursued to maximise the economic and social benefits of historic buildings."[4] |
| 2008 (February) | Dismantling of Queen's Pier is complete. |
| 2008 (February) | Development Bureau (DevB) launches the Revitalisation of Historic Buildings Through Partnership Scheme (Revitalisation Scheme). |
| 2008 (April) | Commissioner for Heritage's Office (CHO) is established within the Development Bureau (DevB) to coordinate government initiated adaptive reuse (revitalization) projects. |
| 2008 (August) | Development Bureau (DevB) launches the Financial Assistance for Maintenance Scheme on Built Heritage (Maintenance Scheme). |

3. Since the establishment of the UNESCO Asia-Pacific Awards for Cultural Heritage Conservation in 2000, Hong Kong has won 20 awards collectively under the Conservation and New Design in Heritage Contexts categories. See the full list at: "Asia-Pacific Heritage Awards: Winning Projects," UNESCO Bangkok, accessed October 28, 2019, https://drupal.unescobkk.org/content/winning-projects.
4. Office of the Chief Executive, 2007–08 Policy Address (Hong Kong: Hong Kong SAR Government, October 10, 2007), http://www.policyaddress.gov.hk/07-08/eng/policy.html.

| 2010 | Savannah College of Art and Design (SCAD) Hong Kong, the adaptive reuse of the former North Kowloon Magistracy (built in 1960) in Sham Shui Po, opens as a school for art and design. (This is one of the five Hong Kong case studies.) |
| --- | --- |
| 2012 (February) | Asia Society Hong Kong Center, the adaptive reuse of the former Explosives Magazine Compound (built in stages starting in the mid-19th century into the early 20th century) in Admiralty, opens as an educational center for art and culture. |
| 2012 | Buildings Department (BD) publishes the first edition of the *Practice Guidebook for Adaptive Re-use of and Alteration and Addition Works to Heritage Buildings 2012*. |
| 2014 (April) | Development Bureau (DevB) commissions the *Consultancy Study on the Heritage Conservation Regimes in Other Jurisdictions* as the key reference for the Review of the Built Heritage Conservation Policy to be launched in the same year and led by the Antiquities Advisory Board (AAB). |
| 2014 (June) | As a part of the Review of the Built Heritage Conservation Policy, the Antiquities Advisory Board (AAB) produces a consultation document, *Respecting Our Heritage While Looking Ahead: Policy on Conservation of Built Heritage*, to facilitate public consultation on the review. |
| 2014 (December) | Antiquities Advisory Board (AAB) issues the *Report on the Policy Review on Conservation of Built Heritage*. |
| 2016 | Prince Edward Road West Shophouses (built in the 1930s), in Mong Kok, are adapted for mixed commercial and cultural uses related to the visual arts and flower-trade. (This is one of the five Hong Kong case studies.) |
| 2016 (November) | Development Bureau (DevB) announces the enhancement of the Financial Assistance for Maintenance Scheme on Built Heritage (Maintenance Scheme) by increasing the ceiling of the grant from the previous HK$1 million to 2 million. |
| 2017 | Blue House Cluster, the adaptive reuse of three shophouses (built from the 1920s to the 1950s) in Wan Chai, opens as a residential and community complex. (This is one of the five Hong Kong case studies.) |
| 2017 (May) | Tai Kwun – Centre for Heritage and Arts, the adaptive reuse of the former Central Police Station Compound (built from the 1850s until the 1930s) in Central, opens as a center for heritage and arts. |
| 2017 (November) | Blue House Cluster is the first Hong Kong project to receive the highest honor, Award of Excellence, in the 2017 UNESCO Asia-Pacific Awards for Cultural Heritage Conservation. |
| 2018 (December) | The Mills, the adaptive reuse of three disused textile mills (built from the 1950s to the 1970s) in Tseun Wan, opens as a textile-based creative industry incubator. |
| 2019 (October) | Tai Kwun – Centre for Heritage and Arts receives the highest honor, Award of Excellence, in the 2019 UNESCO Asia-Pacific Awards for Cultural Heritage Conservation. This is Hong Kong's largest and most important adaptive reuse project to date.[5] |
| 2019 (October) | The Mills receives a New Design in Heritage Contexts award in the 2019 UNESCO Asia-Pacific Awards for Cultural Heritage Conservation. This is arguably Hong Kong's largest privately initiated and funded adaptive reuse project on a privately-owned property.[6] |

5.  The Hong Kong Jockey Club, "Phased-opening of Tai Kwun to mark a major milestone for heritage revitalisation in Hong Kong," The Hong Kong Jockey Club press release (May 9, 2018), https://corporate.hkjc.com/corporate/corporate-news/english/2018-05/news_2018050902057.aspx.

6.  Vivienne Chow, "Developer plans to spend HK$700m on new home for design creativity," *South China Morning Post*, December 9, 2014, https://www.scmp.com/news/hong-kong/article/1658157/developer-plans-spend-hk700m-new-home-design-creativity.

# Adaptive Reuse: Reincarnation of Heritage Conservation and Its Evolution in Shanghai

Hugo Chan and Ho Yin Lee

## Introduction

As the prefix "re-" suggests, adaptive reuse of heritage buildings involves a two-step process—the first step is the conservation of the building or site, which gives rise to the second step, the reuse of the building or site. The reuse action would not be possible without the conservation intervention. Heritage conservation focuses primarily on protecting and managing a heritage asset, but adaptive reuse takes it one step further—what to do with the place in its next life. Thus, adaptive reuse can be seen as the reincarnation of heritage places. This chapter looks at adaptive reuse in the context of China, specifically examining its rise and use in Shanghai.

## Historical Development of Conservation in China and Shanghai

While adaptive reuse is a relatively new concept in China, heritage conservation per se has a long history in the country. As early as the 1920s, isolated historic structures and sites were protected and preserved under piecemeal governmental efforts. At the same time, and in contrast, historic fabric and heritage were damaged or destroyed by frequent warfare and the zealous pursuit of modernization. With the founding of the People's Republic of China (PRC) in 1949, unparalleled tension developed between urban conservation and socialist industrialization, especially during the Cultural Revolution (1966–1976). Later, propelled by economic reform and the 1982 "open door" policy, China gained unprecedented momentum in infrastructural development and a heightened awareness of cultural heritage conservation. Following in the footsteps of developed countries, China became a signatory to UNESCO's Convention concerning the Protection of World Cultural and Natural Heritage in 1985. This marked China's entry into the world of international conservation planning and practice, and comprehensive conservation policies and regulations were developed on national, provincial, and local levels. From the late 1990s onward, as urban populations increased and property markets heated up, historic fabric and sites in cities across China have been subject to the growing pressure exerted by economic restructuring and redevelopment.

Shanghai, historically and currently, has been heavily influenced by the West.[1] This influence has extended into areas of heritage conservation and adaptive reuse as

---

1. After the defeat in the Opium War, the Qing government of China was compelled by the British expedition to sign the Treaty of Nanking on August 29, 1842, which listed Shanghai, alongside Canton

well as the sustainability of its built heritage. All these aspects have become increasingly important with seismic shifts in the city's development agenda and its urban landscape since the turn of the millennium. This phenomenal urban spatial change, together with a wide array of conservation efforts, has made Shanghai a compelling case study for understanding heritage conservation and adaptive reuse in the ever-changing context of China, as well as Asia.

Shanghai, as the dragon head of China's economy, has always been an arena for the cutthroat race between heritage conservation and urban development. The adoption of its "open door" policy, the designation of the Pudong New Area in 1990, and the opening up of China and Shanghai to foreign corporations and businesses catalyzed the economic transformation of modern China. Propelled by boosterism and development policies in the early 1990s, the Shanghai Municipal People's Government initiated the famous 365 Plan (365 *wei peng jian gai zao*), which explicitly stated a target of demolishing 365 hectares of substandard or illegal properties in the city center by the year 2000.[2] Shanghai, as the engine of national economic development, started to experience massive demolition and redevelopment in its core urban areas where land values were about to increase exponentially.

Meanwhile, the sale of land assets was made possible through the formalization of land leases[3] and housing marketization, as housing units became commodities for transaction in a free market, instead of for allocation by state-owned work units (*dan wei*) to their employees, which had been the standard practice since the 1950s.[4] Land sales increasingly became the major source of income for cities in China. To entice foreign investment, promote growth, and achieve the goal set by the aforementioned 365 Plan, the Shanghai municipal government further reduced the land leasing fee and offered incentives to private developers. As expected, the government of Shanghai announced that the 365 Plan was successfully accomplished in 2000, though at a high price, which was only realized in hindsight. Despite being a national-level Famous Historical and Cultural City (*Lishi wenhua mingcheng*),[5] historic buildings and neighborhoods were bulldozed under the 365 Plan in the name of redevelopment.

Due to the extensive loss of heritage assets during the 1990s, the Shanghai government placed greater emphasis on conservation during the first decade of the twenty-first century. It turned out to be a decisive period for the legislation of heritage conservation in Shanghai. In 2000, the China National Committee of the International Council on Monuments and Sites (ICOMOS China) issued the Chinese version of *The Principles for the Conservation of Heritage Sites in China* (also known as *The China Principles*)—a document that sets out general conservation principles, intervention guidelines, and management planning for heritage buildings and sites. In 2003, Wu Jiang, a respected professor of architectural history at Tongji University (Shanghai), was appointed the deputy director general of the Shanghai Municipal Urban Planning Administration Bureau. His task was to oversee the management and care of historic buildings and sites in the city. In September of the same

(current-day Guangzhou), Amoy (Xiamen), Foochow (Fuzhou), and Ningpo (Ningbo), as treaty ports to be opened to foreign trades, and it was agreed that fair tariff rates would be imposed. In the decades that followed, Shanghai saw an upsurge in population from Western countries.

2. Qi Yu, *Zhuan xing qi Shang Hai cheng shi ju zhu kong jian de sheng chan ji xing tai yan jin* [The production and morphological evolution of urban living space in transitional Shanghai] (Nanjing: Southeast University Press, 2011), 103.

3. The Ordinances on Urban Land Management on the national level (1986) and The Shanghai Municipal Ordinances on Urban Land Management on the city level (1992) were enacted to allow for land redevelopment in the central built-up areas.

4. Jiemin Zhu, "A Transitional Institution for the Emerging land Market in Urban China," *Urban Studies* 42, no. 8 (2005): 1369–90.

5. Shanghai was named one of the national-level Famous Historical and Cultural Cities by the State Council of China in 1986.

year, twelve Areas with Historical Cultural Features in the city center were designated (based on a list first drafted in 1991). Heritage protection plans for these areas were completed in 2005, covering almost one-third (27 square kilometers) of Shanghai's inner-city area. Another thirty-two Areas with Historical Cultural Features were added in Pudong and other outer districts in 2005, with implementation plans issued in 2007.[6] In addition, in 2004, the Shanghai Municipal People's Government announced the fourth batch of the city's Excellent Historical Buildings, bringing the total number of such buildings to 617, up from a mere 61 sites in the first batch.[7]

With these initiatives, the Shanghai government shifted its urban conservation policies from small-scale, piecemeal efforts at conserving individual buildings (monuments) in the late 1980s to a more holistic approach of designating historic areas, composed of commercial and vernacular architecture as well as industrial heritage, in the 2000s and beyond. Heritage conservation, including adaptive reuse projects, secured its legitimacy and priority in the urban development agenda of Shanghai. The following slogan epitomizes the value now placed on conservation within the context of development: "Building new is development, conserving the old is also development" (開發新建是發展，保護改造也是發展) delivered by Han Zheng, the mayor of Shanghai in 2004.[8]

## Adaptive Reuse Takes Time: Nurturing and Revealing Heritage Values

The paradigm shift at a crossroads between heritage conservation and development saw market-led adaptive reuse efforts, ranging from small-scale ad hoc interior renovation projects to large-scale urban redevelopment and regeneration projects, undertaken around the turn of the century. To understand how adaptive reuse became popular in Shanghai, it is important to consider one specific project—the conversion of a former rice warehouse at 1305 South Suzhou Road into a design studio by Taiwanese architect, interior designer, and visionary artist Deng Kun-yan in 1997 (Fig. 8.1).

---

6. "Notice of Shanghai Municipal People's Government on Approving and Transmitting Some Suggestions on the Administration of Planning Work for Preservation-of-Historical-Look Streets (Alleys/Lanes) in This Municipality Drawn up by the Municipal Urban Planning Administration Bureau," PKULaw, accessed December 12, 2019, http://en.pkulaw.cn/display.aspx?cgid=7ee0f90988b60be1966806d707aee5d8bdfb&lib=law.

7. "Public Announcement of the Fourth Batch of Excellent Historical Buildings in Shanghai," Shanghai Municipal People's Government, October 25, 2004, accessed November 29, 2019, http://www.shanghai.gov.cn/nw2/nw2314/nw2319/nw12344/u26aw2359.html.

8. "Han Zheng and Deputies of the National People's Congress Discuss the Protection of Historical Architecture, Etc.," Shanghai Municipal People's Government, August 3, 2004, accessed January 25, 2019, http://www.shanghai.gov.cn/nw2/nw2314/nw2315/nw4411/u21aw90759.html.

**Figure 8.1:** Interior view of the adapted rice warehouse at 1305 South Suzhou Road. (Source: Ian Babbitt.)

A believer in Daoism, Deng Kun-yan applied Chinese philosophies to his interior design. He was inspired by his experience at nostalgic-themed restaurants in Taiwan during the 1980s[9] as well as his living experience while sojourning in New York and various parts of Europe during the 1990s. His approach was to simply take away the chaff and preserve the essence, or in material terms, to make the place more suitable for contemporary use. From a pragmatic standpoint, given the minimal design budget, the level of intervention was also minimal. Apart from removing age-old stains by utilizing high-pressure air and water guns, the original structure of the building was largely retained, except for reinforcement of the timber structure and removal of old flooring materials to reduce the load. Repainting was kept to a

---

9.   Deng designed a coffee shop named and themed Jiu Qing Mian Mian (loosely translated as "Lingering feelings for an old flame") in Taipei in the 1980s.

minimum. The most drastic spatial changes made by Deng were the installation of a wide skylight to illuminate the main floor and removal of three existing staircases to optimize space for an upper-floor design studio.

Deng's design was motivated by practicality rather than the possible heritage value of the place. Given the derelict condition and lack of restrictions (the structure was not graded), he was able to be innovative with design solutions. He retrieved the historic layers and stories behind the ailing warehouse and gave it new meaning and values. As stated in his own words, he attempted to "give life to junk."[10] Unlike photogenic monuments, whose architectural character and historical value are generally easy to grasp, it can take time to see through an aging façade and develop an appreciation for the heritage value of a seemingly mundane vernacular typology.

Recognized with an Honourable Mention at UNESCO's Asia-Pacific Awards for Cultural Heritage Conservation in 2004, this pioneer project subsequently spawned the conservation of many old and abandoned factory buildings and warehouses along the riverbanks of Suzhou Creek. It also inspired the adaptive reuse of numerous underutilized industrial heritage assets dotted across the historical neighborhoods of the former concession areas. Deng's work demonstrated to the public and to government officials the viability of reusing aging and neglected buildings for contemporary purposes. By lobbying for conserving the historic warehouse, the adaptive reuse project prompted the local government to designate the area as one of Shanghai's key protected heritage areas.

While Deng Kun-yan's adaptive reuse effort set a trend to transform dilapidated neighborhoods along Suzhou Creek in the former British Settlement Area, another artist was disturbing the status quo in the former French Concession area. In 1999, world-renowned Shanghainese painter Chen Yi-fei (陳逸飛) moved into a renovated studio at Nos. 2–3, Lane 210 of Taikang Road in the historic factory locale of Tianzifang (Fig. 8.2) (a project further elaborated in the case study section of this book). It was an art commune set up by art veteran Wu Mei-sen and local resident Zheng Rong-fa. Similar to Deng Kun-yan, Chen Yi-fei applied his overseas experience (living and working in a factory-converted-studio in New York in the 1980s and 1990s) to design and renovate his studio space. As one of the pioneer tenants and uncertain about the feasibility of the lease structure and the concept of an art commune, he was cautious, and his budget for this adaptive reuse project was limited. Yet the minimal intervention approach worked well with the existing physical and social fabric, and well-established Chinese artists flocked to the place to set up their galleries, music schools, and studios. With a synergistic effect, boutique shops and cafes were gradually attracted to the area, and, before long, Tianzifang became a popular cultural hub and tourist destination.[11]

10. Jun Wang, "'Art in Capital': Shaping Distinctiveness in a Culture-Led Urban Regeneration Project in Red Town, Shanghai," *Cities* (December 2009): 320.
11. Yibo Xu and Zuliang Weng, *Vibrant Lanes in Shanghai: Tianzifang* (Shanghai: Shanghai People's Fine Arts, 2011), 21–23.

**Figure 8.2:** A former mixed-use precinct is revitalized as Tianzifang, one of Shanghai's creative industry clusters. (Source: Ian Babbitt.)

Prior to these two initiatives, the neighborhoods in both Suzhou Creek and Tianzifang were deemed derelict and were included at the top of the local government's agenda and private developers' wish lists. Suzhou Creek was perceived as a slum area, heavily polluted by industrial establishments and sea trade, and populated by the lower class. The significance of the aging factories and warehouses was often overlooked. Similarly, the residential neighborhood where Tianzifang is located was generally viewed as congested and rapidly deteriorating. A sizeable portion of the two neighborhoods was included in the aforementioned 365 Plan in the 1990s.[12]

These early adaptive reuse initiatives by Deng and Chen demonstrated to government officials and the general public not only the economic potential of heritage buildings but the widespread appeal of vernacular and industrial buildings. In other words, by retrieving, repackaging, and romanticizing heritage values, even everyday vernacular structures can sell. The most valuable lesson of all: it is not necessarily expensive to realize the financial potential embedded in heritage places. This change of mentality paved the way for the subsequent adaptive reuse of a number of industrial legacies, such as M50 Art Industry Park (Fig. 8.3); Red Town (as elaborated in the case study section); and 1933 Shanghai (Fig. 8.4), as well as the comprehensive conservation-led redevelopment projects, such as Xintiandi, that were underway almost at the same time as the Tianzifang initiative.

**Figure 8.3:** A former mill revitalized into a contemporary art district known as M50. (Source: Ho Yin Lee.)

---

12. Qi Yu, *Zhuan xing qi Shang Hai cheng shi ju zhu kong jian de sheng chan ji xing tai yan jin*, 103.

**Figure 8.4:** A former slaughterhouse, built in 1933, revitalized into a restaurant and shopping complex known as Shanghai 1933. (Source: Ho Yin Lee.)

## Adaptive Reuse Takes Understanding: Representing and Monetizing Heritage Values

While the two aforementioned projects were low budget and low key to begin with, as the public and private sectors started to see the profitability of conservation and adaptive reuse projects, a number of high-end adaptive reuse projects were undertaken. With experience from M at the Fringe, a gourmet restaurant housed in a restored colonial building in the commercial district of Hong Kong, Australian restaurateur Michelle Garnaut applied the same formula to Shanghai and established M on the Bund (Fig. 8.5). She converted one floor of the handsome Nishin Navigation Building (built in 1925) into a fine-dining restaurant with a spectacular view of the Bund, including the ever-soaring skyscrapers in Lujiazui Financial District across the Huangpu River. Since its opening in 1999, this upmarket restaurant has helped to energize a once run-down neighborhood and restore the Bund to its former glory as a cultural and financial hub.[13]

**Figure 8.5:** M on the Bund, adaptive reuse of the top floor of the Nishin Navigation Building as a fine-dining restaurant. (Source: Hugo Chan.)

13. The Bund, an Anglo-Indian term for the embankment of a muddy waterfront, is referred to as Waitan (meaning "outer shore" in Chinese) or officially as Zhong Shan Dong Lu (Zhongshan Road East). In the colonial days, it was "Shanghai's Wall Street," with neoclassical architectural wonders of banks, clubs, hotels, and offices built around the early twentieth century flanking the western side of Huangpu River.

Around the corner from M on the Bund, there is Three on the Bund (Fig. 8.6), a privately funded commercial project using a leasing model. This building was conserved on the exterior and dramatically changed on the interior. Designed by world-renowned architect Michael Graves and opened in 2004, this high-profile adaptive reuse project reignited the public's interest in the Bund's potential in cultural and monetary terms. Conservation projects along the Bund, such as Bund 18 and The Waterhouse at South Bund (both elaborated in the case study section), became financially viable solutions for developers and investors, following these early projects.

**Figure 8.6:** The former Union Building, built in 1916, revitalized as a luxury retail and food and beverage destination known as Three on the Bund. (Source: Hugo Chan.)

As small-scale adaptive reuse efforts mushroomed across Shanghai, large-scale conservation-led redevelopment projects also became increasingly popular. As the first of its kind in the country, the economic triumph of Xintiandi shifted Shanghai's urban development policies from demolition to conservation. Since its completion in the early 2000s, it has spawned numerous revitalization projects of different scales across the city and the nation, such as The Cool Docks (Fig. 8.7) (located near The Waterhouse at South Bund) and Sinan Mansion in Shanghai; as well as Xihu Tiandi in Hangzhou; Wuhan Tiandi in Wuhan; and Lingnan Tiandi in Foshan.

**Figure 8.7:** Cool Docks, adaptive reuse of riverside docks for commercial and recreational uses. (Source: Hugo Chan.)

Similar to their lower-end counterparts, these high-end adaptive reuse projects at divergent scales demonstrate that history and historic buildings can be repackaged and marketed for profit. The wide range of adaptive reuse projects (from Three on the Bund's interior "make-over" to Xintiandi's "wholesale" reconstruction) have once again demonstrated that the economic viability of heritage properties does not always lie in the authenticity or integrity of the project. What users (in these cases, customers and shoppers) seem to value the most is the ambience or "mood." For commercial projects like these, users are the drivers. Investors and developers are happy and will continue to engage in such conservation-led redevelopment projects as long as consumers are drawn to them. Above all, what matters most in heritage conservation and adaptive reuse efforts are the soft qualities, the human aspects. Or, simply put, the culture of the place as well as its economic, environmental, and social aspects, as expressed in the New Urban Agenda on sustainable urban development.[14]

Xintiandi's designer, Benjamin Wood, admits he is a modernist architect and maybe a romanticist but definitely not a preservationist, and he undertook the Xintiandi project "not for a love of old buildings, but for a love of culture." Similar to interior designer Deng Kun-yan in the Suzhou Creek warehouse project and artist Chen Yi-fei in the Tianzifang art studio project, Wood also made use of his experiences from overseas projects (among others, the revitalization of two historic market buildings in Boston: Quincy Market and Faneuil Hall) and applied them to the former colonial city of Shanghai, which was under Western influence for many years.

14. United Nations Habitat, New Urban Agenda, A/RES/71/256 (October, 2016), http://habitat3.org/the-new-urban-agenda/.

As Wood emphasizes in his TED Talk (August 2016), "Xintiandi is the first place in a post-Cultural Revolution society, [that] the rising middle class, the people in Shanghai could go and hear and see. . . . They are literally creating culture at the same time they are consuming it."[15] He is a firm believer that heritage value does not really lie in the physical realm; it is more about the cultural significance that has been cultivated and nurtured by historic buildings and settings. Culture, as manifested in the renewed sustainability paradigm, is composed of values not merely from the environmental but also from the economic and social dimensions. To realize the heritage value of a place to its fullest, it is imperative to see through its physicality to its economic and social aspects in order to realize the economic value and social capital that are embedded in the heritage asset.

Since its completion, Xintiandi has received criticism as a "fake antique," notably from well-respected pioneer conservationist from Tongji University, Professor Ruan Yi-san. To this Wood responds, "You can be a critic of the commercialization of a historic neighborhood, but Xintiandi did change China. And it changed it by holding out a promise of a better life and a better city."[16] Like it or not, economic viability is an indispensable part in the equation of an adaptive reuse project. There is a fine line between realizing the economic value of a heritage property and its overcommercialization, yet at least the physical shell of such places has been kept, for now. More opportunities will arise for adaptive reuse projects in the future, the next round of reuse or the "after-afterlife" of heritage architecture.

With the shift of governmental mentalities and policies, the cultural and historic significance of specific places in Shanghai was revealed, together with the financial potential of such architectural legacies. Indeed, if not for these low- and high-end adaptive reuse endeavors by various artists and designers bringing the wide range of heritage values of these places to the attention of government officials, the policies and laws conducive to conservation would not have been integrated into the city's urban development plans and agenda. In fact, many of the subsequent adaptive reuse projects and comprehensive conservation-led redevelopment projects would never have been embraced by the local government if not for these early projects.

## Adaptive Reuse Takes Determination: Understanding and Realizing True Heritage Values

Subsequent to the commercial success of these adaptive reuse projects, in a matrix of scales and budgets, ranging from small-scale endeavors, such as M on the Bund, Three on the Bund, and Bund 18, to large-scale projects, such as Xintiandi and Tianzifang, private developers and government officials detected the economic potential of adaptive reuse projects and comprehensive urban conservation approaches, along with their possible contributions to the city's sustainable development. With this progress, there was a seismic change in the government's policy and developmental mentality, as manifested in the aforementioned public policy address in 2004 by Han Zheng, mayor of Shanghai, "Building new is development, conserving the old is also development."[17]

This paradigm shift from "development versus conservation" to "development with conservation" is a beneficial and mutual learning process for both the public and private sectors, as well as for the general public and the architects involved in these

---

15. Benjamin Wood, "A Commercial Block That Changed China," TEDxXiguan video, 17:59, August 2016, https://www.youtube.com/watch?v=8mB3-f0z0xI.
16. Benjamin Wood, "A Commercial Block That Changed China."
17. "Han Zheng and Deputies of the National People's Congress Discuss the Protection of Historical Architecture,".

adaptive reuse efforts. More often than not, developers may see only the shell (or the physical fabric) of heritage buildings and are willing to invest only enough to keep the shell intact. The quality and authenticity of the conservation effort is often sacrificed because of budget and time constraints. However, architects and designers engaged in adaptive reuse projects are oftentimes too idealistic to acknowledge the price tag behind such projects. Perfectionists, as many architects can be, have to learn when to persist and when to compromise in the best interest of the place.

In an interview Andrea Destefanis of Kokaistudios admits, even with a long track record of successful adaptive reuse projects (notably, Bund 18 and Huai Hai Lu 796, as discussed in the case study sections), committing to adaptive reuse projects is a continuous and ceaseless learning experience for the firm.[18] Unlike generic high-rise towers or expansive shopping malls populating most Asian cities today, every adaptive reuse project is distinct and challenging in its own right; each heritage building or site has its unique history and layers of stories behind it; and each deserves specific attention, care, and treatment that inevitably translates into a higher cost and longer timeframe. Therefore, when approached by clients of adaptive reuse projects, his first question will always be, "Are you sure about this? We are going to cause you trouble!" Indeed, engaging in adaptive reuse projects is a testament to the dedication of both the architects and developers.

There have been both successful and unsuccessful adaptive reuse projects in Shanghai, but to consider the range in a positive light, architects and developers can learn from all of these projects. The public and private sectors as well as the direct users of these sites increasingly value historic architecture and places, which makes adaptive reuse a more logical and desirable path. Government officials have realized the importance of heritage conservation, and private developers have discovered the financial potential of heritage buildings.

According to both Benjamin Wood and Andrea Destefanis, in recent years, many developers have been actively seeking architecture firms specializing in conservation and adaptive reuse projects. Oftentimes, it seems as though the local government encourages the developers to do so, which indicates that the government increasingly values architectural heritage as well as the professional input of the discipline.[19] For example, Kokaistudios was approached by the Overseas Chinese Town (OCT), a Chinese developer, to engage in the adaptive reuse of an abandoned warehouse in a mixed-use redevelopment project along Suzhou Creek. Ben Wood of Studio Shanghai was invited by Shui On Group, the Hong Kong developer behind Xintiandi, to participate in Xintiandi-esque projects in Hangzhou, Chongqing, and Foshan as well as government-led streetscape conservation efforts in Wuhan.

From repackaging and selling nostalgia to the realization and legitimization of true heritage values (both hard and soft qualities of the heritage building or site), as well as the speculation on the financial potential of the heritage values of buildings or blocks or historic areas, there has been an increased number of "façadism,"[20] "fake antique," or "pseudo-conservation" projects. With the property market boom in Shanghai, such projects have been growing in number. Presently, the overcommercialization of the cultural significance of heritage places and the plethora of adaptive reuse endeavors are posing imminent threats to the intactness of the historic fabric and streetscape.

---

18. Andrea Destefanis, interview by author, Kokaistudios office, Shanghai, December 2016.
19. Andrea Destefanis, interview by author; and Ben Wood, interview by author, BWSS office, Shanghai, December 2016.
20. "Façadism" is the conservation approach that involves preserving merely the façade of a historic building while demolishing or drastically altering the remainder of the structure.

## Adaptive Reuse Takes Heart: The Complete Picture of Sustainability

While the economic and spatial aspects of heritage conservation in Shanghai have gone through significant changes in the past decade, the cultural and social milieu of adaptive reuse efforts have also been transformed. Following the land market reform and economic restructuring in the 1990s, many state-owned enterprises were dismantled and privatized. They subsequently consolidated their assets and relocated their operations to the urban fringe, leaving behind several abandoned or underutilized industrial heritage buildings and compounds in the prime urban core area. It should be noted that Shanghai was the economic engine of the nation during the socialist industrialization.

In 2004, UNESCO launched the Creative Cities Network with an aim to "promote the social, economic and cultural development of cities in both the developed and the developing world."[21] In light of the rising market for creative industries in the global circuit, and having realized the economic value of its abundant industrial heritage legacies, the national and local governments of China set out conducive policies and measures to encourage adaptive reuse of industrial legacies into creative industrial uses. Shortly after, China's Ministry of Culture announced the first batch of National Cultural Industrial Demonstration Parks.[22]

Shanghai acted promptly and proactively to this opportunity and, in the same year, established a quasi-governmental department—the Shanghai Creative Industry Center—under the Shanghai Municipal Economic and Information Technology Committee (SHEITC). In 2005, the center designated its first batch of eighteen creative industry clusters by making use of a number of abandoned or underutilized factories and warehouses, mostly built in the 1920s and 1930s, including Tianzifang and Red Town (as discussed in the case study section).[23] In 2005, Xi'an hosted the Fifteenth General Assembly and Scientific Symposium of ICOMOS where the *Xi'an Declaration on the Conservation of the Setting of Heritage Structures, Sites and Areas*[24] was adopted. A year later the State Administration of Cultural Heritage (SACH) organized the first international forum focusing on industrial heritage— Wuxi Forum on the Conservation of China's Cultural Heritage, and Shanghai played host to the International Creative Industry Week. In 2010, Shanghai became the seventh City of Design, joining the UNESCO Creative Cities Network.[25] By the end of 2013, Shanghai was home to 87 creative clusters, more than 4,000 innovative design-related agencies and institutions, 283 art institutions, 239 art and cultural community centers, 100 museums, 25 libraries, and 743 archive institutions, covering a total floor area of more than 2.68 million square meters, many of which were housed in repurposed industrial heritage sites.[26]

Apart from the cultural policies that have been instrumental in the revitalization of vernacular architecture and industrial heritage sites throughout Shanghai, the national and local governments have also increasingly realized the importance

21. UNESCO Creative Cities Network, *Mission Statement* (Paris: UNESCO, 2004), https://en.unesco. org/creative-cities/sites/creative-cities/files/Mission_Statement_UNESCO_Creative_Cities_ Network_1.pdf.

22. Fei Liu et al., *The Yearbook of China's Cultural Industries 2011: Editorial Board of the Yearbook of Chinas Cultural Industries* (South Australia: Time AACP, 2017), 415.

23. "Shanghai's creative industry is clustering," Shanghai Municipal People's Government, accessed April 3, 2020, http://www.shanghai.gov.cn/nw2/nw2314/nw2315/nw4411/u21aw114779.html.

24. ICOMOS, *Xi'an Declaration on the Conservation of the Setting of Heritage Structures, Sites and Areas* (Xi'an: ICOMOS General Assembly, October 21, 2005), accessed May 15, 2020, https://www.icomos. org/xian2005/xian-declaration.htm.

25. "Shanghai," UNESCO Creative Cities Network, accessed April 4, 2017, https://en.unesco.org/ creative-cities/shanghai.

26. "Shanghai," UNESCO Creative Cities Network.

of social aspects in the planning process and development agenda. These now play a decisive role in the undertaking of adaptive reuse projects.

As a corollary to the national land market reform since the 1990s, the central planning system was decentralized, and local governments became responsible for the financial well-being of their cities.[27] Oftentimes, this was simply driven by a desire for economic and urban growth. Government officials and decision makers equated growth with sharp rises in the rate of urbanization and land sale revenue. Parcels of land in built-up central areas were made available to satisfy the growing appetite of private developers and pseudo-developers comprising former state-owned enterprises.

To facilitate the central city's redevelopment, the local government promised remuneration for affected residents and parties with vested interests in the redevelopment process, including options of participation in a house replacement program and financial compensation, even though such policy measures often favored the private sector. As one of the pioneering social policies of its kind, the Interim Provisions of Shanghai Municipality on the Replacement of the State-Owned House in Waitan Area (the Bund) was promulgated in 1994, with the redevelopment of the Bund area as an experimental case. The evicted tenants were entitled to a resettlement allowance in the transition period and were presented with an option to be resettled in ready-made replacement housing units where "the original construction area shall not be reduced and the housing condition shall not be lowered."[28]

Regarding financial compensation, the first formal legal document that explicitly set out the amount of compensation for relinquishing land use rights was the Rules of Shanghai Municipality on the Implementation of the Administration of Demolition and Relocation of Urban Houses, which was issued by the Shanghai municipal government in October 2001.[29] It stipulated that evicted tenants in residential areas were entitled to a compensation package equivalent to 80 percent of the prevalent market value of the demolished properties, while the remaining 20 percent would go to the "owner" or "provider" (an organization or a *dan wei*, or work unit).[30]

To counter the rise in the speculative real estate market in the latter half of the decade, the national government passed the Property Law of the People's Republic of China in 2007. This law covers the creation, transfer, and ownership of property, legitimizing ownership rights, use rights, and security rights. As pointed out by Tongji University Professor of Architecture Chang Qing, the enactment of this law considerably increased the development cost and compensation package for existing residents' relocation implicitly. It offered timely protection for many aging but valuable vernacular buildings in the urban areas of Shanghai (which are not listed and might otherwise be demolished) and halted many large-scale redevelopment efforts by private developers.[31]

In the years leading up to hosting the Expo 2010 Shanghai, the local government actively initiated, invested, and subsidized a slew of community-level face-lifting urban transformations, neighborhood upgrading, and street amelioration projects in lieu of

27. Jiemin Zhu, "From Land Use Right to Land Development Right: Institutional Change in China's Urban Development," *Urban Studies* 41, no. 7 (2004): 1250.
28. Shanghai Municipal People's Government, *Interim Provisions of Shanghai Municipality on the Replacement of the State-Owned House in Waitan Area (the Bund)* (Shanghai: Shanghai Municipal People's Government, August 23, 1994), Articles 11 and 12.
29. "Rules of Shanghai Municipality on the Implementation of the Administration of Demolition and Relocation of Urban Houses," Laws of the Shanghai Province, AsianLII, accessed December 12, 2019, http://www3.asianlii.org/cn/legis/sh/laws/rosmotiotaodarouh1092/.
30. Zhu, "From Land Use," 1254.
31. Qing Chang, "Jiu Gai Zhong De Shang Hai Jian Zhu Ji Qi Du Shi Li Shi Yu Jing: The Conservation of Shanghai and its Urban Historical Context," *Architectural Journal*, no. 10 (2009): 23–28.

a top-down wholesale demolition and redevelopment approach. As a result, many of the derelict residential blocks in the inner-city area were saved and revitalized.

Increasingly, government officials, private developers, and the general public viewed heritage conservation and adaptive reuse endeavors from a different perspective: they were not only "physical" matters and opportunities for financial returns but more importantly "cultural" and "social" endeavors. Conservation was seen as more than preservation or restoration of the urban fabric for aesthetic, historical, or tourist reasons or just improving the physical environs to make a neighborhood more livable; it was also recognized as important for its potential social value and how the space could be reused and adapted to the needs of the present day. Conservation was no longer simply concerned with protecting and restoring a single monument or landmark. The more holistic outlook toward a historic site or a cluster of buildings sheds new light on the practice of conservation where the cultural, economic, and social values of a place were equally emphasized and "adaptability" or its ability to withstand change were considered.

## Promise of Adaptive Reuse in Shanghai

Today, there is still a need for improvement in conservation practice, including adaptive reuse projects in Shanghai by government and professionals. While *bao hu* (protection) or *gai zuo* (change or renovation or, more implicitly, change of use or reuse) have already surfaced in some legal planning documents and regulations, the keyword "adaptive" is still missing. Nonetheless, two particular events, outlined below, point to a promising future.

To a certain degree, the revitalization of the Hongkou River Area (Fig. 8.8), an ongoing decade-long conservation effort initiated by the local district government in collaboration with the Shanghai Centre under UNESCO's World Heritage Institute of Training and Research for the Asia and the Pacific (WHITRAP), has served (since 2006) as a good example of adaptability of a community-wide conservation effort that has withstood changes with the passage of time. By embracing the Historic Urban Landscape approach, this grassroots revitalization effort has managed to improve poor facilities in historic buildings and to mend some of the damage in building structures. Additionally, it has addressed economic and social issues in the area by reusing many of the vacated factories and providing job opportunities to the growing low-income population as well as by mitigating and halting urban redevelopment projects, such as road-widening and real estate development, which pose a threat to the historic buildings.[32]

---

32. UNESCO, *The HUL Guidebook: Managing Heritage in Dynamic and Constantly Changing Urban Environments* (Shanghai: WHITRAP, 2016), 28.

**Figure 8.8:** A view of the Hongkou River and the range of architectural forms being revitalized. (Source: Ian Babbitt.)

Another noteworthy event took place in 2008, when the Shanghai government relaxed the regulations against the conversion of residential properties to nonresidential uses (popularly known as *ju gai fei*, loosely translated as "residence changed to nonresidence"), specifically to enable the adaptive reuse of Tianzifang's residential properties for commercial use. It was a major government initiative that had the potential to impact policies not only in Shanghai but also at the national level. This showed how planning regulations could adapt to changing environments.

As it appears to be the case from such landmark adaptive reuse projects in Shanghai, the ongoing success of adaptive reuse projects largely depends on people—the local community. Neither the government officials and private investors involved in planning and funding of such projects nor the architects and designers involved in the adaptive reuse process are as important as the people who live in and interact with the city day in and day out, those who care about the city. Fortunately for Shanghai, most adaptive reuse projects have been undertaken by individuals who care about the city. Similar to the old concession days when Shanghai was renowned for its *hai pai* culture, its open-mindedness and cultural tolerance, which made it a cosmopolitan metropolis, the city has once again been blessed with an influx of talent and returning Chinese from around the globe reclaiming its former glory as the cultural and financial fulcrum of the Far East. While these individuals may be foreigners or may have spent an extensive period of time sojourning and absorbing inspiration abroad, many have chosen to stay behind (in China) upon completion of their projects and started their own practices locally. In fact, some have become so attached to the city that they have started their families in Shanghai. "Because we care!" was the reason Andrea Destefanis of Kokaistudios chose to stay behind after the Bund 18 and Huai Hai Lu 796 projects wrapped up.

Architecture is a living matter, and the meaning of its life is given through its interactions with its users. One meaning may fade with the passage of time; however, adaptive reuse attempts to give a second life to a place and a new meaning to its reincarnation. This new meaning has to be renewed and validated by its new users. Consequently, adaptive reuse projects should also be living, flexible, and adaptable, so as to be regenerated over time. Such places need to be nurtured and cared for by generations of people with their heart and soul, to ensure their ongoing relevance and significance to their communities.

## Bibliography

Appleyard, Donald. *The Conservation of European Cities*. Cambridge, MA: MIT Press, 1979.

Chang, Qing. "Jiu Gai Zhong De Shang Hai Jian Zhu Ji Qi Du Shi Li Shi Yu Jing: The Conservation of Shanghai and its Urban Historical Context," *Architectural Journal*, no. 10 (2009): 23–28.

"Han Zheng and Deputies of the National People's Congress Discuss the Protection of Historical Buildings." Shanghai Municipal People's Government. Last modified August 3, 2004. Accessed January 25, 2019. http://www.shanghai.gov.cn/nw2/nw2314/nw2315/nw4411/u21aw90759.html.

Liu, Fei, Huang, Lin, Zheng, Hong, Chen, Hu Yangyu, and Cui, Xuan, *The Yearbook of China's Cultural Industries 2011: Editorial Board of the Yearbook of Chinas Cultural Industries*. Adelaide, Australia: Time AACP, 2017.

Qi Yu, Qi. *Zhuan xing qi Shang Hai cheng shi ju zhu kong jian de sheng chan ji xing tai yan jin* [The production and morphological evolution of urban living space in transitional Shanghai]. Nanjing: Southeast University Press, 2011.

Shanghai Municipal People's Government. "Shanghai's creative industry is clustering." Accessed April 3, 2020. http://www.shanghai.gov.cn/nw2/nw2314/nw2315/nw4411/u21aw114779.html.

United Nations Habitat. New Urban Agenda. A/RES/71/256. October, 2016. http://habitat3.org/the-new-urban-agenda/.

UNESCO Creative Cities Network. *Mission Statement*. Paris: UNESCO, 2004. https://en.unesco.org/creative-cities/sites/creative-cities/files/Mission_Statement_UNESCO_Creative_Cities_Network.pdf.

UNESCO. *The HUL Guidebook: Managing Heritage in Dynamic and Constantly Changing Urban Environments*. Shanghai: WHITRAP, 2016.

Wang, Jun. "'Art in Capital': Shaping Distinctiveness in a Culture-Led Urban Regeneration Project in Red Town, Shanghai." *Cities* (December 2009): 318–30.

Wood, Benjamin. "A Commercial Block That Changed China." TEDxXiguan video, 17:59. August 2016. https://www.youtube.com/watch?v=8mB3-f0z0xI.

Xu, Yibo, and Zuliang Weng. *Vibrant Lanes in Shanghai: Tianzifang*. Shanghai: Shanghai People's Fine Arts, 2011.

Yu, Qi. *Zhuan xing qi Shang Hai cheng shi ju zhu kong jian de sheng chan ji xing tai yan jin* [The production and morphological evolution of urban living space in transitional Shanghai]. Nanjing: Southeast University Press, 2011.

Zhu, Jiemin. "From Land Use Right to Land Development Right: Institutional Change in China's Urban Development." *Urban Studies* 41, no. 7 (2004): 1249–67.

Zhu, Jiemin. "A Transitional Institution for the Emerging land Market in Urban China." *Urban Studies* 42, no. 8 (2005): 1369–90.

# Shanghai Timeline

Hugo Chan and Ho Yin Lee

This timeline sets out Shanghai's major conservation-related entities, initiatives, milestones, and regulations from 1978 to 2010, including entries for the five Shanghai case studies outlined in this publication.

| | |
|---|---|
| 1978 (December) | China introduces market-oriented economic reform through its "open door" policy, which has an effect of opening the previously reclusive China to international practices in built-heritage conservation. |
| 1982 (November) | Cultural Relics Protection Law of the People's Republic of China is adopted and comes into effect. |
| 1985 (December) | China ratifies the UNESCO Convention Concerning the Protection of the World Cultural and Natural Heritage. |
| 1986 (December) | Shanghai is listed in the second batch of national-level Famous Historical and Cultural Cities. |
| 1989 (December) | China's first national-level urban planning law, City Planning Law of the People's Republic of China, is issued and comes into effect in April 1990. (It was replaced by the Urban and Rural Planning Law of the People's Republic of China—issued in October 2007 and came into effect in January 2008.) |
| 1991 (December) | Administrative Measures of Shanghai Municipality for the Protection of Excellent Contemporary Buildings (author's translation from 上海市優秀近代建築保護管理辦法) are issued. (They were revised and reissued in December 1997.) |
| 1994 (February) | Procedures of Shanghai Municipality on the Implementation of the Land Administration Law of the People's Republic of China are issued and come into effect in May 1994. |
| 1995 (June) | Regulations of Shanghai Municipality on City Planning are issued and come into effect in July 1995. [They were replaced by the Regulations of Shanghai Municipality on Urban and Rural Planning (issued in November 2010, and came into effect in January 2011).] |
| 1997 | The Taiwanese architect Deng Kun-yan identifies a historic rice warehouse at 1305 South Suzhou Road (built in 1933) for adaptive reuse as his design studio, initiating the trend of adaptive reuse of old warehouses in Shanghai's Suzhou Creek area. |
| 1998 (August) | Shanghai Municipal People's Government implemented the "365 Plan"—to expedite the demolition of 365 hectares of substandard or illegal properties in the city center by the year 2000. |

| | |
|---|---|
| 1999 (January) | M on the Bund, the adaptive reuse of one floor of the Nishin Navigation Building (built in 1925), opens as an upmarket restaurant with a view of the Bund. |
| 1999 (August) | Chen Yi-fei, a Shanghainese painter, moves into an art studio at Lane 210, Taikang Road, Tianzifang, which has been converted from a disused factory. Subsequently, more tenant artists move into this location. |
| 2000 (October) | The China National Committee of International Council on Monuments and Sites (ICOMOS China) issues the Chinese version of the *Principles for the Conservation of Heritage Sites in China* (the first Chinese-English bilingual version of the *China Principles* was published in July 2002). |
| 2001 (May) | China's State Council approves the Overall City Planning of Shanghai Municipality (1999–2020), which attaches equal importance to conservation and development. |
| 2001 (October) | Rules of Shanghai Municipality on the Implementation of the Administration of Demolition and Relocation of Urban Houses are issued, and come into effect in November 2001. |
| 2001 (October) | Xintiandi, the adaptive reuse of a dilapidated residential neighborhood of traditional *shikumen* houses (built between the 1910s and 1930s), opens in time for the Asia-Pacific Economic Cooperation (APEC) forum. |
| 2002 (July) | Regulations of the Shanghai Municipality on the Protection of the Areas with Historical Cultural Features and Excellent Historical Buildings are issued, and come into effect in January 2003. |
| 2004 (August) | In a meeting with municipal representatives of the National People's Congress and Chinese People's Political Consultative Conference on the topic of Strengthening the Protection of this Municipality's Areas with Historical Cultural Features and Excellent Historical Buildings, Shanghai's mayor Han Zheng is quoted to say, "Building new is development, conserving the old is also development." |
| 2004 (September) | Notice of Shanghai Municipal People's Government about Further Strengthening the Protection of this Municipality's Areas with Historical Cultural Features and Excellent Historical Buildings is issued. |
| 2004 (September) | Three on the Bund, the adaptive reuse of the former Union Building (built in 1916) along the Bund, opens as a luxury retail and food and beverage destination. |
| 2004 (October) | Shanghai Municipal People's Government announces the fourth batch of the city's Excellent Historical Buildings, bringing the total number of such buildings to 617, up from a mere 61 sites in the first batch (announced in July 1993). |
| 2004 (November) | The Ministry of Culture (renamed the Ministry of Culture and Tourism in 2018) announces the first batch of National Cultural Industrial Demonstration Parks, paving the way for the adaptive reuse of industrial heritage sites in Shanghai, such as M50, Red Town, and Tianzifang for creative industry uses. |
| 2004 (November) | Bund 18, the adaptive reuse of the former Chartered Bank of India, Australia and China (built in 1923) at Zhongshan East Road, opens as a luxury retail, and food and beverage destination. (This is one of the five Shanghai case studies.) |
| 2004 (November) | Shanghai Municipal Economic and Information Technology Committee (SHEITC) establishes the Shanghai Creative Industry Center (which goes into operation in January 2005) tasked with the repurposing of 18 abandoned or underutilized industrial sites as the first batch of the city's creative industry clusters. |

| | |
|---|---|
| 2005–2006 | Tianzifang is recognized by SHEITC and Shanghai Creative Industry Center as one of Shanghai's top ten most influential creative industry clusters for the year 2005. |
| 2005 (April) | M50 Art Industry Park, the adaptive reuse of a compound of over 50 industrial structures (built from the 1930s to 1990s), is officially listed as a creative industry cluster. |
| 2005 (October) | Xi'an hosts the 15th General Assembly and Scientific Symposium of ICOMOS, where the *Xi'an Declaration on the Conservation of the Setting of Heritage Structures, Sites and Areas* is adopted. |
| 2005 (November) | Shanghai Sculpture Space in Red Town, the adaptive reuse of the cold rolling steel workshop building in a state-owned factory, opens for commercial and creative industry uses, including art and design offices, an exhibition venue, and shops. (This is one of the five Shanghai case studies.) |
| 2006 (April) | State Administration of Cultural Heritage (SACH) organizes the first international forum focusing on industrial heritage—Wuxi Forum on the Conservation of China's Cultural Heritage. |
| 2006 | Community revitalization of the Hongkou River area commences with cooperation by enterprises, local residents, and the sub-district office. |
| 2007 (March) | Property Law of the People's Republic of China is issued, and goes into effect in October 2007. |
| 2007 (November) | 1933 Shanghai, the adaptive reuse of the former Shanghai Municipal Abattoir (built in 1933), is completed as a mixed-use space with commercial and creative industry uses. |
| 2008 (January) | Law of the People's Republic of China on Urban and Rural Planning, is put into effect and the City Planning Law of the People's Republic of China is annulled. |
| 2008 (March) | Shanghai Government relaxes the regulations against the conversion of residential properties to non-residential uses (popularly known as *ju gai fei*, loosely translated as "residence changed to non-residence"), specifically to enable the adaptive reuse of Tianzifang's residential properties for commercial use. (This is one of the five Shanghai case studies.) |
| 2008 (April) | Regulation[s] on the Protection of Famous Historical and Cultural Cities, Towns and Villages is adopted by the State Council. |
| 2008 (September) | Huai Hai Lu 796, the adaptive reuse of two adjacent heritage villas (built in the late 1920s) in the former French Concession area, opens as an exclusive showroom space for luxury brands. (This is one of the five Shanghai case studies.) |
| 2010 (April) | Shanghai hosts the Expo 2010 Shanghai, the preparations for which saw numerous urban transformation and street amelioration projects, continuing to add redevelopment pressure on aging residential neighborhoods. |
| 2010 (May) | The Waterhouse at South Bund, the adaptive reuse of a former warehouse building built in the 1930s and used as the Japanese army headquarters during World War II, opens as a luxury boutique hotel. (This is one of the five Shanghai case studies.) |

# "Adapt and Survive": A Survivalist's Pragmatism and Adaptability Approach to the Adaptive Reuse Paradigm in Singapore

Fredo Cheung and Ho Yin Lee

## Genesis: Singapore's Survivalist Pragmatism

This chapter examines how the pragmatic adaptability of the Singapore government has transformed built heritage conservation into an integral part of the national planning and development agenda. In examining the history of adaptive reuse in Singapore, it has to be understood in the context of "adapt and survive" as it is closely tied to the development framework of the city-state itself.

The city's uncanny ability to adapt and survive can be traced back to its formation as a city-state. To begin, Singapore is a small city-state that has an area of slightly more than 700 square kilometers through successive land reclamation (up from under 600 square kilometers in 1965) and a Chinese majority (about 74 percent in the 2018 census) multiethnic population of about 5.8 million people (2018 census, up from about 1.9 million in 1965).[1] A former British colony, Singapore went through two phases of independence: first in 1963, when it merged with independent Malaya as an autonomous part of the Federation of Malaysia; then in 1965, the city-state became a fully independent nation when it was forced out of the federation because of racial politics that conflicted with the Malay-majority Malaya. The expulsion of Singapore from the Federation of Malaysia in 1965 left the politically isolated and resource-challenged fledgling nation in a survival crisis. The direness of the situation is best epitomized in the speech of the nation's Founding Father, Prime Minister Lee Kuan Yew, for the opening of the Parliament in that same year:

> For us, survival has always been hazardous. We sought to make it less so by seeking the larger framework of Malaysia, but it was not to be. We are on our own, not friendless, not helpless, but nevertheless in the centre of an extremely tumultuous arena of conflict. And our survival depends upon our capacity first, to discern where the dangers are for us as a distinct and separate community in South-East Asia; and second, our ability to convince the bigger powers interested in this region that it is in their interests to ensure our separate survival and, in the end whatever happens, to ensure that we have got enough will and capacity to see that no policies, no solutions are attempted which will destroy our right to be ourselves in this corner of South-East Asia.[2]

---

1. PopulationPyramid, "Population Pyramids of the World from 1950 to 2100: Singapore 1965," accessed February 1, 2019, https://www.populationpyramid.net/singapore/1965/.
2. Lee Kwan Yew, "Speech by the Prime Minister, Mr. Lee Kuan Yew, When He Moved the Motion of Thanks to the Yang Di-Pertuan Negara, for His Policy Speech on the Opening of Parliament on 14th December 1965," *Singapore National Archives*, accessed February 1, 2019, http://www.nas.gov.sg/archivesonline/data/pdfdoc/lky19651214a.pdf.

Cut off from the Federation of Malaysia, the isolated and resource-poor city-state of Singapore was deprived of its access to natural resources in the mainland. The resilient ethos to "adapt and survive" espoused in Lee's speech is what makes Singapore the success story it is today, frequently cited as one of the most sustainable cities in Asia.

## Origins: Singapore's Planning-Based Adaptive Reuse Approach

Singapore's built heritage conservation has its roots in post–World War II challenges, such as the uncertainties associated with increasing self-governance, unrest in the form of Communist insurgency, and overcrowding as a result of the increase in population. The last challenge can be traced to the fact that Singapore was established by the British as a colonial entrepôt. Typical of development strategies pursued by the various administrations of British colonies at the time, urban planning was utilized for the sole purpose of promoting economic development and growth.[3] This laissez-faire approach to planning meant that the primary focus was on economic development at the expense of environmental and social issues.[4] In the context of Singapore, its status as an entrepôt was attractive to migrants from China and other parts of Southeast Asia, and the numbers grew over the course of a century of economic growth. Since the priorities of the colonial administration were focused on economic development, little was done to address increasing problems of overcrowding in the city center, including poor sanitization. The Singapore Improvement Trust (SIT) was set up in 1927 to address this problem but was largely ineffectual in its role, leading to its dissolution in 1960 and replacement with the Housing and Development Board (HDB) in 1960.[5] It is of interest to note that the SIT played an instrumental role in the rehabilitation of buildings damaged during the Japanese occupation. Although not adaptive reuse in the strict sense of the word, rehabilitation of old buildings was a necessity because materials for the construction of new buildings were limited after the war. As noted by Lily Kong in *Conserving the Past, Creating the Future: Urban Heritage in Singapore*:

> The rehabilitation of Trust buildings was reported to be the most important work between 1946 and 1949. Repairs and decoration were undertaken in many parts of Chinatown, in particular the tenements at Banda Street, Albert Street, Trengganu Street, Kreta Ayer, New Bridge and Keong Saik Roads, Tiong Bahru Road, Lavender Street and Madras Street.[6]

Clearly, even in the late 1940s, there was already a subconscious effort to engage in the adaptive reuse of old buildings out of economic and social need but not necessarily for cultural reasons at this point in time.

Another legacy of the SIT was Singapore's first Master Plan of 1958. This master plan is often considered to be the point that marks the end of the laissez-faire approach to urban planning, which had been the norm since 1822, and the beginning

---

3.   Alan Choe, "The Early Years of Nation-Building: Reflections on Singapore's Urban History," in *50 Years of Urban Planning in Singapore*, ed. Heng Chye Kiang (Singapore: World Scientific, 2017), 4.

4.   Laura Bigon, *Garden Cities and Colonial Planning: Transnationality and Urban Ideas in Africa and Palestine* (Manchester: Manchester University Press, 2016), 16. Though the subject of Bigon's research was primarily focused on French and British colonies in Africa and the British Mandatory Palestine, her observation on the development strategy was made in the broader scope of colonialism in a global context.

5.   Michael Hill and Kwen Fee Lian, *The Politics of Nation Building and Citizenship in Singapore* (Oxford: Routledge, 1995), 114.

6.   Lily Kong, *Conserving the Past, Creating the Future: Urban Heritage in Singapore* (Singapore: Urban Redevelopment Authority, 2011), 19.

of a more strategic and systematic urban planning.[7] To facilitate the implementation of the 1958 Master Plan, the ineffectual SIT was dissolved in 1960 and replaced by two new statutory bodies established in 1960. These were the Planning Department and the HDB, with the former tasked with the implementation of the 1958 Master Plan under the direction of the Prime Minister's Office, and the latter with housing the population under the direction of the Ministry of National Development (MND, established in 1959).[8]

The establishment of the HDB is a milestone in the history of urban planning in Singapore because it was set up explicitly to implement the 1958 Master Plan. It marks the beginning of a centralized planning authority to control land development in Singapore. To solve the housing crisis facing the newly independent Singaporean population, the HDB was granted wide-ranging powers that included management of new and existing buildings, clearance and redevelopment of slum/urban areas, and development of rural and agricultural areas. However, it became apparent that the HDB did not have sufficient expertise and personnel to tackle the comprehensive planning and development of the fledgling city-state. As reflected by Alan Choe, the first architect and planner of HDB:

> In Singapore's early years as a young nation, there were hardly any trained architects. For the most part, the transfer of design and planning knowledge was passed down from colonial administrators to local technicians and draftsmen. When the SIT dissolved upon the establishment of HDB, a large number of British architects and town planners left Singapore. However, a small cohort of freshly-qualified architects had just returned to Singapore. I also returned along with this cohort as a graduate of architecture and town planning, and I initially joined a private architecture firm where I was seeking to develop my professional career. Shortly after, however, I was headhunted and invited to join HDB in 1962 as I happened to be the first and only architect then with town planning qualifications in Singapore.[9]

This lack of expertise was remedied in 1962 by the Singapore government in reaching out to the United Nations Development Programme (UNDP) for assistance in evaluating its 1958 Master Plan to better understand how to effectively redevelop its city center. This led to the formation of an advisory panel in 1963, comprising three United Nations (UN) experts: Charles Abrams, Susumu Kobe, and Otto Koenigsberger.[10] In particular, Koenigsberger, an architect and planner, was instrumental in laying the foundation for heritage conservation and the concept of adaptive reuse in Singapore because he clearly defined the urban renewal strategy of the fledgling city-state in three key aspects: rehabilitation, conservation, and rebuilding.[11] This all-inclusive planning approach can be seen as a precursor to today's approach to sustainable development, which balances the economic, environmental, and social-equity needs of a city.[12]

---

7. HistorySG, "First Master Plan is Approved, 8th Aug. 1958," *Singapore Infopedia (Singapore National Library Board e-resources)*, accessed February 1, 2019, http://eresources.nlb.gov.sg/history/events/ef5af33f-bc66-4080-81d4-013564ba3119.

8. NewspaperSG, "2 New Boards Take Over from the S.I.T.," *Straits Times*, February 1, 1960, http://eresources.nlb.gov.sg/newspapers/Digitised/Article/straitstimes19600201-1.2.82. See also Shereen Tay, "Urban Planning Framework in Singapore," *Singapore Infopedia (Singapore National Library Board e-resources)*, accessed February 1, 2019, http://eresources.nlb.gov.sg/infopedia/articles/SIP_1565_2009-09-09.html.

9. Choe, "The Early Years of Nation-Building," 9.

10. NewspaperSG, "UN Experts 'Go Ahead' for Big City Face-Lift," *Straits Times*, August 13, 1963, http://eresources.nlb.gov.sg/newspapers/Digitised/Article/straitstimes19630813-1.2.21.

11. Choe, "The Early Years of Nation-Building," 10.

12. Rayman Mohamed, Robin Boyle, Allan Yilun Yang, and Joseph Tangari, "Adaptive Reuse: A Review and Analysis of Its Relationship to the 3 Es of Sustainability," *Facilities* 35, nos. 3/4 (2017): 138–54.

As observed in an article by Kevin Blackburn and Alvin Tan, "The Emergence of Heritage Conservation in Singapore and the Preservation of Monuments Board (1958–76)," the recommendations of Abrams, Kobe, and Koenigsberger as stated in their self-explanatorily titled report, *Growth and Urban Renewal in Singapore: Report Prepared for the Government of Singapore* (1963), are considered a milestone in the development of modern Singapore as they "laid the groundwork for intensive state involvement in urban planning."[13] This becomes clear when one examines how the objectives of "urban renewal" were defined by Abrams, Kobe, and Koenigsberger:

> It is now generally accepted that the three indispensable elements of urban renewal are (1) conservation (2) rehabilitation and (3) rebuilding. In vesting these three responsibilities in an urban renewal agency and giving it the power to fulfil them, the planning function is automatically highlighted and the need for expanding it into a positive force for change is at once emphasized.[14]

These recommendations led to the formation of the Urban Renewal Team in 1963, which would go on to become a government agency in 1974, known as the Urban Redevelopment Authority (URA). As its name implied, it was responsible for the implementation of redevelopment through planning, land acquisition and clearance, resettlement of affected residents and businesses, improvement on infrastructure and facilities, and land sales to the private sector.[15] Because of the more pressing needs in the 1970s for housing and economic development, built heritage conservation was not among the URA's original mandates. It was not until 1989, when the URA became the national conservation authority, that built heritage conservation shifted into substantial action.

## Convergence of Competing Agendas: Adaptive Reuse for Tourism Development and Urban Renewal

Back in the late 1960s, development for housing and urban renewal was the priority for the newly independent Singapore, as it was a matter of survival for the city-state. Emphasis was placed on new development to address the shortage of housing and the need to develop Singapore's economy. During this time, it was realized that tourism could be a major industry, which Singapore could develop to boost its economy. This led to the decision by the then-minister of culture, Sinnathamby Rajaratnam, to transfer the important tourism portfolio over to the Ministry of Finance in 1963. Rajaratnam's justification was explained in an article in the *Straits Times*, "The Ministry of Finance Would be in a Better Position to Discuss who was to spend What, And Who Was Better Able to Bear and Profit from the Expense of Tourist Promotion."[16]

The Ministry of Finance, in turn, established the statutory body the Singapore Tourist Promotion Board (STPB) in 1964 to coordinate, promote, and regulate the tourism industry. Whether it was intentional or a matter of practicality, STPB set up its office in the historic John Little Building at the heart of Singapore's Central

13. Kevin Blackburn and Alvin Tan, "The Emergence of Heritage Conservation in Singapore and the Preservation of Monuments Board (1958–76)," *South East Asian Studies* 4, no. 2 (2015), 349.

14. Charles Abrams, Susumu Kobe, and Otto Koenigsberger, *Growth and Urban Renewal in Singapore: Report Prepared for the Government of Singapore* (New York: United Nations Programme of Technical Assistance, Department of Economic and Social Affairs, 1963), 121.

15. Shereen Tay, "Urban Redevelopment Authority," *Singapore Infopedia (Singapore National Library Board e-resources)*. Accessed February 1, 2019. http://eresources.nlb.gov.sg/infopedia/articles/SIP_1569_2009-09-18.html?s=urban%20redevelopment%20authority.

16. NewspaperSG, "Finance Ministry to Handle Tourism," *Straits Times*, January 23, 1963, http://eresources.nlb.gov.sg/newspapers/Digitised/Article/straitstimes19630123.2.53.

Business District.[17] However, when the building was slated for demolition in 1973,[18] the STPB moved its office to another historic building known as Tudor Court.[19] The task of adapting this building for the STPB's use was undertaken by the URA, which had not yet become Singapore's national conservation authority at this time. As Blackburn and Tan observed:

> As General Manager of the Urban Redevelopment Authority, Choe [Alan Choe] determined the course of heritage conservation in Singapore by initiating trial restoration and rehabilitation of groups of buildings and whole streets. In co-operation with the Singapore Tourist Promotion Board, the Urban Redevelopment Authority started with the restoration of the Tudor Court buildings in the late 1960s and early 1970s. . . . These were Tudor-styled buildings along Tanglin Road which had been built for government staff during the colonial period. . . . The Urban Renewal Authority, under the 1966 Land Acquisition Act, was given extensive powers to compulsorily acquire land and buildings at a low price; they could then sell them to developers at a higher price. It therefore had access to a level of funding and power over land and buildings that the Preservation of Monuments Board did not.[20]

Though the Preservation of Monuments Board (PMB, renamed the Preservation of Sites and Monuments in 2013) was specifically set up in 1971 as the statutory authority to acquire buildings for conservation and was supported by a trust fund (the Preservation of Monuments Fund), the political and economic realities at the time meant that there were few donations from the general public. Also, most of the funds were allocated for economic development and urban renewal. Therefore, any preservation or adaptive reuse of historic buildings had to be spearheaded by the Urban Redevelopment Authority (URA), which was then part of the Housing Development Board (HDB) and under the Ministry of National Development (MND). As noted by Blackburn and Tan:

> The Preservation of Monuments Board struggled to preserve even single buildings and chose buildings which could still be used for their original function.[21]

The fact that both the PMB and URA were strategically placed under the MND underscored how cultural heritage was perceived as an asset to spur economic development in Singapore. However, the URA at this point was more focused on demolition of old buildings to facilitate new development, and conservation played second fiddle to the primary agenda of urban redevelopment, as noted by Blackburn and Tan:

> It was the Urban Redevelopment Authority that tendered out run-down historic buildings to be demolished and replaced with new concrete multi-storey complexes. Then it published before and after photographs highlighting the changes

17. The John Little Building, built in 1910, was a historic building that stood for 130 years at Raffles Places, which is technically the center of Singapore's CBD. When the John Little Department Store moved out of the premises in 1955, it was purchased by the Robinson Group and adapted into an office/shopping center. This predates the adaptive reuse of Tudor Court in the 1970s, which had often been cited by many to be one of the earliest examples of the adaptive reuse of a heritage building in Singapore.

18. It should also be pointed out that the destruction of the historic John Little Department Store building was perceived as an example of how the administration at the time prioritized new development over conservation/adaptive reuse. This led to the destruction of many iconic and historic building in Raffles Place during the 1970s.

19. Tudor Court was originally a row of 1920s terrace houses used as civil servants' quarters and built in the mock-Tudor style, hence its name.

20. Blackburn and Tan, "The Emergence of Heritage Conservation in Singapore," 360. The Preservation of Monuments Board was established in 1971 with its powers stemming from the Preservation and Monuments Act.

21. Blackburn and Tan, "The Emergence of Heritage Conservation in Singapore," 350.

in its annual report as "progress." The Urban Redevelopment Authority also high-lighted its pilot studies that allowed it to acquire and restore historic areas. A row of 17 shophouses at Cuppage Road was restored and refurbished for new businesses in 1976. These restored shophouses were previously retail shops, sun-dry shops, and a fishmongery, but upon their restoration became antique shops and stores selling local craft and art items. Next to the restored shophouses was the nine-storey concrete Cuppage Complex, which replaces other old shophouses and roadside hawkers. The Urban Redevelopment Authority was clearly more engaged in the demolition of historic buildings than their conservation during the 1970s.[22]

Even within the development-prioritized atmosphere of the 1960s and 1970s, it should also be pointed out that a social agenda to create a "national identity" through the conservation of heritage buildings was already emerging. However, owing to pri-orities for economic development, the national identity agenda was exploited more for the purpose of tourism "desti-nation" branding than for nation building, as can be seen from the Disneyesque and culturally exploitative tourism promotion campaign slogan "Instant Asia," adopted by the STPB from 1964 to 1977 to market Singapore as a "holiday destination that combined the sights, taste and cultures of Asia's main ethnic groups."[23] There were voices within government that associated Singapore's heritage with the creation of a national identity that in turn could contribute to its economy. As observed by Blackburn and Tan:

> The urban planners on Christopher Hooi's committee [the 1967 committee formed within the Ministry of Culture for creating a national monuments trust] emphasized the value of national trust to tourism and its contribution to the development of an identity for a new nation which had only gained full independ-ence in 1965. For them, "this need for preservation was not only significant in the face of the tourism industry" but also "the very basis of a country's history and heritage and will contribute to the formation of a national identity."[24]

The formation of a national identity with the dual purpose of serving Singaporeans for nation building and tourists for economic development was a tall order. Given the dire economic situation of Singapore from 1965 through the 1970s, attracting tour-ists had to come first. However, a major hindrance to brand potential sites as tourist destinations was the dilapidated state of such sites, such as along the Singapore River. The 1971 Concept Plan defined the Central Area in which the Singapore River was to become the focal point. As detailed in Stephen Dobb's book, *Singapore River: A Social History, 1819–2002*, the Singapore River had been the economic hub of the city before the emergence of container shipping, with cargo ferrying lighters known as "bumboats" being the dominant presence along the river. Along with the industry, many makeshift dwellings and food stalls sprang up along the banks, which became a major source of river pollution. As this was counter to the vision of the 1971 Concept Plan, in 1977, Prime Minister Lee Kuan Yew tasked the Ministry of the Environment with cleaning up the Singapore River and Kallang Basin (into which the Singapore River flows) as part of a ten-year Clean Rivers Campaign that lasted from 1977 to 1987. The scale and complexity of the campaign were evident in the

22. Blackburn and Tan, "The Emergence of Heritage Conservation in Singapore," 360.
23. Stephanie Ho, "Singapore Tourism Board," *Singapore Infopedia (Singapore National Library Board e-resources)*, last modified February 5, 2015, accessed February 1, 2019, http://eresources.nlb.gov.sg/infopedia/articles/sip_31_2005-01-31.html. See also Brenda Yeoh, Tan Ern Ser, Jennifer Wang and Theresa Wong, "Tourism in Singapore: An Overview of Policies and Issue," in *Tourism Management and Policy: Perspective from Singapore*, ed. Tan Ern Ser, Brenda Yeoh, and Jennifer Wang (Singapore: World Scientific, 2001), 3–15.
24. Yeoh et al., "Tourism in Singapore," 357.

involvement of Singapore's two key government agencies for national development, the HDB and URA, which were respectively tasked with resolving the resettlement and urban renewal issues involved.[25]

An important part of this massive cleanup operation was to clear the squatters and food stalls along the riverfronts and relocate them to public housing and designated food centers.[26] At first glance, the concerted effort involved in cleaning up the Singapore River may not seem directly relevant to heritage conservation, but it actually informed the URA of its future concept of Historic Districts, and two of such future Historic Districts would be along the Singapore River—Boat Quay and Clarke Quay.

## False Start: Adaptive Reuse for Tourism Development

In the Singapore government's ten-year economic development plan, announced in 1981 by the then-minister of trade and industry, the pillars of growth in the 1980s were "manufacturing, trade, tourism, transport and communications and brain services."[27] By the 1980s the tourism industry of Singapore was well established as a pillar of growth for Singapore's economy. However, in 1982 and 1983, the industry suffered its first major decline since the nation's independence in 1965. The then-minister for finance and trade and industry, Tony Tan, established a Tourism Task Force in 1984 to identify the causes, which he summarized: "As a result of our modernisation programme, we have removed aspects of our Oriental mystique and charm which are best symbolised in old buildings, traditional activities and roadside activities."[28] The Tourism Task Force pointed out that "Singapore's negative image as a tourist destination has two different aspects—the vanishing mystique and romance sought by visitors from developed countries and the unfulfilled fun and excitement desired by regional visitors."[29] To remedy the situation, the task force recommended "bring[ing] back Oriental mystique and idyllic tropical romance by enhancing existing landmarks like Chinatown, Haw Par Villa and Sentosa, and by restoring our diverse manifestations."[30] The recommendations by the Tourism Task Force marked the beginning of the path toward adaptive reuse as the strategy to revitalize the built heritage of Singapore to boost the economy through the tourism industry.

The tourist-oriented conservation approach for Chinatown and Haw Par Villa turned out to be a false start that highlighted the folly of misusing adaptive reuse for foreign tourists instead of local citizens. In the case of Chinatown, the relocation of street hawkers and residents to clear the streets and to free up the many heritage buildings for restoration and adaptive reuse for tourist-friendly upmarket shopping proved to be a conservation disaster. In a lengthy *Sunday Times* article authored by unidentified members of the Singapore Heritage Society, the authors criticized the Singapore Tourism Board's S$97.5 million revitalization plan as simplistic cultural reengineering that had "dislocated a lifestyle and ultimately drained the area of life

25. Cecilia Tortajada, "Clean-Up of the Singapore River," *Lee Kuan Yew School of Public Policy*, April 5, 2012, accessed February 1, 2019, https://lkyspp.nus.edu.sg/gia/article/clean-up-of-the-singapore-river-before-and-after.

26. Tortajada, "Clean-Up of the Singapore River."

27. NewspaperSG, "The Ten-Year Plan," *Business Times*, March 7, 1981, accessed February 1, 2019, http://eresources.nlb.gov.sg/newspapers/Digitised/Article/biztimes19810307-1.2.28.

28. Singapore Tourism Task Force, *Report of the Tourism Task Force* (Singapore: Ministry of Trade and Industry, Government of Singapore, November 1, 1984), 15.

29. Singapore Tourism Task Force, *Report of the Tourism Task Force*, 20.

30. Singapore Tourism Task Force, *Report of the Tourism Task Force*. Haw Par Villa is a 1937 theme-park-like garden owned by a philanthropist and open free of charge to the public, while Sentosa is a small island to the south of the Singapore main island that was formerly a British military base and later designated for tourism development.

and energy."[31] In the 2000s, many of the elements that gave Chinatown its character and identity were gradually reintroduced, such as the street hawker activities and local small businesses and offices that had previously been banned from the area.[32] In the words of the authors, "The tourist experience, local or foreign, never has been, and should not be, the basis of a renewal of Chinatown."

In the same article, the authors also criticized other tourist-oriented adaptive reuse attempts. One example was Lau Pa Sat (Hokkien for "old market"), an 1838 cast-iron market structure that had been gazetted as a National Monument in 1973 and was adapted by a developer in 1991 as an upmarket food court with tourist-oriented retail stalls. Dismissed by the authors as "re-engineering a wholly artificial entity," which was the main reason leading to the failure of the project, as it attracted neither locals nor tourists. In 2014, after a major renovation, the market reopened—this time more successfully—as a "hawker center" (the local name for a cooked food center) for local people.

A similar fate befell Haw Par Villa (also known as Tiger Balm Gardens) in the ambitious attempt to adapt the place as a Chinese-themed, Disneyland-like amusement park. Stipulated by its philanthropist owner Aw Boon Haw shortly before his death in 1954, the property "should be opened to the public free of charge and not be sold or converted into a private possession for twenty years."[33] However, with the patriarch's passing, the garden fell into disrepair and was eventually taken up by the Singapore Tourism Board to rebrand and repurpose as an S$80 million Chinese mythological theme park known as the Dragon World, which opened to much fanfare in 1990.[34] However, the theme park failed to meet expectations as a tourist attraction, and after incurring severe financial losses, the operator gave up in 2001. Among the many reasons for its failure is that by the 1990s, China was establishing itself as a global tourism destination, and under such circumstances, the recreation of a faux "instant China" outside China became embarrassingly outmoded.[35] To bring back the authors' comment in the aforementioned Chinatown article, which applies aptly in the case of Haw Paw Villa, "What Singapore does not need is an Orientalist caricature of itself."[36]

## Enter the URA: Re-orienting the Goals of Adaptive Reuse

By the late 1990s there was increasing public concern about the conservation approach undertaken by the Singapore Tourism Board (STB, renamed from Singapore Tourist Promotion Board in 1997). This concern is best summed up by the members of the Singapore Heritage Society in their article "Chinatown as Theme Park?": "The Board must understand that what Singaporeans (or even tourists) seek today is not another theme park on the Exotic East, but an experience of how life was, and is, lived in a country and in a historic quarter."[37]

The initial revitalization of Clarke Quay, undertaken by DBS Land, is a case in point. The area, described as a "festival village," was an attempt to evoke a sense of old Singapore by creating an ambiance that had little to do with the quay's history. The

31. "Chinatown as Theme Park?" *Sunday Times*, November 22, 1998. The full article is included in the appendix of Kwok Kian Woon et al., *Rethinking Chinatown and Heritage Conservation in Singapore* (Singapore: Singapore Heritage Society, 2000), 71–72.
32. Brenda S. A. Yeoh, "Singapore's Chinatown: Nation Building and Heritage Tourism in a Multiracial City," *Localities* 2 (2012): 141.
33. Jianli Huang and Lysa Hong, "Chinese Diasporic Culture and National Identity: The Taming of the Tiger Balm Gardens in Singapore," *Modern Asian Studies* 41, no. 1 (2007): 52.
34. Huang and Hong, "Chinese Diasporic Culture and National Identity," 60–63.
35. Huang and Hong, "Chinese Diasporic Culture and National Identity," 74.
36. "Chinatown as Theme Park?"
37. "Chinatown as Theme Park?"

revitalization attempt was a failure, as explained by Heng Chye Kiang and Vivienne Chan in their article, "The 'Night Zone' Storyline: Boat Quay, Clarke Quay and Robertson Quay":

> The net result has been to establish a tourist zone that has little appeal to local people either in terms of services offered or identification with the past. This is evident in the fact that the area is all but deserted most of the day, and only comes to life in the evening and on weekends.[38]

Clearly, it was time to rethink the priorities of conservation—for tourism branding or for nation building? This brings back the recommendation of the 1967 Ministry of Culture committee regarding the need for conservation, as it "was not only significant in the face of the tourism industry but also the very basis of a country's history and heritage and will contribute to the formation of a national identity."[39] By the end of the 1980s, Singapore's economic problems had been largely resolved, and with growing prosperity, the purpose of creating a national identity through heritage conservation shifted from tourism branding to nation building. This paradigm shift was marked by two particular events in 1989: the Urban Redevelopment Authority (URA) becoming the national conservation authority[40] and URA's Conservation Master Plan (first announced in 1986, finalized in 1989) for the city's first batch of conservation areas. These areas, gazetted in the same year, were three Historic Districts that represented the respective working-class people of Singapore's three major ethnic groups: Chinatown (traditionally a Cantonese-Chinese enclave), Kampong Glam (for Muslims of Arab and Malay ethnicities), and Little India (traditionally a Tamil-Indian enclave); two Residential Historic Districts of Cairnhill and Emerald Hill; and two Historic Districts for traditional maritime trade known as Boat Quay and Clarke Quay.

In the same year the URA also announced a S$4.09 million pilot project to restore 220 state-owned shophouses in the Tanjong Pagar Conservation Area (part of the Chinatown Historic District). Notably, the aim of this pilot restoration project, as stated by the URA, was to "educate the public and industry on the importance of heritage conservation . . . , so that the planned gazette of our first conservation areas would receive public buy-in."[41] The tourism priority was obviously gone, and social interest was on the agenda.

The 1989 Conservation Master Plan was concurrently backed by an amendment to the Planning Act to provide the legislative frame for the conservation of the Historic Districts. In anticipation of the more prominent role as the conservation authority of Singapore, the URA released its first draft conservation manuals for providing guidance on the restoration and adaptive reuse of shophouses in the Historic Districts of Chinatown, Kampong Glam, and Little India. By 1991 the draft manuals matured into a comprehensive and regularly updated document entitled *Conservation Guidelines* that stipulated conservation principles, planning parameters, and restoration guidelines for conserved buildings in gazetted conservation areas (which are divided into four categories: Historic Districts; Residential Historic Districts; Secondary Settlements; and Bungalows).[42]

---

38. Chye Kiang Heng and Vivienne Chan, "The 'Night Zone' Storyline: Boat Quay, Clarke Quay and Robertson Quay," *Traditional Dwellings and Settlements Review* 11, no. 2 (Spring 2000): 46.
39. Blackburn and Tan, "The Emergence of Heritage Conservation in Singapore," 357.
40. Tay, "Urban Redevelopment Authority."
41. "The House before Restoration," Urban Redevelopment Authority, last modified March 2009, accessed February 1, 2019, https://www.ura.gov.sg/services/download_file.aspx?f=%7B185BBF60-1AB8-4FB2-8429-06E799AEFFEF%7D.
42. Urban Redevelopment Authority, *Conservation Guidelines* (Singapore: Urban Redevelopment Board, December 2017), https://www.ura.gov.sg/Corporate/Guidelines/Conservation/-/media/E20551594A1C4A899F12E5F124ECE008.ashx.

Notably, the document provides the basis for adaptive reuse by stating that "old buildings may often have to be restored and upgraded to meet modern living needs or to accommodate new uses."[43] Detailed explanation of the key elements of the two main types of conserved buildings—the shophouse and the bungalow—are provided in the document "to retain the intrinsic character and historical values of the building" while undergoing restoration and adaptive reuse.[44] The conservation guidelines, while not statutory regulations, are enforced under Singapore's Planning Act (Chapter 232) (revised edition 1998, which is the current edition), as the statute states that the condition for obtaining Conservation Permission to carry out restoration or adaptive reuse work on conserved buildings within a conservation area is in "compliance with any conservation guidelines [which specifically referred to those issued by the URA under Section 11 of the Act] or any other requirements related to conservation,"[45] and this, therefore, marks the formalization of adaptive reuse as an integrated part of Singapore's urban planning framework.

An even clearer sign of reorienting conservation from tourists to the local community came in the form of incentives. In 1991, the Voluntary Conservation Scheme (originally known as the Conservation Initiated by Private Owners Scheme) was launched to encourage public participation in the conservation of heritage buildings under private ownership. Though the URA does not provide financial incentives to land and property owners for voluntary conservation, incentives are provided in the form of "development charge due to enhancement from change-of-use [a key aspect of adaptive reuse] will be exempted for the conserved GFA [gross floor area], similar to all other conservation properties."[46] In 1995, an annual URA Architectural Heritage Awards (AHA) was established to recognize exemplary conservation efforts in the private sector. The public participation agenda of this award is stated by the URA:

> Over two decades ago, after the successful gazette of Singapore's Historic Districts, it was felt that best-practices adopted in Government restoration projects would not be sufficient to bring about a positive change in the wider heritage environment. The community also needed to come on board the journey to carry out best-practices in private sector restoration projects.[47]

The first awards in 1995 were given for the restoration and rehabilitation of a single row house unit and a cluster of shophouses, and there was no adaptive reuse involved. Similarly, there was no adaptive reuse involved among the winning projects of 1995, 1996, and 1999. However, the 1997 and 1998 awards went to two adaptive reuse projects, which were among the first in Singapore, and they were the adaptive reuse of the former Convent of the Holy Infant Jesus (a Catholic convent and school) (Fig. 10.1) as food and beverage facilities collectively renamed CHIJMES (a play on the abbreviation of the original name), and the adaptive reuse of the former Tao Nan School (a Chinese primary school) as the Asian Civilisation Museum (converted into the Peranakan Museum in 2008 after the original museum moved to bigger premises).[48]

---

43.  Urban Redevelopment Authority, *Conservation Guidelines*, Part 1, Item 3.
44.  Urban Redevelopment Authority, *Conservation Guidelines*, Part 2, Items 3–5.
45.  Attorney-General's Chambers, *Planning Act (Chapter 232)*, rev. ed., 1998, Section 15(2)(a), Singapore Statutes Online statue, https://sso.agc.gov.sg/Act/PA1998#pr11.
46.  Urban Redevelopment Authority, "Circular on Extra Gross Floor Area (GFA) for All Bungalows Conserved in Future on Sites with Gross Plot Ratio (GPR) Control," circular no.: URA/PB/2004/13-CUDD, June 7, 2004, Item 3, accessed on February 1, 2019, https://www.ura.gov.sg/Corporate/Guidelines/Circulars/dc04-13.
47.  Urban Redevelopment Authority, *Architectural Heritage Awards: 20 Years of Restoration Excellence* (Singapore: Urban Redevelopment Authority, 2015), https://artsandculture.google.com/exhibit/tAKy0X_IIG-FKQ.
48.  Urban Redevelopment Authority, *Architectural Heritage Awards*.

Figure 10.1: The former Convent of the Holy Infant Jesus complex, built in stages beginning in the 1840s and extending through the 1850s, 1900s, and 1950s, revitalized as an entertainment, dining, and shopping venue known as CHIJMES. (Source: Ho Yin Lee.)

Into the twenty-first century, adaptive reuse projects became regular winners of the AHA. The 2000 and 2001 awards, respectively, went to the adaptive reuse of the former Rendezvous building (an ornate shophouse famous for its restaurant) as a hotel and the former House of Tan Yeok Nee (a traditional Chinese mansion) as a business school. Two adaptive reuse projects received the award in 2005 and 2006: respectively, a heritage center adapted from the former Istana Kampong Glam (a modest-looking palace of the former local sultan) and a restaurant adapted from the former Water House (a water-supply station) (Fig. 10.2).

Figure 10.2: The former Water House, built in 1919, revitalized as a trendy restaurant known as the Fullerton Waterboat House. (Source: Ho Yin Lee.)

From then on, award winners were more frequently adaptive reuse projects, such as those in 2007, 2009, 2011, and 2012, a number of which were hotel adaptive reuse projects.[49] More recent award winners include the 2016 adaptive reuse of the former Capitol Theatre (a cinema) (Fig. 10.3) as a hotel and shops, the 2017 adaptive reuse of an old godown (anglicized Malay word for "warehouse") into a hotel,[50] and the 2018 adaptive reuse of a prewar SIT Flat (Fig. 10.4) as another hotel.[51]

**Figure 10.3:** The former Capitol Theatre, built in 1929, revitalized as a hotel and shops. (Source: Ho Yin Lee.)

49.  Urban Redevelopment Authority, *Architectural Heritage Awards*.
50.  Urban Redevelopment Authority, "Architectural Heritage Awards," 2019, accessed February 1, 2019, https://www.ura.gov.sg/Corporate/Get-Involved/Conserve-Built-Heritage/Architectural-Heritage-Season/Architectural-Heritage-Awards.
51.  Indesignlive, "URA Unveils the Winners of Architectural Heritage Awards 2018," accessed February 1, 2019, https://www.indesignlive.sg/happenings/architectural-heritage-award-aha-2018.

**Figure 10.4:** A former Singapore Investment Trust (SIT) apartment building, built in the 1930s, revitalized as a hotel known as the Great Madras. (Source: Ho Yin Lee.)

## Wider Scope: From Building-Based to Area-Based Adaptive Reuse

Up until the late 1990s, heritage conservation in Singapore was very much a top-down affair with no public consultation. But in 1998, public discontent with the process was evident when the Urban Redevelopment Authority (URA) announced that the 1960 old National Library Building, a building identified with the early statehood of Singapore (it was opened by Singapore's first president), would be demolished to make way for the new campus of the Singapore Management University (SMU) and the construction of the Fort Canning Tunnel. The library was closed on March 31, 2004, and subsequently demolished, despite widespread and sustained public petition to retain it.[52] The saga showed that Singaporeans were no longer satisfied with a top-down approach to heritage conservation and that greater public participation was needed. Moreover, the unprecedented public display of collective attachment to the old National Library Building seemed to indicate the success of the government's effort in the 1990s to use built heritage as a means for fostering national identity.

The demolition of the old National Library Building raised the Singaporean public's demand to have a stake in matters relating to conservation, and this led the Singapore government to introduce reforms to incorporate public consultation into the decision-making process for built heritage. One such reform is the involvement of local professionals in the periodical review of URA's conservation guidelines. In 2000, the URA and the Singapore Institute of Architects (SIA) jointly released a set of revised conservation guidelines providing professionals with greater flexibility in design and planning for adaptive reuse of heritage buildings.[53] Another reform was the establishment of a public-represented advisory body in 2002, known as the Conservation Advisory Panel (CAP), whose role would be expanded in 2018 to become the Heritage and Identity Partnership (HIP).[54] It is noteworthy that the

52. Terry Xu, "Was the Demolishing of the Old National Library a Well-Thought [Out] Decision?," *Online Citizen*, accessed February 1, 2019, https://www.theonlinecitizen.com/2015/02/03/was-the-demolishing-of-the-old-national-library-a-well-thought-decision/.

53. Urban Redevelopment Authority, *Annual Report 2000/01* (Singapore: Urban Redevelopment Authority, 2001), 5, https://www.ura.gov.sg/-/media/Corporate/Resources/Publications/Annual-Reports/PDFs/AnnualReport_2000-2001.pdf.

54. Urban Redevelopment Authority, "Formation of new partnership on built heritage and identity," Urban Redevelopment Authority, last modified August 7, 2018, accessed February 1, 2019, https://www.ura.gov.sg/Corporate/Media-Room/Media-Releases/pr18-49.

press release for the URA's announcement of the HIP was titled "Formation of a New Partnership on Built Heritage and Identity."[55]

Since 2000, an important outcome of the URA's public engagement process on built heritage–related matters is the Identity Plan. Introduced by the URA in 2002 to conserve localities that have strong heritage character and identity, the plan recognized that there should be a development strategy to "retain the charm and character of places that had evolved over time and which held a special place within the hearts of the local communities."[56] Among the fifteen areas identified in the plan is a locality known as the Gillman Village, a sprawling 6.4-hectare former army camp site that had been repurposed unsuccessfully in 1996 for commercial use (mainly food and beverage businesses and furniture retail). The site is historically significant for its wartime memories as well as the collective memory of past national service soldiers (Fig. 10.5). The URA's ambitious plan for the site was to adapt it for a bigger national purpose—as a place for developing Singapore's contemporary art scene. This became a S$10 million two-year project jointly undertaken by three government agencies and completed in 2012, with the site's name reverting back to the original Gillman Barracks (as discussed in greater detail in the case study section of this book).[57] What is significant about the Identity Plan is that, in the same year it was launched, public feedback was sought and incorporated into the URA's Master Plan 2003, a statutory land-use plan, reviewed every five years, for guiding Singapore's physical development over the following ten to fifteen years.[58] Hence, the national identity agenda in Singapore's built heritage conservation goes beyond the adaptive reuse of individual buildings into an area-based adaptive reuse strategy that will ultimately shape the physical and social environment, leading to an integrated and holistic approach to heritage.

**Figure 10.5:** Part of the former Gillman Barracks, built in 1936, showing the former Block 7, which was used as the Regal Cinema by the Army Kinema Corporation (AKC) after the Second World War. Its AKC logo is still preserved on the exterior of the building. This and the numerous other blocks on site have been revitalized as an art center. (Source: Ho Yin Lee.)

55. Urban Redevelopment Authority, "Formation of New Partnership on Built Heritage and Identity."

56. Elaine Tan and Tan Xin Wei Andy, "Place-making and Identity in Singapore: The Role of Integrated Planning and Our Built Heritage," *Cultural Connections* 4 (2019): 161–170, accessed March 26, 2020, https://www.clc.gov.sg/docs/default-source/contributions/bc-105-cultural-connections-clc.pdf#page=162.

57. The three government agencies were the Singapore Economic Development Board, JTC Corporation (a state-owned real estate company and statutory board), and National Arts Council. See Valerie Chew, "Gilman Village," *Singapore Infopedia (Singapore National Library Board e-resources)*, accessed March 14, 2017, http://eresources.nlb.gov.sg/infopedia/articles/SIP_1395_2008-12-06.html.

58. Urban Redevelopment Authority, "Speech by Dr Vivian Balakrishnan, Minister of State for National Development, at the Launch of Draft Master Plan 2003 Exhibition (West Region), at the URA Centre Atrium," press release (February 28, 2003), accessed February 1, 2019, https://www.ura.gov.sg/Corporate/Media-Room/Speeches/pr03-09a.

## The Future: Towards Self-Sustainability

As discussed earlier in this chapter, the Urban Redevelopment Authority (URA) has been the driving force behind Singapore's built heritage conservation, especially through rigorous implementation of the 1989 Conservation Master Plan, in which adaptive reuse has become the main conservation approach and the scope expanded from individual buildings to areas. However, in an evaluation of the URA's conservation effort published in the 1994 paper "Urban Conservation in Singapore: A Survey of State Policies and Popular Attitudes" by sociologists Lily Kong and Brenda Yeoh, it was found that

> the URA has been too "heavy-handed": the public has largely been uninvolved and their opinions unsolicited or unheeded; the private sector has not been given sufficient free rein; and the commercial intent has been too overriding.[59]

As previously mentioned, in the late 1990s to the early 2000s, the strong show of public sentiment against the demolition of the old National Library Building led the URA to become aware of the need for public participation in the decision-making process for built heritage conservation, resulting in the 2002 Conservation Advisory Panel (CAP). The URA probably realized that the active involvement of the citizenry in conservation could better serve the national-identity building agenda, and the manifestation of this awareness is clearly demonstrated in the 2002 Identity Plan and, more recently, the 2018 Heritage and Identity Partnership (HIP). Whether by circumstances or by design, these public inclusion initiatives have expanded the scope of adaptive reuse from building based to area based. With this extended role of adaptive reuse, the stage is set for the transformation of community-involved area-based adaptive reuse into an effective enabler of sustainable development.

The approach to built heritage conservation as the means to achieve sustainable development is by closely engaging stakeholders to ensure the sustainability of Singapore's heritage assets. In this regard, a significant program is the URA's "stakeholder-led place management" of a community through a Business Improvement District (BID) mechanism, announced by the Minister for National Development and Second Minister for Finance Lawrence Wong in 2017. In its current pilot stage (as of early 2019), the URA is inviting communities to form legislated BIDs where "the legislation will require every eligible stakeholder in the BID to contribute funds to enhance the precinct to increase footfall."[60] It should be noted that the formation of BIDs is voluntary and requires more than half of a potential BID precinct's stakeholders to buy into the business plan on which the BID is based. At first glance, the focus of this initiative seems to be on economics since its intention is to create BIDs to enhance business opportunities:

> [The BID] is to allow the government to garner interest and support from the private sector for Singapore to adopt a formalised place management framework through legislation—a recommendation made by the Committee on the Future Economy (CFE) with the intention to create opportunities for businesses to innovate and initiate ground-up efforts, as stakeholders are better placed to respond to rapid changes in the economic environment.[61]

59. Lily Kong and Brenda Yeoh, "Urban Conservation in Singapore: A Survey of State Policies and Popular Attitude," *Urban Studies* 31, no. 2 (March 1994): 263.
60. Urban Redevelopment Authority, "Moving towards Stakeholder-Led Place Management," press release (September 5, 2017), accessed February 2, 2019, https://www.ura.gov.sg/Corporate/Media-Room/Media-Releases/pr17-58.
61. Urban Redevelopment Authority, "Moving towards Stakeholder-Led Place Management."

As the URA acknowledges, there is an existing mechanism similar to the BID organized by community-based business associations, but because the funding contribution is not legislatively required for a collective sign-in by the community, the mechanism limits contributors and benefits noncontributing free riders.[62] The idea behind URA's BID model is to ensure widespread participation within a community, and when applied to a community in a conservation area, the stakeholders can decide the form of adaptive reuse for their community's heritage assets and collectively raise the corresponding funding.

It is clear that economic and social factors to ensure the livelihood of the stakeholders are paramount considerations for adaptive reuse, which will in turn help to achieve economic and social stability. This is best accomplished through an inclusive planning system that empowers stakeholders to take ownership of their own community and enables them to assume management responsibility, which is evidently the goal of URA's BID program. Such a sustainable goal is implicitly connected with the Sustainable Development Goals (SDGs) set by the United Nations (UN) General Assembly in 2015, in which Goal 11 for sustainable cities and communities targets, "by 2030, [to] enhance inclusive and sustainable urbanization and capacity for participatory, integrated and sustainable human settlement planning and management in all countries."[63]

Such holistic thinking as well as an integrated approach to participatory urban planning and conservation that reinforces national identity and ensures cultural, economic, and social livelihood is what sets Singapore apart as one of the most sustainable cities in Asia. The success of Singapore in regard to the repurposing of its heritage assets lies in its ability to adapt and change according to contextual realities. The holistic thinking about adaptive reuse ties in seamlessly with the national policy to promote design as a means to spur economic growth, a sector first identified by the Economic Review Committee (established by the Ministry of Trade and Industry) in 2003, and which led to the formation of the Design Singapore Council (by the Ministry of Communications and Information) in the same year. In 2016, such efforts culminated in the Design 2025 vision for Singapore, where design is seen as "a key driver of innovation and value creation for business and economy," "an effective approach for solving complex societal problems," and "contributes to national identity and nation buildings."[64]

This emphasis on good design and design as a means to contribute to national identity is best reflected in the National Gallery Singapore (Fig. 10.6, elaborated in the institutional case study section), which opened in 2015, shortly before the announcement of the Design 2025 vision for Singapore. The National Gallery is a conservation project where innovative design is utilized for adaptive reuse of two side-by-side gazetted National Monuments—the former City Hall and former Supreme Court—as a united new facility for fostering appreciation of art and design. The most important lessons to be learned from Singapore are the importance of holistic thinking and flexibility when it comes to the adaptive reuse of heritage buildings. As well, there needs to be a coherent vision within the context of national policies that ensures the long-term sustainability of heritage assets on a macro level—and, indeed, the sustainability of the city itself.

62.  Urban Redevelopment Authority, "Moving towards Stakeholder-Led Place Management."

63.  United Nations Development Programme, "Goal 11 Targets," accessed February 2, 2019, http://www.undp.org/content/undp/en/home/sustainable-development-goals/goal-11-sustainable-cities-and-communities/targets.html.

64.  Design Singapore Council, *Design 2025* (version2) (Singapore: Design Singapore Council, 2016), accessed March 26, 2020, https://www.designsingapore.org/~/media/corp/documents/Design 2025Masterplan_v2.pdf.

**Figure 10.6:** The former City Hall (right), built in 1929, and the former Supreme Court (left), built in 1939, revitalized as an art gallery and museum, known as the National Gallery Singapore. (Source: Ho Yin Lee.)

Through a long and winding learning process, during which mistakes were made and lessons learned, the desperate quest for solutions to the survival problems of a fledging Singaporean nation has led to a survivalist's pragmatism and adaptability in dealing with the urgent agendas for housing, urban renewal, tourism development, and national-identity building. From a Third World beginning, the convergence of economic, land, and socio-cultural development toward built heritage conservation, facilitated by a determined and visionary government, has ultimately produced a world-class sustainable development model.

## Bibliography

Abrams, Charles, Susumu Kobe, and Otto Koenigsberger. *Growth and Urban Renewal in Singapore: Report Prepared for the Government of Singapore*. New York: United Nations Programme of Technical Assistance, Department of Economic and Social Affairs, 1963.

Attorney-General's Chambers. *Planning Act (Chapter 232)*. Rev. ed., 1998. Singapore Statutes Online statue. https://sso.agc.gov.sg/Act/PA1998#pr11.

Bigon, Laura. *Garden Cities and Colonial Planning: Transnationality and Urban Ideas in Africa and Palestine*. Manchester: Manchester University Press, 2016.

Blackburn, Kevin, and Alvin Tan. "The Emergence of Heritage Conservation in Singapore and the Preservation of Monuments Board (1958–76)." *South East Asian Studies* 4, no. 2 (2015): 341–64.

Chew, Valerie. "Gillman Barracks." *Singapore Infopedia (Singapore National Library Board e-resources)*. July 2017. Accessed February 1, 2019. http://eresources.nlb.gov.sg/INFOPEDIA/articles/SIP_1395_2008-12-06.html.

Choe, Alan. "The Early Years of Nation-Building: Reflections on Singapore's Urban History." In *50 Years of Urban Planning in Singapore*, edited by Heng Chye Kiang, 3–22. Singapore: World Scientific, 2017.

Design Singapore Council. *Design 2025 (version 2)*. Singapore: Design Singapore Council, 2016. Online report. Accessed March 26, 2020. https://www.designsingapore.org/~/media/corp/documents/Design2025Masterplan_v2.pdf.

Heng, Chye Kiang, and Vivienne Chan. "The 'Night Zone' Storyline: Boat Quay, Clarke Quay and Robertson Quay." *Traditional Dwellings and Settlements Review* 11, no. 2 (Spring 2000): 41–49.

Hill, Michael, and Kwen Fee Lian. *The Politics of Nation Building and Citizenship in Singapore*. Oxford: Routledge, 1995.

HistorySG. "First Master Plan Is Approved, 8th Aug. 1958." *Singapore Infopedia (Singapore National Library Board e-resources)*, 2019. Accessed February 1, 2019. http://ere-sources.nlb.gov.sg/history/events/ef5af33f-bc66-4080-81d4-013564ba3119.

Ho, Stephanie. "Singapore Tourism Board." *Singapore Infopedia (Singapore National Library Board e-resources)*. Last modified February 5, 2015. Accessed February 1, 2019. http://eresources.nlb.gov.sg/infopedia/articles/sip_31_2005-01-31.html.

Huang, Jianli, and Lysa Hong. "Chinese Diasporic Culture and National Identity: The Taming of the Tiger Balm Gardens in Singapore." *Modern Asian Studies* 41, no. 1 (2007): 41–76.

Indesignlive. "URA Unveils the Winners of Architectural Heritage Awards 2018." Accessed February 1, 2019. https://www.indesignlive.sg/happenings/architectural-heritage-award-aha-2018.

Kong, Lily. *Conserving the Past, Creating the Future: Urban Heritage in Singapore*. Singapore: Urban Redevelopment Authority, 2011.

Kong, Lily, and Brenda Yeoh. "Urban Conservation in Singapore: A Survey of State Policies and Popular Attitude." *Urban Studies* 31, no. 2 (March 1994): 247–65.

Kwok, Kian Woon, C. J. Wee Wan-Ling, and Karen Chia. *Rethinking Chinatown and Heritage Conservation in Singapore*. Singapore: Singapore Heritage Society, 2000.

Lee, Kwan Yew. "Speech by the Prime Minister, Mr. Lee Kuan Yew, When He Moved the Motion of Thanks to the Yang Di-Pertuan Negara, for His Policy Speech on the Opening of Parliament on 14th December 1965." *Singapore National Archives*. Accessed February 1, 2019. http://www.nas.gov.sg/archivesonline/data/pdfdoc/lky19651214a.pdf.

Mohamed, Rayman, Robin Boyle, Allan Yilun Yang, and Joseph Tangari. "Adaptive Reuse: A Review and Analysis of Its Relationship to the 3 Es of Sustainability." *Facilities* 35, nos. 3/4 (2017): 138–54.

PopulationPyramid. "Population Pyramids of the World from 1950 to 2100: Singapore 1965." Accessed February 1, 2019. https://www.populationpyramid.net/singapore/1965/.

Singapore Tourism Task Force. *Report of the Tourism Task Force*. Singapore: Ministry of Trade and Industry, Government of Singapore, November 1, 1984.

Tan, Elaine, and Tan Xin Wei Andy. "Place-making and Identity in Singapore: The Role of Integrated Planning and Our Built Heritage." *Cultural Connections* 4 (2019): 161–170. Accessed March 26, 2020. https://www.clc.gov.sg/docs/default-source/contributions/bc-105-cultural-connections-clc.pdf#page=162.

Tay, Shereen. "Urban Planning Framework in Singapore." *Singapore Infopedia (Singapore National Library Board e-resources)*, 2009. Accessed February 1, 2019. http://eresources.nlb.gov.sg/infopedia/articles/SIP_1565_2009-09-09.html.

Tay, Shereen. "Urban Redevelopment Authority." *Singapore Infopedia (Singapore National Library Board e-resources)*. Accessed February 1, 2019. http://eresources.nlb.gov.sg/infopedia/articles/SIP_1569_2009-09-18.html?s=urban%20redevelopment%20authority.

Tortajada, Cecilia. "Clean-Up of the Singapore River: Before and After." *Lee Kuan Yew School of Public Policy*. Last modified April 5, 2012. Accessed February 1, 2019. https://lkyspp.nus.edu.sg/gia/article/clean-up-of-the-singapore-river-before-and-after.

Urban Redevelopment Authority. *Annual Report 2000/01*. Singapore: Urban Redevelopment Authority, 2001. Accessed March 26, 2020. https://www.ura.gov.sg/-/media/Corporate/Resources/Publications/Annual-Reports/PDFs/Annual-Report_2000-2001.pdf.

Urban Redevelopment Authority. "Architectural Heritage Awards." Accessed February 1, 2019. https://www.ura.gov.sg/Corporate/Get-Involved/Conserve-Built-Heritage/Architectural-Heritage-Season/Architectural-Heritage-Awards.

Urban Redevelopment Authority. *Architectural Heritage Awards: 20 Years of Restoration Excellence*. Singapore: Urban Redevelopment Authority, 2015. https://artsandculture.google.com/exhibit/tAKy0X_IIG-FKQ.

Urban Redevelopment Authority. "Circular on Extra Gross Floor Area (GFA) for All Bungalows Conserved in Future on Sites with Gross Plot Ratio (GPR) Control." Circular no. URA/PB/2004/13-CUDD, June 7, 2004. Accessed February 1, 2019. https://www.ura.gov.sg/Corporate/Guidelines/Circulars/dc04-13.

Urban Redevelopment Authority. *Conservation Guidelines*. Singapore: Urban Redevelopment Authority, December 2017. https://www.ura.gov.sg/Corporate/Guidelines/Conservation/-/media/E20551594A1C4A899F12E5F124ECE008.ashx.

Urban Redevelopment Authority. "Formation of New Partnership on Built Heritage and Identity." Last modified August 7, 2018. Press release (August 7, 2018). Accessed February 1, 2019. https://www.ura.gov.sg/Corporate/Media-Room/Media-Releases/pr18-49.

Urban Redevelopment Authority. "The House before Restoration." Online brochure (March 2009). Accessed February 1, 2019. https://www.ura.gov.sg/services/download_file.aspx?f=%7B185BBF60-1AB8-4FB2-8429-06E799AEFFEF%7D.

Urban Redevelopment Authority. "Moving towards Stakeholder-Led Place Management." Press release (September 5, 2017). Accessed February 2, 2019. https://www.ura.gov.sg/Corporate/Media-Room/Media-Releases/pr17-58.

Urban Redevelopment Authority. "Speech by Dr Vivian Balakrishnan, Minister of State for National Development, at the Launch of Draft Master Plan 2003 Exhibition (West Region), at the URA Centre Atrium," Press release (February 28, 2003). Accessed February 1, 2019. https://www.ura.gov.sg/Corporate/Media-Room/Speeches/pr03-09a.

United Nations Development Programme. "Goal 11 Targets." Accessed February 2, 2019. http://www.undp.org/content/undp/en/home/sustainable-development-goals/goal-11-sustainable-cities-and-communities/targets.html.

Xu, Terry. "Was the Demolishing of the Old National Library a Well-Thought [Out] Decision?" *Online Citizen*. Accessed February 1, 2019. https://www.theonlinecitizen.com/2015/02/03/was-the-demolishing-of-the-old-national-library-a-well-thought-decision/.

Yeoh, Brenda. "Singapore's Chinatown: Nation Building and Heritage Tourism in a Multi-racial City." *Localities* 2 (2012): 117–59.

Yeoh, Brenda, Tan Ern Ser, Jennifer Wang, and Theresa Wong. "Tourism in Singapore: An Overview of Policies and Issue." In *Tourism Management and Policy: Perspective from Singapore*, edited by Tan Ern Ser, Brenda Yeoh, and Jennifer Wang, 3–15. Singapore: World Scientific, 2001.

# Singapore Timeline

Fredo Cheung and Ho Yin Lee

This timeline sets out Singapore's major conservation-related entities, initiatives, legislation, and milestones from 1951 to 2018, including entries for the five Singapore case studies outlined in this publication.

| | |
|---|---|
| 1951 (September) | Singapore is conferred *city* status by King George VI. |
| 1951 (September) | Municipal Commission, established in 1887 to oversee local urban affairs, is renamed as the City Council. |
| 1958 (August) | State of Singapore Act is passed, marking the transition of Singapore from a colony into a self-governing state. |
| 1958 (August) | Singapore's first Master Plan is approved. |
| 1959 (July) | Ministry of National Development (MND) is formed to progressively take over the functions of the City Council, particularly those of national land use and development. |
| 1960 (January) | Singapore Improvement Trust (SIT), a government agency formed in 1927 to carry out the urban services of urban development and public housing, is dissolved. |
| 1960 (January) | Planning Department is formed to take over the urban planning function of the Singapore Improvement Trust (SIT), and to implement the first Master Plan. |
| 1960 (February) | Housing and Development Board (HDB) is formed to take over the public housing function of the Singapore Improvement Trust (SIT). |
| 1962 | Town planning experts from the United Nations (UN) are invited by the Singaporean government to review Singapore's first Master Plan. |
| 1963 (January) | Singapore's tourism portfolio is transferred from the Ministry of Culture to the Ministry of Finance. |
| 1963 (September) | Federation of Malaysia is formed, with Singapore as a member. |
| 1963 | United Nations (UN) experts' advisory panel is formed to define Singapore's urban renewal strategy under the Master Plan, introducing three key aspects: rehabilitation, conservation, and rebuilding. |
| 1964 (January) | Singapore Tourist Promotion Board (STPB, renamed as Singapore Tourism Board in 1997) is formed as a statutory body in accordance with the Tourism Board Ordinance (1963). |
| 1965 (August) | Singapore leaves the Federation of Malaysia to become an independent nation. |

| | |
|---|---|
| 1970 (October) | Singapore Tourist Promotion Board's (STPB) headquarters, the adaptive reuse of Tudor Court, a row of terrace houses (built in the 1920s) at Tanglin Road, opens. |
| 1971 (January) | Preservation of Monuments Board (PMB) is formed under the Preservation of Monuments Act, as the statutory authority to acquire buildings for conservation. |
| 1971 | Singapore's first Concept Plan is formulated as a long-term urban development framework. |
| 1973 (July) | First batch of eight National Monuments is gazetted by the Preservation of Monuments Board (PMB). |
| 1974 (April) | Urban Redevelopment Authority (URA) is formed as an agency of the Ministry of National Development (MND) to carry out urban development and renewal, and, later, conservation through adaptive reuse. |
| 1977 (February) | Ten-year-long Clean Rivers Campaign is launched to clean up the Singapore River and the Kallang Basin, which were the two areas identified in the first Concept Plan as focal points for urban development. The campaign paved the way for the future revitalization of Boat Quay and Clarke Quay, two future Historic Districts along the Singapore River. |
| 1977 | Urban Redevelopment Authority (URA) completes the refurbishment of fourteen shophouses in Food Alley at Murray Street and seventeen shophouses at Cuppage Terrace. |
| 1981 (March) | Singapore government announces a ten-year economic development plan, in which tourism is defined as one of the five key pillars of economic growth for the 1980s. |
| 1981 (August) | Urban Redevelopment Authority (URA) announces the Emerald Hill Conservation Area, Singapore's first large-scale urban conservation project including 184 pre-war terrace houses. |
| 1984 (November) | Tourism Task Force is formed, marking the beginning of adaptive reuse as a strategy to boost the economy through tourism. |
| 1986 (December) | Urban Redevelopment Authority (URA) announces the Conservation Master Plan for the city's historic areas. Six areas are identified: Chinatown, Kampong Glam, Little India, Singapore River, Emerald Hill, and the Heritage Link (comprising of the interlinked colonial civic and cultural areas of Empress Place, Fort Canning Park, and Bras Basah Road). The plan was finalized in 1989. |
| 1986 | Singapore Heritage Society, a nongovernmental organization, is established. It went on to play a significant role in critiquing the Singapore government's early conservation plans. |
| 1986 | Singapore Tourist Promotion Board (STPB) unveils its first tourism master plan—the Tourism Product Development Plan (1986 to 1990). |
| 1987 | Clean Rivers Campaign is completed. |
| 1989 (March) | A new Planning Act is enacted, in which the Urban Redevelopment Authority (URA) is appointed as the Conservation Authority, and "conservation areas" become statutory designations. |
| 1989 (July) | Tanjong Pagar Conservation Area is gazetted and becomes the Urban Redevelopment Authority's (URA) pilot project in area-based restoration. |
| 1991 (November) | Urban Redevelopment Authority (URA) publishes the first edition of the *Conservation Guidelines* for carrying out conservation in designated conservation areas (updated from the draft version of July 1988). |

| | |
|---|---|
| 1991 | Voluntary Conservation Scheme (originally known as the "Conservation Initiated by Private Owners Scheme") is launched to encourage public participation in the conservation of heritage buildings under private ownership. |
| 1992 | Clarke Quay, the adaptive reuse of former godowns and warehouses (built between the 1850s and 1950s) along the Singapore River, opens as a family-oriented Festival Village. (This is one of the five Singapore case studies.) |
| 1993 (August) | National Heritage Board (NHB) is formed as a statutory board under the Ministry of Culture, Community and Youth (MCCY), and is tasked with the management of national museums and heritage institutions as well as the setting of policies relating to heritage sites. |
| 1995 (January) | Urban Redevelopment Authority's (URA) annual Architectural Heritage Awards (AHA) are launched to give recognition to exemplary restoration of monuments and buildings. |
| 1997 (April) | Preservation of Monuments Board (PMB) is transferred from the Ministry of National Development (MND) to the Ministry of Information and the Arts, which was renamed several times, from the Ministry of Information, Communications and the Arts (MICA) to the current Ministry of Communications and Information (MCI). |
| 1998 (December) | Government announces the location of a third university, the Singapore Management University (SMU), which requires the demolition of the old National Library Building. |
| 2001 (July) | Urban Redevelopment Authority (URA) announces its third concept plan, Concept Plan 2001, which mentions that more heritage buildings would be identified for conservation in order to create a city with rich character, diversity, and heritage. |
| 2002 (October) | Public consultation for the Urban Redevelopment Authority's (URA) Identity Plan is completed. |
| 2002 | Conservation Advisory Panel (CAP) is formed, in response to the widespread public discontent regarding the demolition plan for the old National Library Building, as a platform to incorporate public consultation in the decision-making process for built heritage conservation. (CAP morphed into the Heritage and Identity Partnership [HIP] in 2018.) |
| 2003 (December) | Master Plan 2003, which supported the Concept Plan 2001 and incorporated the Identity Plan (2002), is approved by Ministry of National Development (MND) and is gazetted. |
| 2004 (March) | Old National Library Building is closed for demolition. |
| 2006 | Clarke Quay, the adaptive reuse of former godowns and warehouses (built between the 1850s and 1950s) along the Singapore River, re-opens as a mixed-use dining and entertainment venue after its initial adaptive reuse in 1992 as a family-oriented Festival Village. (This is one of the five Singapore case studies.) |
| 2009 (July) | Preservation of Monuments Board (PMB), originally under the Ministry of National Development (MND), merges with the National Heritage Board (NHB). |
| 2011 (November) | Space Asia Hub, the adaptive reuse of a former villa and shophouse (built in the late 1800s) at Bencoolen Street, opens as a premium furniture showroom. (This is one of the five Singapore case studies.) |
| 2012 | Gillman Barracks, the adaptive reuse of a former military camp (built in 1936) at Lock Road, opens as a cultural arts center. (This is one of the five Singapore case studies.) |

| | |
|---|---|
| 2013 (July) | Preservation of Monuments Board (PMB) is renamed the Preservation of Sites and Monuments (PSM), a division under the National Heritage Board (NHB). |
| 2015 | National Gallery Singapore, the adaptive reuse of the former City Hall and Supreme Court (built in 1929 and 1939 respectively) at St. Andrew's Road, opens as a museum and art gallery. (This is one of the five Singapore case studies.) |
| 2017 (January) | The Warehouse Hotel, the adaptive reuse of a former warehouse complex (built in 1895) at Robertson Quay, opens as a boutique hotel. (This is one of the five Singapore case studies.) |
| 2018 (August) | Urban Redevelopment Authority (URA) announces the Heritage and Identity Partnership (HIP), which supports collaborations between the public and private sectors in shaping Singapore's built heritage and identity. |

# Case Studies

# Industrial Case Studies

**Table 12.1:** Industrial case studies.

| Project Name | Location | Nature | New Use | Original Use | Timeframe |
|---|---|---|---|---|---|
| Cattle Depot Artist Village | Hong Kong | Government project | Cultural (artist village) | Industrial (quarantine depot and slaughterhouse) | 2000–2001 |
| Red Town | Shanghai | Government and private partnership project | Creative industries/ Commercial (art and design offices, art galleries, exhibition venue, and retail outlets) | Industrial (steel manufacturing plant) | 2004–2005 (Shanghai Sculpture Space); 2007 (Redtown Culture and Art Community) |
| The Warehouse Hotel | Singapore | Private project | Commercial (boutique hotel) | Industrial (warehouse complex) | 2013–2017 |

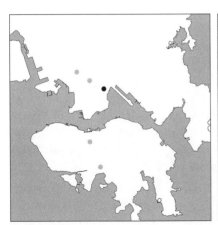

**Figure 12.1:** Location plan of Cattle Depot Artist Village, Hong Kong. (Drawn by Wai Shing Ng.)

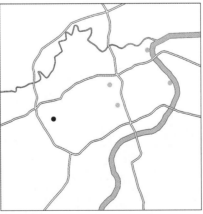

**Figure 12.2:** Location plan of Red Town, Shanghai. (Drawn by Wai Shing Ng.)

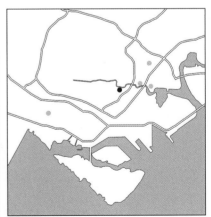

**Figure 12.3:** Location plan of The Warehouse Hotel, Singapore. (Drawn by Wai Shing Ng.)

# Cattle Depot Artist Village, Hong Kong

Tiffany Tang

## Project Information

**Table 13.1:** Basic details of Cattle Depot Artist Village.

| | |
|---|---|
| Address | 63 Ma Tau Kok Road, To Kwa Wan, Kowloon, Hong Kong |
| Old use | Industrial (quarantine depot and slaughterhouse) |
| New use | Cultural (artist village) |
| Heritage status | Grade 2 Historic Building |
| Area | 7,541 square meters (artist village); 6,000 square meters (rear portion) |
| Project cost estimate | US$2.95 million (HK$23 million)[i] |
| Operator | Development Bureau (DevB), Hong Kong SAR government |
| Developed/Funded by | Architectural Services Department (ArchSD), Hong Kong SAR government |
| Architect | N/A |
| Contractor | N/A |
| Start and completion date | 2000–2001 |

i.   The Hong Kong dollar is pegged to the US dollar at about US$1=HK$7.8.

**Figure 13.1:** Main entrance to Cattle Depot Artist Village from Ma Tau Kok Road. (Source: Curry Tse.)

## Vision

To carry out the adaptive reuse of the front portion of the former Ma Tau Kok Animal Quarantine Depot, also known as the Cattle Depot, as an artist village, to house artists relocated from Oil Street.

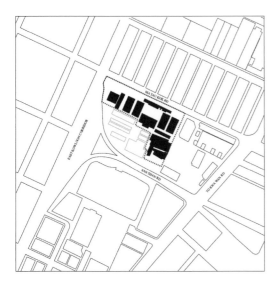

**Figure 13.2:** Site plan showing the front and rear portions of Cattle Depot Artist Village. (Drawn by Wai Shing Ng based on materials from AMO.)

**Figure 13.3:** Cattle Depot Artist Village with the slaughterhouse— to the left. (Source: Curry Tse.)

## Site History

The Cattle Depot is the only surviving prewar cattle slaughterhouse in Hong Kong. Purpose-built in 1908 as a quarantine station and abattoir, it was a large complex of animal sheds and yards, with a capacity to hold around 120 cows, 200 sheep, and 400 pigs. At the time, Ma Tau Kok was not densely populated, and hygiene problems associated with an abattoir would not have been an issue.

The complex was originally composed of five blocks built in red brick with tiled roofs. The main block, a one- and two-story building, facing Ma Tau Kok Road, had offices, stores, a kitchen, and toilets, while the other buildings served as animal sheds. A structure with a vented pitched roof and Dutch gable ends was the actual slaughterhouse. The complex, "a rare collection of Victorian style farm buildings,"[1] features brick façades with brick chimneys, double pan-and-roll Chinese tiled roofs, the aforementioned Dutch gable walls, and segmental arches. The use of fair-face red brick is one of the major characteristics contributing to the architectural significance of the place.

The Cattle Depot's slaughter function was relocated to Cheung Sha Wan in 1969. The site continued to serve for the quarantine and trading of cattle until 1999 when a modern centralized abattoir was set up in Sheung Shui. In 2001, the former slaughterhouse on Mau Tau Kok Road was revitalized as the present Cattle Depot Artist Village for use by an artist community originally occupying the former Government Supplies Department Headquarters on Oil Street, North Point. Although some renovation work was carried out during this period, the external appearance of the complex remains close to its original.

Table 13.2: Timeline of Cattle Depot Artist Village.

| 1908 | Cattle Depot, a cattle quarantine depot and slaughterhouse, is built in To Kwa Wan |
|---|---|
| 1956 | Rear portion of Cattle Depot is constructed |
| 1969 | Cattle Depot's slaughter function is relocated to Cheung Sha Wan; the site continues to function as a quarantine depot and for cattle trade |
| 1994 | Antiquities Advisory Board (AAB) recognizes the site as a Grade 3 Historic Building |
| 1999 | Cattle Depot permanently closes |
| 2001 | Architectural Services Department (ArchSD) renovates the front portion of the site, adapting it into the Cattle Depot Artist Village. Its units are leased to artists who have been relocated from the artist community in the former Government Supplies Department Headquarters on Oil Street, North Point |
| 2009 | Cattle Depot is recognized as a Grade 2 Historic Building. The Development Bureau (DevB) appoints the Hong Kong Arts Development Council (HKADC) to carry out a study concerning the future development of the site[i] |
| 2011 | Management of the Cattle Depot is passed from the Government Property Agency (GPA) to the Commissioner for Heritage's Office (CHO) under DevB. |
| 2013 | Hong Kong SAR Government grants HK$100 million through the Signature Project Scheme for the Kowloon City District Council to revitalize the rear portion of the Cattle Depot into a public open space themed on arts and culture |
| 2015 | ArchSD publishes a Heritage Impact Assessment and Conservation Management Plan for the rear portion of the Cattle Depot |
| 2019 | Rear portion of Cattle Depot opens as an Art Park[ii] |

i.   Hong Kong Arts Development Council, *Research on Future Development of Artist Village in Cattle Depot* (Hong Kong: Development Bureau Hong Kong SAR Government, July 2010), https://www.heritage.gov.hk/en/doc/conserve/CDAV_finalversionjun10.pdf.

ii.  Antiquities Advisory Board, *Historic Building Appraisal, Ma Tau Kok Animal Quarantine Depot, No. 63 Ma Tau Kok Road, To Kwa Wan, Kowloon* (Hong Kong: Hong Kong SAR Government, 2009), http://www.aab.gov.hk/historicbuilding/en/230_Appraisal_En.pdf.

1.   Antiquities Advisory Board, *Historic Building Appraisal, Ma Tau Kok Animal Quarantine Depot, No. 63 Ma Tau Kok Road, To Kwa Wan, Kowloon* (Hong Kong: Hong Kong SAR Government, 2009), http://www.aab.gov.hk/historicbuilding/en/230_Appraisal_En.pdf.

## Revitalization Concept

* Preserving the site's original architecture, facilities, and industrial character, while allowing for new use as an artist village.
* Improving accessibility to the site to enable more public appreciation and enjoyment of the unique historic site.

## Process and Partnership

The revitalization of the former slaughterhouse, the Cattle Depot, was inspired by another heritage site: the former Government Supplies Department Headquarters. In 1998, the government complex on Oil Street was vacated, and while waiting for redevelopment plans to materialize, the government rented out its units on short-term leases. The combination of affordable rents, good location, heritage value, and spacious and flexible floorplans made the units an instant success as studio and gallery spaces for the artist community. Oil Street became Hong Kong's first organic art community. The vibrancy of the Oil Street complex ended in 1999 when the government announced that the site would be sold for redevelopment. Consequentially, all leases, albeit short-term, were terminated. As compensation, the former slaughterhouse near the old airport in To Kwa Wan was offered as a replacement arts venue. In 2000, the Architectural Services Department (ArchSD) carried out renovation work at the front portion of the former slaughterhouse for artists relocating from Oil Street.

The site was renamed Cattle Depot Artist Village and, soon after, both established and emerging artists from the Oil Street community took up the space and started organizing art exhibitions and events. As with Oil Street, the government took a pragmatic approach to adaptive reuse—leases were affordable and short, and renovations to the building were minimal. This time the government's property bureau, the Government Property Agency (GPA), also levied restrictions on opening hours and public access. As a result, the artist community was considerably less vibrant than its predecessor was, and out of the twenty available units, five remained vacant.

In 2007, the Hong Kong Arts Development Council (HKADC) consulted artists about the future development of the Cattle Depot Artist Village, and in 2011, the site's management passed from the GPA to the Commissioner for Heritage's Office (CHO), under the Development Bureau (DevB). The latter intended to adopt a more flexible approach to the management of the site to facilitate its organic growth and increase public accessibility.

Of note: Eventually, the Oil Street facility redevelopment fell through, and in 2010, the government's Leisure and Cultural Services Department (LCSD) converted the site into a base for promoting community arts. It opened in 2013 under the management of the LCSD's Art Promotion Office (APO), albeit with none of the original tenants involved.

## Development Environment

In 2001, nineteen tenants moved into the Cattle Depot Artist Village, including art groups, creative industry practitioners, and individual artists. Initially, all tenants were on three-year leases, but in 2004 this was shortened to three months, making the property less attractive for tenants. No new tenants were recruited after the spaces were vacated. Additionally, the Government Property Agency (GPA) adopted a stringent estate management approach for the administration of the property, including limiting public access (compulsory registration) and restricting the opening hours to 10 a.m. to 8 p.m.

In 2008, some of the institutional members formally registered the Cattle Depot Arts Festival Association and applied for funding from the Hong Kong Arts Development Council (HKADC) to organize art festivals and promotional events. They argued for the artist village to be further developed into a contemporary art hub, which would bring energy to the district and also to form a nonprofit foundation for the operation and management of the site. Unfortunately, this proposal did not materialize.

All of these factors impeded the development of the Cattle Depot Artist Village into a thriving art community. As of 2017, there were fourteen tenants occupying the artist village, who were either independent artists or artist groups.[2] There is no collective management structure that stipulates operational guidelines or a direction for further development of the site.

## Commercial Sustainability

Twelve units are occupied by long-term tenants while eight units are available for short-term leases (from one day to three months). The Development Bureau (DevB) is responsible for ongoing repair and maintenance of the complex and the Government Property Agency (GPA) is responsible for monitoring and collecting rents.

The rent is below HK$2 per square meter,[3] which is relatively affordable compared to most other art/cultural spaces in similar city locations. To be able to pay rent, most art groups receive grants (ranging from project grants to yearly grants) from the Hong Kong Arts Development Council (HKADC). The DevB is considering a sustainable financial management model, complementary to the recent Kai Tak District revitalization project.[4]

## Key Success Factors

+ The Cattle Depot adaptive reuse project was initiated to accommodate relocated artists from Oil Street.
+ Tenants have organized a variety of cultural activities over the years, such as the Art Basel, Berlin Fest (2014), Cattle Depot Arts Festival, Cattle Depot Book Fair, and the M+ exhibition (2014)

## Key Challenges

+ The temporary nature of tenancy agreements makes commitment, coordination, and trust between the different parties a challenge.
+ In the absence of a community marketing and management structure, there is little added value for tenants. This also limits the potential for cultivation of young artists or interaction between local and international artists.
+ Proximity of the site to the gasometer nearby and current zoning restrictions limit its development potential.

---

2.  Department of Architecture of Hong Kong Chinese University, *Historical cum Social Study on Kowloon City District in Connection with Kai Tak Area* (Hong Kong: Development Bureau, Hong Kong SAR Government, December 2008), 46, https://www.heritage.gov.hk/en/doc/conserve/kowlooncityfinalreport.pdf.
3.  Commissioner for Heritage Office, Fee Chargeable Short-Term Lease of Vacant Units at Cattle Depot (Hong Kong: Commissioner for Heritage's Office, Development Bureau, Hong Kong SAR Government, July 1, 2019), https://www.heritage.gov.hk/en/doc/conserve/Fee_table_(new_rate_effective_on_1_July_2019)EN.pdf.
4.  Department of Architecture of Hong Kong Chinese University, *Historical cum Social Study.*

- Local residents feel disconnected from the Cattle Depot Artist Village. Experimental art and culture is not necessarily high on their agenda, and many of the older residents still perceive the site as the old slaughterhouse.
- The site is not freely accessible to the public, it is hard to reach by public transport, and parking facilities are limited. There are no ancillary food and beverage, leisure, or recreational services on site, and emergency access, fire safety installations, hygiene facilities, and lighting are below standard.

## Keeping Heritage Alive

The Cattle Depot is a unique place owing to the retention of its character and layout. In Hong Kong's competitive urban environment most elements of the slaughterhouse (i.e., the feeding troughs, red brick columns, shed, water pond, water tank, and well) have survived intact. Unfortunately, the outstanding historic value of the Cattle Depot Artist Village is not well articulated on site. There are no interpretation displays available to visitors that communicate the heritage significance of the place.

**Figure 13.4:** Inside one of the animal sheds adapted as an artists' studio. (Source: Tiffany Tang.)

## Value Creation

Cultural: Cattle Depot Artist Village is an important space provider for local alternative contemporary arts, ideas, and theater. It is home to two of Hong Kong's most influential visual artists—Kwok Mang Ho and Kum Chi Keung— and a number of prominent experimental art spaces including, 1a Space, Artist Commune, On & On Theatre, and Videotage.

Economic: In its current configuration, the site fills a much-needed gap in affordable art spaces in Hong Kong but provides little economic benefit to nearby residents and the community at large.

Social: The art fairs and festivals are positive events and draw crowds to the Cattle Depot Artist Village. In addition, the tenants undertake a wide variety of educational programs for schoolchildren, which nurtures young talent. In 2017, Hong Kong Baptist University (HKBU) Visual Arts Department and six other art initiatives organized a PlayDepot project to help integrate the local community and the artist village.

> Artists should be inspired by the surrounding neighborhood while the community should feel welcome to create art together.
>
> —*Artist Wong Wing Tong*

## Bibliography

Antiquities Advisory Board. *Historic Building Appraisal: Ma Tau Kok Animal Quarantine Depot, No. 63 Ma Tau Kok Road, To Kwa Wan, Kowloon* (Hong Kong: Hong Kong SAR Government, 2009. http://www.aab.gov.hk/historicbuilding/en/230_Appraisal_En.pdf.

Architectural Services Department and AGC Design Ltd. *Revitalisation of the Rear Portion of the Cattle Depot at To Kwa Wan, Kowloon, Hong Kong: Heritage Impact Assessment; Conservation Management Plan.* Hong Kong: ArchSD, Hong Kong SAR Government, 2015.

Commissioner for Heritage Office. *Fee Chargeable Short-Term Lease of Vacant Units at Cattle Depot.* Hong Kong: Commissioner for Heritage's Office, Development Bureau, Hong Kong SAR Government, July 1, 2019. https://www.heritage.gov.hk/en/doc/conserve/Fee_table_(new_rate_effective_on_1_July_2019)EN.pdf.

Department of Architecture of Hong Kong Chinese University. *Historical cum Social Study on Kowloon City District in Connection with Kai Tak Area.* Hong Kong: Development Bureau, Hong Kong SAR Government, December 2008. https://www.heritage.gov.hk/en/doc/conserve/kowlooncityfinalreport.pdf.

Development Bureau, Hong Kong SAR Government. "Ex-Ma Tau Kok Animal Quarantine Depot—Cattle Depot." Last modified December 23, 2016. https://www.heritage.gov.hk/en/conserve/cattleDepot.htm.

Hong Kong Arts Development Council. *Research on Future Development of Artist Village in Cattle Depot.* Hong Kong: Development Bureau Hong Kong SAR Government, July 2010. https://www.heritage.gov.hk/en/doc/conserve/CDAV_finalversionjun10.pdf.

# Red Town, Shanghai

## Hugo Chan

## Project Information

**Table 14.1:** Basic details of Red Town.

| | |
|---|---|
| Address | No. 570, Huai Hai West Road, Changning District, Shanghai |
| Old use | Industrial (steel manufacturing plant) |
| New use | Creative industries/Commercial (art and design offices, art galleries, exhibition venue, and retail outlets) |
| Heritage status | Shanghai Sculpture Space—Site Protected for its Historical and Cultural Value at the City Level. Other structures—not graded |
| Area | 55,000 square meters (site area); 46,000 square meters (total floor area)—including 11,400 square meters for Shanghai Sculpture Space and 34,600 square meters for Red Town |
| Project cost estimate | Undisclosed |
| Operator | Various operators |
| Developed/Funded by | Shanghai Redtown Culture Development Co. Ltd. |
| Architect | Various architects (for individual industrial buildings); Deshaus Architecture Office (master plan and architectural design); BAU (architectural design for Shanghai Sculpture Space); W&R Group (architectural design); Taranta Creations (Red Town Sculpture Space office building) |
| Contractor | Various contractors |
| Start and completion date | September 2004–November 2005 (Shanghai Sculpture Space); June 2007 (Redtown Culture and Art Community) |

**Figure 14.1:** Exterior open space of Red Town before it closed for redevelopment in 2018. (Source: Ho Yin Lee.)

## Vision

To build "an international sculpture art center that combines the functions of creation, production and exhibition"[1] as well as to introduce a new operation model for art institutes, in which "the government sets up the stage and private enterprises put on the show."[2]

**Figure 14.2:** Site plan of Red Town. (Drawn by Wai Shing Ng based on Google Earth.)

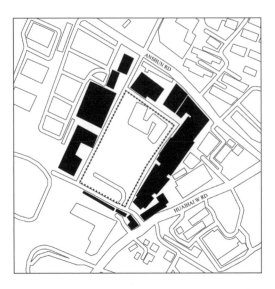

**Figure 14.3:** Interior view of the Shanghai Sculpture Space in Red Town. (Source: Ian Babbitt.)

## Site History

A branch of the Shanghai Steel Company, No. 10 Steel Plant, was established in 1956 on Huai Hai West Road along the eastern edge of Changning District, an urban fringe in proximity to Xujiahui (one of the commercial and business hubs in downtown Shanghai). The company's cold rolling workshop building (later Shanghai Sculpture Space) was completed in 1958, while the other buildings spread around

1.    Redtown, "Redtown," accessed February 4, 2019, http://www.redtown570.com/en/eng.html.
2.    Redtown, "Redtown."

an extensive open space were constructed at various times amid the socialist indus-trialization, notably in the 1950s and 1960s.[3] The compound consisted of a number of dormitory buildings, factories, mills, warehouses, and workshops. In 1998, with the restructuring of the Shanghai Steel Company, its operations were relocated. The plant and various buildings in the compound were subsequently abandoned.

**Table 14.2:** Timeline of Red Town.

| | |
|---|---|
| 1956 | No. 10 Steel Plant is established as a branch of the Shanghai Steel Company on Huai Hai West Road |
| 1958 | Construction of the plant's cold rolling workshop building begins |
| 1950s to 1960s | Other plant buildings are constructed within a compound |
| 1998 | Shanghai Steel Company undergoes restructuring—No. 10 Steel Plant and various buildings in the compound cease operation |
| 2004 | Tender for the "Shanghai Sculpture Space" opens; Dingjie Investment Ltd. wins the bid with a ten-plus-ten-year right of management contract |
| 2005 | Renovation of the former cold rolling workshop building as the Shanghai Sculpture Space is complete |
| 2007 | Dingjie Investment Ltd. wins the contract to renovate all the other buildings in the compound; second phase of the (Red Town) project opens to the public |
| 2014 | Shanghai Steel Company decides to liquidate their assets and sells the land for redevelopment (with 10 percent of the redeveloped area designated for art and cultural uses) |
| 2018 | Red Town closes for redevelopment |

## Revitalization Concept

+ Adhering to the concept of "city birth," which called for reasonable use of limited land and environmental resources in compliance with the vision of sustainable development along with "reutilization of historic architecture" and creation of an "open cultural space" and "public art buildings."[4]
+ Emphasizing the conservation of the extensive open space on site along with the reuse and rehabilitation of the built industrial heritage.
+ Introducing a variety of uses through adaptive reuse of the heritage architecture and open space by combining the functions of art and cultural exhibitions and self-sustained commercial activities to strike a balance between art and business.

## Process and Partnership

In September 2004, as a key component in the Shanghai Urban Sculpture Master Plan[5] (as approved by the municipal government of Shanghai), tenders were invited for the Shanghai Sculpture Space. By this time, the compound of No. 10 Steel Plant

---

3.  Zong Xuan, "The Elegant Turn of 10th Steel Factory of Shanghai: The Renovation Practice of Shanghai Red Town," *Urbanism and Architecture* (August 2011): 53.
4.  Redtown, "Redtown."
5.  The Shanghai Urban Sculpture Master Plan was compiled under the framework of the Shanghai Master Plan. It takes urban public spaces within the administrative jurisdiction of Shanghai as the main planning scope. The plan determines the layout of key districts for urban sculptures from two different geographic levels of the city level (*shiqu*) and central city level (*zhongxin cheng*). See Zhe Liu, Pieter Uyttenhove, and Xin Zheng, *Moving Urban Sculptures towards Sustainability: The Urban Sculpture Planning System in China* (Basel, Switzerland: MDPI, December 2018), 11.

had been left abandoned by the restructuring of the Shanghai Steel Company in 1998. After nine months of evaluations and revisions, out of nine developers, Dingjie Investment Ltd. won the bid for this project. The tender contract stipulated that the developer would be responsible for the renovation work, upon the completion of which a ten-plus-ten-year right of management would be granted. It also specified that two high-level exhibitions would have to be staged per year in the premises. The first two years of operation the Shanghai Municipal Planning Bureau would pay a rent subsidy to the land owner, Shanghai Steel Company.[6] In November 2005, conservation of the Shanghai Sculpture Space (the former cold rolling workshop building) was completed. After that, Dingjie Investment Ltd. won the contract to renovate all the other buildings in the compound as a predominately private commercial project and to redevelop the compound into what would be later known as the Redtown Culture and Art Community (popularly known as Red Town). The company was formally renamed as Redtown Culture Development Co. Ltd. in January 2006. In June 2007, the second phase of Redtown Culture and Art Community opened to the public. In the same year, the Redtown Culture Development Co. Ltd. received an award at the Creative Industry Annual Awards.[7]

In December 2014, Shanghai Steel Company decided to liquidate its assets and sold the Red Town property (essentially the land) to Rong Qiao Real Estate. As stipulated in the sales agreement, the plot ratio of the land will be augmented from 0.9 to 2.7. The Site Protected for Its Historical and Cultural Value at the City Level (the former cold rolling workshop building) and its use as the Shanghai Sculpture Space will be preserved. Including this 6,000–square meter structure, a total of 13,000 square meters will be designated as arts and cultural uses, accounting for 10 percent of the total floor area in the redevelopment scheme.[8]

At present (as of 2019), the entire compound of Red Town has been closed for redevelopment. Whether the function of the Shanghai Sculpture Space and other cultural uses can be maintained after the redevelopment is still somewhat uncertain.

## Development Environment

Following then-mayor Han Zheng's famous slogan, "Building new is development, conserving the old is also development," in September 2004, Chen Liangyu, then secretary general of Shanghai Chinese Communist Party, delivered a speech on Shanghai's cultural policy, stressing the equal importance of cultural facilities and industries, thereby formally legitimizing the creative industry. Later that year, the Master Plan for Cultural Spaces was published, and the Shanghai Creative Industry Center was set up.[9] The national and local governments' emphasis on creative industries in the development agenda was unprecedented.

Based on the outline of the Shanghai Urban Sculpture Master Plan, the idea of converting a disused industrial building into the Shanghai Sculpture Space was conceived in 2004 as part of the Shanghai Municipal Planning Bureau's promotion of urban sculpture—an experimental effort to demonstrate possible ways to restore the city's rich industrial heritage and to reuse facilities of the Expo 2010 Shanghai after the mega-event.[10] In regard to Red Town, it was envisaged that the repurposing effort

6.   Jun Wang, "'Art in Capital': Shaping Distinctiveness in a Culture-Led Urban Regeneration Project in Red Town, Shanghai," *Cities*, December (2009): 322.

7.   Redtown, "Redtown."

8.   Qing Ma (assistant to CEO, Shanghai Redtown Culture Development Co. Ltd.), in discussion with the author, May 2017.

9.   Shanghai Municipal Commission of Economy and Information, accessed July 10, 2019, http://english. sheitc.sh.gov.cn/.

10.  Wang, "Art in Capital," 321.

would create a platform for showcasing city sculpture, a place embracing both art and business.[11] Through creatively reusing and renovating old industrial structures, the government sought to transform the compound and its environs into a dynamic public art space in the urban center. The project was also seen as a way to rejuvenate the decaying urban neighborhood and enhance Shanghai's city image.

## Commercial Sustainability

Since its opening in late 2005, most usable spaces in the compound (including art galleries, event spaces, food and beverage outlets, offices, and retail and entertainment venues) were rented out at an occupancy rate of 98–100 percent, and the project generated a healthy return on investment.[12] In particular, the office and event/exhibition spaces commanded an above-average rent as compared with similar properties nearby, attracting high-profile tenants (including the 4A advertising firm) and hosting launch events for luxury brands, such as Chivas, Omega, and Swarovski.[13]

By mid-2008, less than three years after the opening of Phase 1 and one year after the opening of Phase 2, Redtown Culture Development Co. Ltd. had become one of the major contributors to the tax revenue of the Changning district government. In early 2017, despite some turnover, most original tenants continued to occupy the site. However, with the looming redevelopment plan (demolition commenced in June 2017) and the retention of only a fraction of the spaces related to cultural and creative industry uses, the future of Red Town is up in the air.

## Key Success Factors

- Right timing—the project was made possible at a time when the national and local governments increasingly emphasized the importance of creative industries and also of innovatively reusing industrial heritage in urban areas, which resulted from the market reform and economic restructuring in the 1990s.
- Development team—with previous experience in art and design as well as conservation projects, the team recognized the cultural significance and economic potential in repurposing the abandoned industrial heritage site.
- Clear market niche—from the outset, the development team understood its position well and tapped into an emerging market that integrated art and cultural industries with real estate and commercial activities.

## Key Challenges

- Industrial buildings and manufacturing plants, especially those constructed during the socialist industrialization era in China (1950s–1970s), followed standardized designs; conveying and manifesting their individual architectural and cultural values was a challenging task for the project team.
- With regard to the former cold rolling workshop building (Shanghai Sculpture Space), issues of authenticity were raised as the historic elements were not as distinctive as those typically seen in monuments or other heritage architectural typologies. The architect chose to preserve and expose the original industrial elements, such as the large steel trusses, pillars with concrete brackets, and pitched

---

11. Wang, "Art in Capital," 322.
12. Qing Ma (assistant to CEO, Shanghai Redtown Culture Development Co. Ltd.), in discussion with the author, May 2017.
13. Wang, "Art in Capital," 325.

roofs. Most original materials and finishes were retained and received minimal treatment. The building's spatial configuration was altered drastically—to increase rentable floor areas, a series of rectangular concrete structures were inserted in the middle of the building to create additional levels of rentable office space.

+ As stipulated in the original tender document, Shanghai Sculpture Space was envisioned as a communal sculpture space to serve as an incubator for up-and-coming artists. It was a challenge to strike a balance between showcasing work by renowned artists and displaying sculptures by young or unknown artists. As such, Red Town designated a permanent exhibition space for established artists while reserving yearly/temporary exhibition spaces for emerging artists and students.

+ Given a market position that relied on a fusion of arts, creative industries, and commercial viability, finding and maintaining the right tenant mix was a challenging task since inception

+ The lease structure for the development was ten plus ten years, meaning there existed uncertainty at the end of the first term (the first ten years). As it turned out, the landowner decided to redevelop the plot after ten years. Despite the fact that the Shanghai Sculpture Space building will be retained and that 10 percent of the overall floor area in the redevelopment will be designated as art and creative industry–related uses, the future of Red Town as an art and creative industry hub is unclear.

## Keeping Heritage Alive

The extensive compound of the former No. 10 Steel Plant occupied a prime location along the urban fringe of Shanghai and became an integral part of the local community, which includes former workers and their dependents. In lieu of a massive redevelopment, the conserved open space of Red Town and adjacent low-rise industrial buildings provided spatial and cultural continuity and helped preserve some "breathing space" amid the densely developed neighborhood. Opening the place to the public enabled the enjoyment of both the open space and a range of art installations, and created a social hub for artists, businesses, local residents, and visitors. The project provided government and developers with a working business model as well as a technical benchmark for the adaptive reuse of industrial heritage assets, most of which still remain underutilized and hidden in the city of Shanghai.

**Figure 14.4:** An internal pathway in Red Town showing the low-rise industrial buildings. (Source: Ho Yin Lee.)

## Value Creation

Cultural: As an exemplary project initiated in anticipation of Expo 2010 Shanghai and with Shanghai playing host to the International Creative Industry Week in 2005 and 2006, Red Town was considered one of the city's most popular cultural and creative industry sites and received visitors and delegations from around the world.

Economic: Red Town set an impressive example of reusing abandoned and deteriorating industrial heritage sites in an economically viable manner. As one of the early adaptive reuse efforts in Shanghai for transforming industrial heritage into spaces for creative industries, the economic success of this project helped trigger other projects of a similar nature, together contributing to a robust growth of creative industries in Shanghai as well as in China. The developer behind Red Town has since been engaged in a number of similar and well-received projects in Chongqing, Fuzhou, and Wuhan.[14]

Environmental: The financial viability of Red Town demonstrated to developers, government officials, and the general public that such industrial compounds can be beneficially repurposed for the public. More specifically, the conservation of low-rise industrial buildings with open space helped to create a "green lung" amid intense urban development (including flyovers), facilitate natural ventilation, and enhance the cityscape.

Social: After renovation, the compound was open to the public and easily accessible by public transportation. With a welcoming open space in the middle of the compound, Red Town contributed to the local environment and served as a community hub for social interaction, fostering social networks.

> **We believe each [adaptive reuse] project should have its own theme, needs to have its market niche to form its core competitive edge. For Red Town, it has its own theme, a very distinctive theme, with two major uses: a venue for cultural and visual arts, and also as an exemplary site for creative industries.**
>
> 〔我們認為每個項目都必須要有它自己的主題，都需要錯位的競爭，形成自己的核心競爭力。作為紅坊，它有自己的主題，它的主題非常清晰，它的產業主要體現在兩個方面，一是文化視覺藝術，另外是獲得了創意產業聚集區的示範產業基地。〕
>
> —*Zheng Pei-guang, CEO of Shanghai Redtown Culture Development Co. Ltd.*[15]

---

14. Qing Ma (assistant to CEO, Shanghai Redtown Culture Development Co. Ltd.), in discussion with the author, May 2017.
15. Sohu, "Zheng Pei-guang," last modified July 6, 2017, http://www.sohu.com/a/154862332_423538.

## Bibliography

Redtown. "Redtown." Accessed February 4, 2019. http://www.redtown570.com/en/eng.html.

Sohu. "Zheng Pei-guang." Last modified July 6, 2017. http://www.sohu.com/a/154862332_423538.

Wang, Jun. "'Art in Capital': Shaping Distinctiveness in a Culture-Led Urban Regeneration Project in Red Town, Shanghai." *Cities* (December 2009): 318–30.

Zhe, Liu, Pieter Uyttenhove, and Xin Zheng. *Moving Urban Sculptures towards Sustainability: The Urban Sculpture Planning System in China*. Basel, Switzerland: MDPI, December 2018.

Zong, Xuan. "The Elegant Turn of 10th Steel Factory of Shanghai: The Renovation Practice of Shanghai Red Town." *Urbanism and Architecture* (August 2011): 52–55.

# The Warehouse Hotel, Singapore

Debbie Wong

## Project Information

**Table 15.1:** Basic details of The Warehouse Hotel.

| | |
|---|---|
| Address | 320 Havelock Road, Robertson Quay, Singapore 169628 |
| Old use | Industrial (warehouse complex) |
| New use | Commercial (hotel) |
| Heritage status | Conservation building |
| Area | 1,536.2 square meters |
| Project cost estimate | Undisclosed |
| Operator | Lo & Behold Group |
| Developed/Funded by | I Associated Company (owner) |
| Architect | Zarch Collaboratives (restoration), Asylum Studio (interior design consultants) |
| Contractor | Towner Construction Pte. Ltd. |
| Start and completion date | 2013–2017 |

**Figure 15.1:** Exterior view of The Warehouse Hotel. (Source: Lo & Behold Group.)

## Vision

To transform a historic warehouse complex (composed of three structures) into a thirty-seven-room boutique hotel focusing on heritage and local culture.

**Figure 15.2:** Site plan of The Warehouse Hotel. (Drawn by Lavina Ahuja based on Google Earth.)

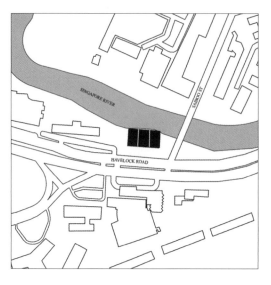

## Site History

The Warehouse Hotel, which is consists of three conserved warehouse buildings originally built in 1895, reflects Singapore's trading history. Located along the Singapore River as part of the Straits of Malacca trade route, it was positioned in the heart of the red-light district, known for various liquor distilleries, secret societies, underground activities, and vices.

Originally built as warehouses (called "godowns" in East Asia), the site later housed the Warehouse Disco, the biggest disco in Singapore when it opened in 1986.[1] It closed down in 1995, and the site was put to intermittent uses until the Urban Redevelopment Authority (URA) released the site for sale under the Reserve List[2] of the Government Land Sales (GLS) program.[3] In 2015, Lo & Behold Group was selected to develop the warehouse complex as a boutique hotel.[4]

1.  STProperty, "Former Warehouse to be Transformed into Hotel," last modified July 1, 2013, https://www.stproperty.sg/articles-property/financial-guide/former-warehouse-disco-to-be-transformed-into-hotel/a/125354.
2.  STProperty, "Former Warehouse to be Transformed into Hotel."
3.  Government Land Sales (GLS) Programme releases state land for development by private developers. The GLS Programme is an important mechanism for achieving key planning objectives in the long-term development of Singapore. GLS Programmes are planned and announced every six months. The GLS comprises sites on the Confirmed List and Reserve List. See: "FAQ," Urban Redevelopment Authority, accessed May 30, 2019, https://www.ifaq.gov.sg/URA/apps/Fcd_faqmain.aspx#FAQ_122407.
4.  Melissa Mok, "Warehouse Hotel at Heritage Site," *Straits Times*, June 21, 2015, http://www.straits-times.com/lifestyle/food/warehouse-hotel-at-heritage-site.

**Table 15.2:** Timeline of The Warehouse Hotel.

| | |
|---|---|
| 1895 | Warehouse complex is built and used as a godown |
| 1950s | Premise is used to produce soaps |
| 1986 | Site is converted into the Warehouse Disco |
| 1995 | Warehouse Disco closes down |
| 2013 | Urban Redevelopment Authority (URA) releases the site for sale under the Reserve List of the Government Land Sales (GLS) program |
| 2015 | Lo & Behold Group takes charge of its redevelopment |
| 2017 | The Warehouse Hotel opens |

## Revitalization Concept

+ Endorsing the 3R Principle—maximum Retention, sensitive Restoration, and careful Repair—to turn the derelict warehouse buildings into a boutique hotel.
+ Demonstrating the area's historic past and the original industrial nature of the buildings through the conserved physical fabric.
+ Reinforcing the area as a popular dining, entertainment, and social district through the establishment of the hospitality project.

**Figure 15.3:** Interior view of The Warehouse Hotel showing the entrance and double-height lobby space. (Source: Lo & Behold Group.)

## Process and Partnership

The property was acquired by I Associated Company and is operated by Lo & Behold Group, a leading hospitality specialist in Singapore. It is the first hotel venture by Lo & Behold, and together with Asylum Studio, which led the interior design, new meaning has been given to the warehouse repurposed as a hotel.

Inspired by the lineage of locals who built the warehouse and their entrepreneurial endeavors, The Warehouse Hotel highlights Singapore's local culture and heritage through thoughtful collaboration with Singapore designers and homegrown companies, and maintains that heritage by ensuring the hotel is operated and owned by Singaporeans. For example, in-room crockery was commissioned to Mud Rock, a local ceramic studio.[5]

---

5.  "A Look Inside the Warehouse Hotel Singapore," *Urdesignmag,* last modified January 26, 2017, http://www.urdesignmag.com/architecture/2017/01/26/warehouse-hotel-singapore/.

## Development Environment

The site was released for sale under the Reserve List of the Government Land Sales (GLS) program and cannot be subdivided or strata subdivided, and the individual warehouses are not to be demolished. The site has a sixty-year tenure compared to the usual ninety-nine years. The conservation status of the warehouses also meant that the project needed to comply with existing building specifications within a stipulated budget.

## Commercial Sustainability

The commercial sustainability of the project is dependent on the occupancy rates for the thirty-seven rooms and income generated from the food and beverage outlets, partnerships with and marketing of local designers and products and space rental for events.

## Key Success Factors

- Famous for creating unique food and beverage experiences, the operator, Lo & Behold Group, has ensured an enriched hotel experience through creative interpretation of the historic warehouse buildings.
- Relevance of conservation has been conveyed through a tailored experience for a contemporary audience.
- Determination creating an authentic Singapore experience in The Warehouse Hotel through partnerships with local designers has reinforced Singapore's cultural identity.

## Key Challenges

- As Lo & Behold Group's first hotel project, in comparison to their extensive experience in operating restaurants, the adaptive reuse project was a much longer process. Unlike the usual six-month lead time for restaurants, The Warehouse Hotel took two years.
- Aside from the challenge to comply with numerous regulations related to the restoration of the warehouses, there was also a need to redefine "industrial heritage" and to articulate the approach to protecting the heritage and ambience of the space while changing its use.[6]

## Keeping Heritage Alive

The new use as a boutique hotel combined the three warehouses internally as one seamless space with double-height ceilings and pitched roofs. The space allowed for thirty-seven luxurious rooms, each with a unique theme. The Urban Redevelopment Authority (URA) was actively involved in determining the configuration of the rooms and their spatial quality. The distinctive symmetrical façade, jacked roofs, and original character-defining elements, such as the cornices, doors, louvered windows, and moldings, were carefully restored. Additional effort was made to find the records

---

6.  Daven Wu, "Wee Teng Wen Shares His Vision for New Venture, The Warehouse Hotel," *Peak Magazine* (January 9, 2017), http://thepeakmagazine.com.sg/interviews/interview-wee-teng-wen-shares-his-vision-for-newly-launched-the-warehouse-hotel-2/?slide=7-07--Eating-In-Its-restaurant--Po--features-a-moder.

for the original floor construction methods that enabled the floor structure/layout to be retained "as is." An unobstructed view and access to the Singapore River remained per the original design. The URA recommended reinstating the original plasterwork of the buildings and in the process discovered the original "Ho Hong Oil Factory Building" (和豐油較有限公司) signage on the left gable, which was conserved and is now a prominent part of the main façade. A new extension features an elevated infinity pool with riverbank views, strengthening the visual connection with the waterfront.[7]

The former industrial nature of the place was referenced by featuring its original architectural features, such as exposed ceiling trusses, masonry walls, and midcentury-style furniture. Artwork, in-room minibars, uniforms, and other items used on the premises were all locally sourced to provide an authentic Singapore experience.

**Figure 15.4:** River view suite of The Warehouse Hotel. (Source: Lo & Behold Group.)

## Value Creation

Cultural: The adaptive reuse project retells the history of the Singapore River as a significant part of the Malacca Straits trade route. The Warehouse Hotel illustrates the industrial heritage of the former warehouse complex and includes interpretation about the district's intriguing past—with all its secret societies and vices.

Economic: The partnerships showcasing goods by local designers help to nurture Singapore's cultural identity and also provide opportunities for marketing and business development for home-grown talents and brands.

Social and Environmental: The Warehouse Hotel further contributes to the already vibrant entertainment and social scene of Robertson Quay.

7.  Zarch, "The Warehouse Hotel," accessed June 20, 2017, http://zarch.com.sg/portfolio/the-warehouse-hotel/.

> **Our focus has been to protect the property's legacy, while creating a fresh perspective on the term industrial.**[8]
>
> —*Chris Lee, Head Designer and Founder of Asylum Studio*

## Bibliography

BLLNR (Billionaire). "Fancy Staying in A Heritage-Listed Warehouse?" Last modified June 17, 2017. http://www.bllnr.sg/travel/hotels/93/fancy-staying-in-a-heritage-listed-warehouse.

Cardelo. "The Forgotten Side of Singapore River." *Singapore Lost and Filed* (blog). May 1, 2013. https://lostnfiledsg.wordpress.com/2013/05/01/the-forgotten-side-of-singapore-river/.

EssentialSingapore. "Historical Boutique Chic in the Warehouse Hotel." Last modified January 24, 2017. http://www.essentialsingapore.com/historical-boutique-chic-in-the-warehouse-hotel/.

Gibson, Eleanor. "Asylum and Zarch Collaboratives Transform Singapore Spice Warehouse into Boutique Hotel." *Dezeen*. Last modified February 6, 2017. https://www.dezeen.com/2017/02/06/spice-warehouse-hotel-asylum-singapore-river-mid-century-furniture/.

Hong, Xinying. "5 Design Details You Should See at the Warehouse Hotel." *Singapore Tatler*, February 2, 2017. Accessed June 20, 2017. http://sg.asiatatler.com/homes/interiors/5-design-details-we-love-at-the-warehouse-hotel.

"A Look Inside the Warehouse Hotel Singapore." *Urdesignmag*. Last modified January 26, 2017. http://www.urdesignmag.com/architecture/2017/01/26/warehouse-hotel-singapore/.

McDonald, Andrew. "Secret Society Turned Boutique Hotel." Indesignlive. Last modified November 7, 2016. http://www.indesignlive.com/the-work/the-warehouse-hotel.

Robertson Quay. "The Warehouse Hotel." Accessed June 20, 2017. http://www.robertsonquay.com/the-warehouse-hotel.html.

Seet, Adrian Eugene. "The Warehouse Hotel in Photos." *Superadrianme* (blog). January 15, 2017. https://www.superadrianme.com/travel/accommodation/photos-warehouse-hotel-singapore/.

STProperty. "Former Warehouse Disco to Be Transformed into Warehouse Hotel." Last modified July 1, 2013. http://www.stproperty.sg/articles-property/financial-guide/former-warehouse-disco-to-be-transformed-into-hotel/a/125354.

Warehouse Hotel. "About." Accessed June 20, 2017. http://www.thewarehousehotel.com/about.

Wu, Daven. "Wee Teng Wen Shares His Vision for New Venture, The Warehouse Hotel." *Peak Magazine*, January 9, 2017. http://thepeakmagazine.com.sg/interviews/interview-wee-teng-wen-shares-his-vision-for-newly-launched-the-warehouse-hotel-2/?slide=7-07--Eating-In-Its-restaurant--Po--features-a-moder.

Zarch. "The Warehouse Hotel." Accessed June 20, 2017. http://zarch.com.sg/portfolio/the-warehouse-hotel/.

---

8.    "A Look Inside the Warehouse Hotel Singapore," *Urdesignmag*.

# Institutional Case Studies

**Table 16.1:** Institutional case studies.

| Project Name | Location | Nature | New Use | Original Use | Timeframe |
|---|---|---|---|---|---|
| Savannah College of Art and Design (SCAD) | Hong Kong | Government and private partnership project | Institutional (art and design education) | Institutional (courthouse) | 2009–2010 |
| Bund 18 | Shanghai | Private project | Commercial (galleries, restaurants, and shops) | Institutional (bank) | 2002–2004 |
| Singapore National Gallery | Singapore | Government project | Institutional/Cultural (art gallery and museum) | Institutional (city hall and courthouse) | 2011–2015 |

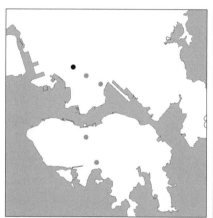

**Figure 16.1:** Location plan of SCAD, Hong Kong. (Drawn by Wai Shing Ng.)

**Figure 16.2:** Location plan of Bund 18, Shanghai. (Drawn by Wai Shing Ng.)

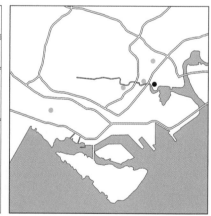

**Figure 16.3:** Location plan of National Gallery Singapore, Singapore. (Drawn by Wai Shing Ng.)

# Savannah College of Art and Design (SCAD), Hong Kong

Tiffany Tang

## Project Information

**Table 17.1:** Basic details of SCAD.

| | |
|---|---|
| Address | 292 Tai Po Road, Sham Shui Po, Kowloon, Hong Kong |
| Old use | Institutional (courthouse) |
| New use | Institutional (art and design education) |
| Heritage status | Grade 2 Historic Building |
| Area | 7,530 square meters |
| Project cost estimate | US$10.51 million (HK$82 million)[i, ii] |
| Operator | Savannah College of Art and Design (SCAD) Foundation Hong Kong Ltd. |
| Developed/Funded by | Savannah College of Art and Design (SCAD) Foundation Hong Kong Ltd., Development Bureau (DevB), Hong Kong SAR government |
| Architect | LWK & Partners (HK) Ltd. |
| Contractor | Hsin Chong Construction Group Limited |
| Start and completion date | December 2009–September 2010 |

i. The Hong Kong dollar is pegged to the US dollar at about US$1=HK$7.8.
ii. Legislative Council, *SCAD Foundation (Hong Kong) Limited: Remarks for the Legislative Council Panel on Education* (Hong Kong: LEGCO Hong Kong SAR Government, February 2015), https://www.legco.gov.hk/yr14-15/english/panels/ed/papers/ed20150207cb4-428-6-e.pdf.

**Figure 17.1:** External view of SCAD Hong Kong from Tai Po Road. (Source: SCAD Hong Kong.)

## Vision

To establish the former North Kowloon Magistracy (NKM) as a preeminent historic site for the study of art and design in Asia.

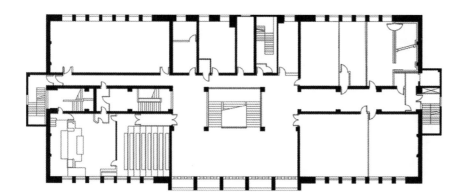

**Figure 17.2:** First-floor plan of SCAD Hong Kong. (Drawn by Wai Shing Ng based on materials from the SCAD Hong Kong Student Guide 2018–19.)

## Site History

Constructed during the 1960s, the former North Kowloon Magistracy (NKM) is one of the few surviving historic magistracy buildings of its kind. It represents the development of the administration of law and order in Hong Kong as well as the continuous economic and social changes in the Sham Shui Po District. The magistracy closed in 2005 because of consolidation of the city's magistracies. The seven-story postwar building adopts a neoclassical architectural style, the only surviving example in Hong Kong.[1]

**Table 17.2:** Timeline of SCAD.

| | |
|---|---|
| 1960 | North Kowloon Magistracy (NKM) is built |
| 2005 | NKM ceases operation due to the consolidation of magistracies from nine to six |
| 2008 | NKM is included in Batch I of the Revitalisation Scheme[i] |
| 2009 | Savannah College of Art and Design (SCAD) Foundation Hong Kong Limited wins the bid to revitalize the magistracy into an art and design institution |
| 2010 | SCAD Hong Kong opens |
| 2011 | SCAD Hong Kong is acknowledged with an Honourable Mention at the UNESCO Asia-Pacific Awards for Cultural Heritage Conservation |

i.  Conserve and Revitalise Heritage in Hong Kong, "Batch I of Revitalisation Scheme Result of Selection," *Development Bureau*, accessed January 30, 2019, https://www.heritage.gov.hk/en/rhbtp/ProgressResult_North_Kowloon_Magistracy.htm.

## Revitalization Concept

+ Revitalizing a historic site to provide 1,500 students tertiary-level education in art and design, specifically in digital media, including advertising, animation, game development, graphic design, photography, and visual effects.
+ Conserving the building's authenticity and integrity with minimum intervention, use of reversible additions, and enhancement of heritage value.

---

1.  SCAD Hong Kong, "Building Highlights (SCAD—Heritage Public Tour, 2017)," accessed January 30, 2019, https://visitscadhk.hk/en/building-hightlights.html.

+ Installing up-to-date technology in the forty classrooms as well as in the art gallery, digital studios, lecture hall, and library to create optimal learning, research, and teaching spaces for professors and students.
+ Implementing green design, including high-efficiency lighting and fixtures from sustainable materials.

**Figure 17.3:** Grand staircase of SCAD Hong Kong. (Source: SCAD Hong Kong.)

## Process and Partnership

The Savannah College of Art and Design (SCAD) Hong Kong revitalization project was fully supported by the main SCAD campus in the United States, its parent university. The proposal was selected by Hong Kong's Development Bureau (DevB) under Batch I of the Revitalisation Scheme in 2009.

## Development Environment

The Savannah College of Art and Design (SCAD) Foundation Hong Kong Ltd. was established by SCAD as a local social enterprise. It received full financial and operational support from SCAD without further investment from the Hong Kong SAR government. Surpluses were retained locally for the benefit of the people of Hong Kong.

## Commercial Sustainability

The sustainability of the project operation depends on the target enrollment of students while managing operational costs. As a mature, sophisticated, and iconic institution, established in 1978 in the United States, with two campuses in the US state of Georgia and in the south of France, Savannah College of Art and Design (SCAD) Hong Kong is likely to continue to attract enrollment from talented local and international students in a sustained manner.

## Key Success Factors

Savannah College of Art and Design (SCAD) Hong Kong has more than thirty years of experience in heritage conservation in the United States, Europe, and Asia. Many of SCAD's facilities are housed in rehabilitated heritage buildings with histories of more than one hundred years.

## Key Challenges

+ Minimal change, with the retention of key character defining elements, rather than demolition, whenever possible, such as the grand granite staircase with Grecian motifs, original flooring, and spatial configuration of the former courtroom and detention cells.
+ Original building materials were retained for future reuse.
+ Features were retrofitted to be more environmentally friendly, for example, efficient lighting systems, cooling systems, and solar-reducing technologies.

## Keeping Heritage Alive

Apart from the careful conservation of the original architectural elements of the historic building, the legacy of the heritage building is kept alive as Savannah College of Art and Design (SCAD) Hong Kong opens parts of the institute to the public multiple times annually and has set up a gallery to display the history of the building year-round. A documentary was produced to capture the entire conservation project. The main lecture hall, where original fittings and fixtures of the high-ceiling courtroom were retained, perpetuates the memory of its function while offering a unique learning environment.

**Figure 17.4:** Former courtroom adapted into a lecture hall. (Source: SCAD Hong Kong.)

## Value Creation

Cultural: Savannah College of Art and Design (SCAD) Hong Kong reinforces Hong Kong's competitiveness in global creative industries and increases the city's choices of higher education institutions. In synergy with a fellow creative hub, the Jockey Club

Creative Arts Centre, the institution has revitalized the old community of Sham Shui Po. By the end of 2018, more than 371,500 visitors participated in free public guided tours, exhibitions, and open days.[2]

Economic: In 2014, SCAD paid HK$42.8 million, or 72.1 percent of its operating and capital expenses, to 209 local vendors, demonstrating its support for local businesses.[3] SCAD also provides employment opportunities to local educators.

Social: SCAD actively contributes to the local community, including collaboration with the Child Welfare Scheme Hong Kong to enhance education, health care, and social opportunities for local disadvantaged children and conducting workshops for elderly residents of Sham Shui Po.

> The former courthouse is now home to more than 700 local and overseas SCAD students studying in twenty-two majors ranging from painting and illustration to advertising, animation, and graphic design.[4] It has stood the test of time and is more than suitable for its use as an educational environment to nurture the next generation of creative talents.[5]
>
> —*Project Team*

## Bibliography

Conserve and Revitalise Heritage in Hong Kong. "Batch I of Revitalisation Scheme Result of Selection." Development Bureau. Accessed January 30, 2019. https://www.heritage.gov.hk/en/rhbtp/ProgressResult_North_Kowloon_Magistracy.htm.

Legislative Council. *Progress Report on Heritage Conservation Initiatives.* Hong Kong: LEGCO Hong Kong SAR Government, January 22, 2019. https://www.legco.gov.hk/yr18-19/english/panels/dev/papers/dev20190122cb1-456-5-e.pdf.

Legislative Council. *SCAD Foundation (Hong Kong) Limited: Remarks for the Legislative Council Panel on Education.* Hong Kong: LEGCO Hong Kong SAR Government, February 2015. https://www.legco.gov.hk/yr14-15/english/panels/ed/papers/ed20150207cb4-428-6-e.pdf.

SCAD Hong Kong. "Building Highlights (SCAD—Heritage Public Tour, 2017)." Accessed January 30, 2019. https://visitscadhk.hk/building-highlights.

SCAD Hong Kong. "Student Guide 2018–2019." Accessed May 3, 2019. https://www.scad.edu/sites/default/files/PDF/SCAD-Hong-Kong-student-guide-2018-2019.pdf.

---

2. Legislative Council, *Progress Report on Heritage Conservation Initiatives* (Hong Kong: LEGCO Hong Kong SAR Government, January 22, 2019), https://www.legco.gov.hk/yr18-19/english/panels/dev/papers/dev20190122cb1-456-5-e.pdf.
3. Legislative Council, *Progress Report on Heritage Conservation Initiatives.*
4. Figures provided by SCAD Hong Kong in January 2019.
5. Conserve and Revitalise Heritage in Hong Kong, "Batch I of Revitalisation Scheme Result of Selection," Development Bureau, accessed January 30, 2019, https://www.heritage.gov.hk/en/rhbtp/ProgressResult_North_Kowloon_Magistracy.htm.

# Bund 18, Shanghai

Hugo Chan

## Project Information

**Table 18.1:** Basic details of Bund 18.

| | |
|---|---|
| Address | No. 18, Zhong Shan East Road, Huangpu District, Shanghai |
| Old use | Institutional (bank) |
| New use | Commercial (galleries, restaurants, and shops) |
| Heritage status | Excellent Historical Building, Shanghai City |
| Area | 10,600 square meters |
| Project cost estimate | US$22 million (RMB148 million)[i] |
| Operator | Various operators |
| Developed/Funded by | Shanghai Bund 18 Real Estate Development Ltd. |
| Architect | Kokaistudios and Architectural Design and Research Institute of Tongji University |
| Contractor | Shanghai Construction Decoration Engineering Co. Ltd. |
| Start and completion date | March 2002–November 2004 |

i.   The conversion rate is taken at US$1=RMB6.74; UNESCO, "Bund 18," in *Asia Conserved Volume II: Lessons Learned from the UNESCO Asia-Pacific Awards for Cultural Heritage Conservation (2005–2009)*, ed. Montira Horayangura Unakul (Bangkok: iGroup Press, 2013), 150–52.

**Figure 18.1:** Main entrance of Bund 18. (Source: Hugo Chan.)

## Vision

To achieve a balance between restoring the surviving historical features of Bund 18 and meeting the demands of a modern building, recognizing that such adaptive reuse will invariably entail some transformation in the building's character.[1]

**Figure 18.2:** Site plan of Bund 18. (Drawn by Wai Shing Ng based on Google Earth.)

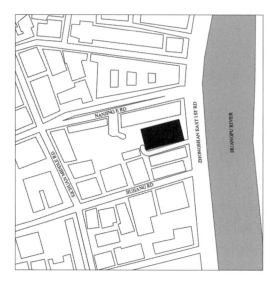

## Site History

The original Bund 18 was constructed in two phases—the front portion was completed in 1923 as the headquarters building for the Chartered Bank of India, Australia and China (one of the earliest foreign banks in China), and the rear portion was completed in 1938.[2] In 1955, the bank building was nationalized, and the bank moved out of the country, together with other foreign banks that formerly operated on the Bund. The Chinese government subsequently assigned the buildings on the Bund to government agencies and state-owned companies.[3]

The front portion of Bund 18 was used as government offices while the rear portion was used as a residential area and staff quarters. The ground floor was originally a high-ceiling space used as the banking hall, but a mezzanine was added in the 1980s to increase the usable floor area.[4] In 1994, the rear portion was largely demolished, and the interior was partially exposed, posing a structural threat to the remaining building.[5]

In the late 1990s, the property was transferred to a state-owned enterprise held by the Shanghai municipal government and was leased to a private developer of Taiwanese background on a twenty-year contract. At the time the restoration project began, the building was in a derelict state, with structural members and building elements exposed for years and in desperate need of repair.[6]

1.  UNESCO, "Bund 18," in *Asia Conserved Volume II: Lessons Learned from the UNESCO Asia-Pacific Awards for Cultural Heritage Conservation (2005–2009)*, ed. Montira Horayangura Unakul (Bangkok: iGroup Press, 2013),
2.  UNESCO, "Bund 18," in *Asia Conserved Volume II*, 154.
3.  UNESCO, "Bund 18," in *Asia Conserved Volume II*, 154.
4.  Michelle Qiao and Xuefei Zhang, *Shanghai Bund Architecture* (Shanghai: Tongji University Press, 2015), 103.
5.  UNESCO, "Bund 18," in *Asia Conserved Volume II*, 154.
6.  Andrea Destefanis (founder/principal architect, Kokaistudios), in discussion with the author, December 2016.

**Table 18.2:** Timeline of Bund 18.

| | |
|---|---|
| 1923 | Front portion of Bund 18 is constructed |
| 1938 | Rear portion of Bund 18 is constructed |
| 1955 | Bund 18 is requisitioned and used as government offices |
| 1994 | Most of the building's rear portion is demolished |
| Late 1990s | Ownership of Bund 18 is transferred to a state-owned enterprise |
| Early 2000s | Twenty-year lease is signed; renovation project commences |
| 2004 | Bund 18 officially opens |
| 2006 | Bund 18 receives an Award of Distinction at the UNESCO Asia-Pacific Awards for Cultural Heritage Conservation |

## Revitalization Concept

+ Respecting and maintaining the building through removal of inconsistent later additions and meticulous restoration of damaged features.
+ Using modern design for new additions to differentiate old and new elements.[7]
+ Adhering to the Nara Document on Authenticity (adopted by UNESCO in 1994) through relying on both European conservation practice and respecting local context and sources of knowledge.
+ Preserving the building's integrity and the spirit of the place by undertaking a series of surveys investigating the building's physical fabric and by considering the wider context (adjacent historic buildings and their inhabitants).
+ Close collaboration between the project team, public sector, and local academia (notably from Tongji University).
+ Applying overseas expertise combined with respect for local materials, building techniques, and craftsmanship by the project team to facilitate knowledge exchange and transmission of traditions.[8]

---

7.  UNESCO, "Bund 18," in *Asia Conserved Volume II*, 156.
8.  UNESCO Bangkok, "2006 UNESCO Asia-Pacific Heritage Awards," accessed January 25, 2019, https://bangkok.unesco.org/sites/default/files/assets/article/Asia-Pacific%20Heritage%20Awards/files/2006-winners.pdf.

## Process and Partnership

The Bund 18 conservation project was a collaboration between the public and private sectors. The building is owned by the public sector, and after the building was left vacant for five years, it was leased to the private sector (Shanghai Bund 18 Real Estate Development Ltd.) for restoration and a commercially viable new use.[9]

In March 2002, the restoration project commenced with a preparatory survey and analysis of building materials, followed by a detailed structural investigation and a stratigraphic survey to reveal changes to the building over approximately eighty years. Later in 2002, two young Italian architects from Venice, Filippo Gabbiani and Andrea Destefanis of Kokaistudios, were invited to Shanghai to lead the adaptive reuse of this landmark project on the Bund. Subsequently, a survey was conducted by Italian specialists in heritage restoration, shedding more light on the building's existing condition and structural integrity, and possible adaptive reuse options were

9. Andrea Destefanis (founder/principal architect, Kokaistudios), in discussion with the author, December 2016.

identified. These options informed the restoration strategy, completed in November 2002.[10] Structural work began in March 2003, followed by restoration work and the construction of new additions that took place between December 2003 and October 2004. Bund 18 officially opened in November 2004 and has since become a prime destination for luxury shopping, fine dining, and cultural events in Shanghai.[11]

## Development Environment

Historically speaking, the Bund, also known as the Wall Street of Asia, was the financial and cultural center of Shanghai. Situated along the western bank of the Huangpu River, the area was distinguished by imposing bank offices and trading houses of foreign companies (largely American and British) built predominately during the 1920s and 1930s. Following the founding of the People's Republic of China in 1949, all the commercial establishments, including those along the Bund, were nationalized and assigned to government agencies and state-owned companies. Up until China's "open door" policy economy in the late 1970s, such architecture on the Bund received minimal maintenance and was becoming derelict. These government offices were oftentimes viewed as dumping grounds or as state warehouses.[12]

Just before the new millennium, the Bund was once again center stage for private developers with the 1999 opening of M on the Bund (a fine-dining venue by Australian restaurateur Michelle Garnaut), which served as an example of a financially viable renovation project.[13] Many restoration and renovation attempts along the Bund soon followed, notably Three on the Bund around the corner from M on the Bund, as well as Bund 18.

## Commercial Sustainability

Since its opening in 2004, Bund 18 has become a popular place for cultural events, fine dining, and luxury shopping in Shanghai. As of 2019, most of the building's spaces are rented out to food and beverage businesses; some of which are recognized with a Michelin star.[14] In spite of some turnover of tenants, the rentable spaces of Bund 18 are always fully occupied and remain in demand. The spaces have been leased to luxury brands and commercial enterprises at a purportedly high rent. The return on the restoration and renovation is considered robust, and the project has demonstrated that sensitive and sensible adaptive reuse of heritage buildings can be beneficial in both economic and social terms.[15]

## Key Success Factors

+ The project helped the local government to realize the value attached to historic buildings: it was one of the very first adaptive reuse projects in the country.
+ It benefited from a formidable market environment that was conducive to foreign investment (rewarded not only in monetary but also cultural terms).

10. UNESCO, "Bund 18," in *Asia Conserved Volume II*, 154.
11. UNESCO, "Bund 18," in *Asia Conserved Volume II*, 154.
12. Susie Gordon, "The Regeneration of Shanghai's Bund," *BBC*, last modified December 23, 2011, http://www.bbc.com/travel/story/20111219-the-regeneration-of-shanghais-bund.
13. Graham Norwood, "Shanghai's Bund Braced for Redevelopment Revolution," *Financial Times*, last modified May 23, 2013, https://www.ft.com/content/09cf365e-bd78-11e2-a735-00144feab7de.
14. Andrea Destefanis (founder/principal architect, Kokaistudios), email message to author, December 30, 2019.
15. UNESCO, "Bund 18," in *Asia Conserved Volume II*, 157.

‣ The dedicated project team and investor made this landmark project an outstanding example of adaptive reuse as well as an international showcase.

## Key Challenges

‣ Before this project, because of a lack of precedent and an absence of practical guidance in the commercial reuse of heritage structures, government agencies and state-owned companies were reluctant to lease heritage buildings to the private sector.

‣ Prior to the restoration effort, the building suffered severe structural damage from decades of negligence. For example, after the demolition of the rear portion in 1994, the structure of the remaining building was at risk, and reinforcement and partial reconstruction were needed in order to strengthen and stabilize the overall structure.

‣ The building façade was in poor condition, and many decorative features had to be reconstructed or replicated to restore the building's former state yet maintain its patina.

‣ Modern fittings were required and various services, such as electrical and plumbing services, required upgrading to suit the building's proposed new uses. Yet these new features needed to respect and complement the building's heritage character.

‣ Five Italian architects worked on site for ten months to oversee the quality of the restoration work, and they had to work closely with Chinese builders and artisans, most of whom were not acquainted with restoration of heritage buildings, and they did not share a common language.[16]

## Keeping Heritage Alive

Bund 18's important surviving heritage features were carefully cleaned and restored, such as the marble columns, the marble mosaic floor, and the wooden balustrades of the main staircase.[17] Partially damaged decorative elements were repaired, while missing decorative details were not replicated in order to reflect the building's multilayered history. For example, some of the decorations on the façade were possibly destroyed during the Cultural Revolution. Their absence becomes an evocative aspect of the building.[18]

Inappropriate later additions, such as the mezzanine floor that had been inserted in the 1980s for additional office floor area, were mostly removed to restore Bund 18's original form and to allow its adaptation to a new use.[19] Only two mezzanine areas around the main ground floor atrium were retained as reminders of that period, as well as to increase the commercial efficiency of the space. Their structures were adjusted to be detachable from the original columns, giving a clear indication that they are later additions.[20]

A detailed investigation of the structural skeleton of the building was carried out, and based on the findings, the building's structural capacity was augmented to meet current building codes and loading requirements for proposed new uses.[21] For

---

16. UNESCO, "Bund 18," in *Asia Conserved Volume II*, 155.
17. UNESCO, "Bund 18," in *Asia Conserved Volume II*, 157.
18. Andrea Destefanis, email message to author, December 30, 2019.
19. Andrea Destefanis (founder/principal architect, Kokaistudios), in discussion with the author, December 2016.
20. Andrea Destefanis, email message to author, December 30, 2019.
21. UNESCO, "Bund 18," in *Asia Conserved Volume II*, 157.

example, after careful study, an anticorrosive treatment was applied to all reinforced concrete slabs and beams to prolong their life span and prevent further decay.[22]

To ensure careful maintenance of the building, the project architects drafted a management plan with specific recommendations, such as routine cleaning and repair work on the windows and façade every five to six years, ensuring dust deposits are removed and a new protective layer is applied when necessary.[23] The architects also offered advice for the tenant mix and tenant selection even years after the project's completion to ensure all proposed new uses adhere to the design intent of the adaptive reuse effort.[24]

The project sets an example for cultural heritage conservation and training in conservation and has provided the authorities with a yardstick for commercially viable adaptive reuse projects as well as a technical benchmark for restoration work.[25] To ensure the accessibility of the lessons learned from the project, all research and building surveys have been translated into Chinese and distributed to related government agencies to serve as a valuable reference.[26]

**Figure 18.4:** External view of Bund 18. (Source: Hugo Chan.)

22. UNESCO, "Bund 18," in *Asia Conserved Volume II*, 157.
23. UNESCO, "Bund 18," in *Asia Conserved Volume II*, 157.
24. Andrea Destefanis (founder/principal architect, Kokaistudios), in discussion with the author, December 2016.
25. UNESCO, "Bund 18," in *Asia Conserved Volume II*, 158.
26. UNESCO, "Bund 18," in *Asia Conserved Volume II*, 158.

## Value Creation

Cultural: Arts and culture have remained key components throughout the renovation project. Not only have the architectural aesthetics and craftsmanship been preserved (or meticulously replicated) and documented, but also art galleries and cultural events have remained an important presence in the overall tenant mix and use of public space. The Bund 18 conservation project won the Award of Distinction at the UNESCO Asia-Pacific Awards for Cultural Heritage Conservation in 2006 for its distinguished contribution to the "overall renaissance of the Bund district" and for "renewing the area's cultural continuum in both tangible and intangible terms." The revival of the Bund, notably led by Bund 18, has helped reclaim Shanghai's former reputation as the cultural fulcrum of the Far East.[27]

Economic: Bund 18 has set an excellent example of reusing an aging heritage building in an economically viable manner. As one of the pioneer adaptive reuse efforts on the Bund, its economic success helped trigger other similar projects, and together they have contributed to a boost in land value and rent for properties in the vicinity.

Environmental: The healthy cost-benefit balance sheet of Bund 18 has caught the attention of fellow private developers, government officials as well as the general public, thereby saving this particular heritage building and its neighbors along the Bund, as well as others, expressing the city's rich history, notably Huai Hai Lu 796 (another successful adaptive reuse project undertaken by Kokaistudios, which is elaborated in the residential case study section of this book).

Social: As a living testament and witness to the building's vicissitude, the security guard who safeguarded the building during its days of abandonment was retained after the reopening of Bund 18, in an attempt to maintain the social fabric and continuity of the place. Public space amelioration and utility upgrades were carried out during the restoration and renovation, which not only benefited the building itself but also Zhong Shan East Road and communities in the neighborhood.

> We succeeded because we bring life back to the building.
>
> —*Filippo Gabbiani of Kokaistudios*[28]

## Bibliography

Qiao, Michelle, and Xuefei Zhang. *Shanghai Bund Architecture*. Shanghai: Tongji University Press, 2015.

Unakul, Montira Horayangura, ed. *Asia Conserved Volume II: Lessons Learned from the UNESCO Asia-Pacific Awards for Cultural Heritage Conservation (2005–2009)*. Bangkok: iGroup Press, 2013.

UNESCO Bangkok. "2006 UNESCO Asia-Pacific Heritage Awards." Accessed January 25, 2019. https://bangkok.unesco.org/sites/default/files/assets/article/Asia-Pacific%20 Heritage%20Awards/files/2006-winners.pdf.

---

27. UNESCO Bangkok, "2006 UNESCO Asia-Pacific Heritage Awards."
28. Michelle Qiao, "No. 18—Strikes Balance between History and Commercial Use," *Shanghai Daily*, last modified January 9, 2013, https://archive.shine.cn/feature/No-18-Strikes-balance-between-history-and-commercial-use/shdaily.shtml.

# National Gallery Singapore, Singapore

Debbie Wong

## Project Information

**Table 19.1:** Basic details of National Gallery Singapore.

| | |
|---|---|
| Address | 1 St. Andrew's Road, Singapore 178957 |
| Old use | Institutional (city hall and courthouse) |
| New use | Institutional/Cultural (art gallery and museum) |
| Heritage status | National Monument |
| Area | Over 64,000 square meters (gross floor area) |
| Project cost estimate | US$392 million (SG$532 million)[i] |
| Operator | National Gallery Singapore |
| Funded by | Singapore Government |
| Developed by | CPG Consultants Pte. Ltd. |
| Architect | studioMilou Singapore; Architectural Restoration Consultants Pte. Ltd. (ARC), Garth Sheldon |
| Contractor | Takenaka-Singapore Piling Joint Venture (TCSP) |
| Start and completion date | 2011–2015 |

i. The conversion rate is taken at US$1=SG$1.35.

**Figure 19.1:** External view of the National Gallery Singapore, showing the two historical buildings and the newly inserted veil. (Source: studioMilou.)

## Vision

To establish the National Gallery Singapore as a major regional institution dedicated to modern and contemporary visual arts for the engagement, enjoyment, and enrichment of Singapore residents and visitors from all over the world. To oversee collaborative research, education, and exhibitions, highlighting the importance of Southeast Asian contemporary art in a global context.[1]

**Figure 19.2:** First-level plan of the National Gallery Singapore. (Drawn by Wai Shing Ng based on materials from studioMilou.)

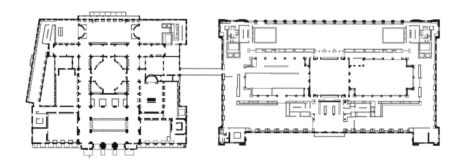

## Site History

Situated in Singapore's Civic District, the National Gallery consists of two National Monuments, the former City Hall and former Supreme Court. Designed by the British municipal architect F. D. Meadows, the former City Hall was built from 1926 to 1929. Originally named the Municipal Building, it formerly housed colonial administration offices and was an important venue for many key events in Singapore's history—notably, Japan's official surrender in 1945 and the swearing in of the first independent government, led by Lee Kwan Yew. From 1963 to 1991, City Hall was home to offices of different government departments and courtrooms. Extensive renovations were carried out to the building between 1987 and 1991, and it was vacated in 2006 in preparation for the National Gallery Singapore.

The former Supreme Court was built on the site of the preexisting Grand Hotel de l'Europe, one of the most palatial hotels in Southeast Asia. It was demolished in 1936 and replaced by the Supreme Court building in 1939, which was designed by Frank Dorrington Ward, chief architect of the Public Works Department. It was one of the last major neoclassical buildings built by the British globally. The Corinthian and Ionic columns, relief panels, and sculptures were created by Italian artist Cavaliere Rudolfo Nolli.[2] The building functioned as the Supreme Court of Singapore until June 2005 when the courthouse was relocated to a new building.

In recognition of their heritage significance, both buildings (City Hall and Supreme Court) were declared National Monuments in 1992. During their use for administrative and legal functions, they were not open to the general public. With the vision of becoming a global city for the arts, Prime Minister Lee Hsien Loong announced the government's plan to convert the two National Monuments into a new national gallery in his National Day Rally speech in 2005.[3] The plan was officially announced by the minister for information, communications and the arts in

1.  "About the Gallery," National Gallery Singapore, accessed June 20, 2017, https://www.nationalgallery.sg/about.
2.  "Courthouse Architecture," Supreme Court Singapore, accessed July 8, 2019, https://www.supreme-court.gov.sg/services/visitor-services/courthouse-architecture.
3.  Prime Minister's Office Singapore, "Prime Minister Lee Hsien Loong's National Day Rally 2005 Speech (English)," last modified August 21, 2005, https://www.pmo.gov.sg/Newsroom/prime-minister-lee-hsien-loongs-national-day-rally-2005-speech-english.

2006, and a steering committee was established for interested parties and stakeholders to contribute their expertise. In February 2007, an international design competition was launched to select a design concept for this project, which studioMilou won, and local engineers CPG Consultants were appointed as the principal consultants for the project. In January 2011, a ground-breaking ceremony marked the beginning of the restoration and construction works to transform the two National Monuments into the National Gallery Singapore. It was officially opened by President Tony Tan on November 27, 2015.

**Table 19.2:** Timeline of National Gallery Singapore.

| | |
|------|-----|
| 1926 | Architect's Department draws up plans for a Municipal Building |
| 1929 | Municipal Building is completed and declared open |
| 1935 | Plans for a new Supreme Court are approved |
| 1939 | Supreme Court building officially opens |
| 1942 | Japanese Occupation of Singapore—the Municipal Building serves as the headquarters of the Japanese government and the Supreme Court is used as the Syonan Supreme Court |
| 1945 | Acceptance of surrender of the Japanese forces at the Municipal Building (City Hall Chamber) |
| 1951 | Singapore is conferred a *city*, and the Municipal Building is renamed as the City Hall building |
| 1959 | Prime Minister Lee Hsien Loong and members of the cabinet take their Oaths of Allegiance and Oaths of Office in the City Hall Chamber |
| 1986 | Additional courtrooms are constructed in the City Hall building |
| 1992 | City Hall and the Supreme Court buildings are declared as National Monuments |
| 2005 | Prime Minister Lee announces plans to convert City Hall and the Supreme Court buildings into the new National Gallery Singapore at the National Day Rally Speech |
| 2007 | An international architectural design competition for the National Gallery is launched and three short-listed schemes are announced |
| 2008 | studioMilou, from France, in collaboration with CPG Consultants Pte. Ltd., is selected as the winner of the architectural design competition |
| 2010 | Takenaka-Singapore Piling Joint Venture (TCSP) is commissioned as the main construction contractor for the project |
| 2011 | Groundbreaking ceremony is held |
| 2012 | Restoration works on the Supreme Court tympanum commences |
| 2015 | Official opening of the National Gallery Singapore by President Tony Tan |

## Revitalization Concept

+ Implementing the 3R Principle—maximum Retention, sensitive Restoration, and careful Repair—throughout the revitalization plan to achieve the simplest and most elegant solutions available to adapt the historic buildings to their new function.
+ Close collaboration of studioMilou's with CPG Consultants and the client to meet the relevant acoustic, energy, and security regulations without compromising the historic character of the sites.
+ Superimposing three key design components (interventions) on the existing buildings—a metal and glass roof structure and veil, which connects the two buildings at the roof level; an underground public concourse that extends longitudinally

across the entire site; and the less obvious but essential additional layer of a wall on the internal face of the exterior façade, which allows for the necessary structural reinforcements for the new gallery's loading and technical requirements.

+ Incorporating green technology to enable the historic buildings to be more energy efficient and sustainable in the future.

**Figure 19.3:** The metal and glass roof structure above the Rotunda Dome of the former Supreme Court building. (Source: Ho Yin Lee.)

## Process and Partnership

The project was initiated and predominately funded by the Singapore government. The Ministry of Information, Communications & the Arts (MICA) began the implementation process by establishing advisory groups (specifically, the Architectural Development and Heritage Advisory, Business and Finance Advisory, Communications, and Museological Development) and launching the international architectural design competition with the Singapore Institute of Architects (SIA).

After winning the competition, studioMilou established a Singapore office. An advisory panel was also formed by the Urban Redevelopment Authority (URA) to act as the appointed technical advisor to the then Preservation of Monuments Board (PMB). CPG Consultants Pte. Ltd. was commissioned as structural consultants, and Takenaka-Singapore Piling Joint Venture (TCSP) as the main contractor for the project, supported by others, such as the architectural restoration expert Garth Sheldon.

In addition to state support, there were also corporate and private donations. A Cultural Matching Fund (CMF), where the government provides dollar-for-dollar matching grants for private cash donations to arts and heritage charities, was set up by the Ministry of Culture, Community and Youth (MCCY) to help nurture the sustainable development of art and heritage in Singapore.

## Development Environment

Both buildings, City Hall and the Supreme Court, were declared National Monuments in 1992 and are subject to preservation guidelines under the authority of the Preservation of Sites and Monuments (PSM).[4] The guidelines state specific requirements for the treatment of the façades, interior finishes, key architectural

---

4. Originally known as the Preservation of Monuments Board (PMB) until the name was officially changed in July 1, 2013.

features, and their spatial quality. The project had to comply with these guidelines and accommodate the new functions of the Singapore National Gallery without compromising the cultural heritage significance of the buildings. Construction regulations covering acoustic and energy performance, antiterrorism, fire safety, and museum-standard conservation benchmarks had to be met with minimal impact on the character and authenticity of the historic fabric.

## Commercial Sustainability

Funding came from the government as well as corporate and private donations. The National Gallery received generous financial support from corporations, such as Accenture, DBS Bank, Far East Organization, Keppel Corporation, Ngee Ann Development, Singtel, Tote Board, and United Overseas Bank, as well as many private individuals. Another source of income is admission fees. The general admission fee is SD\$25 for non-Singaporeans and free entry for all Singaporeans and Permanent Residents. Concession rates are available for children, seniors (sixty years and above), full-time National Servicemen, and overseas students and teachers. Special exhibitions and programs are charged separately. In its first year alone, 1.5 million visitors visited the National Gallery Singapore.[5] In addition, income is generated from the gallery shop/cafe and the rental of ten food and beverage outlets as well as space rentals for a range of events.

## Key Success Factors

+ Architecturally, a significant effort was made by studioMilou to create a radical new experience of these two National Monuments with minimal impact on the buildings' structures.
+ After a thorough study of well-documented records regarding the history and construction of the buildings, the original fabric was carefully restored and retained where possible.
+ While the project was led by the government, there were also numerous opportunities for beneficial collaborations with the private sector in terms of branding, businesses, and programs related to education and research. The project provided extensive opportunities for partnerships across a spectrum of stakeholders through its dynamic programs and related services.
+ National Gallery Singapore successfully reinforced itself as a cultural institution for visual arts in the region and nurtures a sense of national pride for Singaporeans.

## Key Challenges

+ Aesthetically, it was a challenge to unify the two historic buildings and create a clear identity of one institution, while respecting the historical autonomy and sentimental value that the historic buildings embody for Singaporeans.
+ Although they share some similarities, such as façade finishes, the two colonial buildings are structurally quite different. Designed for distinctive uses, the buildings posed a complex set of technical demands to be seamlessly adapted to their new function as an art gallery.

---

5. "National Gallery Shares the Highlights of its First Year with an Immersive Party," *Today Online*, November 25, 2016, http://www.todayonline.com/entertainment/arts/looking-forward-national-gallery-singapore-share-highlights-its-first-year.

♦ City Hall lies on a shallow foundation (marine clay); any movement in the ground has implications on the building itself as a result of compaction. The Supreme Court, however, is stabilized on deep piling anchored in a bolder clay bed, which required minimal reinforcement work. The differences in the height of the foundations demanded tailored design solutions to negotiate the floor levels of the existing structures, which resulted in the introduction of a basement level for the new gallery.

## Keeping Heritage Alive

Significant original spaces of the two National Monuments were carefully restored, such as the wood-paneled courtrooms in the former Supreme Court, its historic lobby, staircase, and the Rotunda Dome of the Law Library with its original materials (marble, terrazzo, and wood paneling). The Board Room of the former City Hall, also remembered as the Surrender Chamber, was restored, including its entrance area and stairway. The impressive neoclassical architecture of City Hall, now restored, evokes memories of its original ceremonial functions. The original penal functions of the Supreme Court are also evident through the internal arrangements of courtrooms and prison cells, which were retained and restored. Free docent-led tours about the buildings' history take place twice daily so the public can gain a better understanding of the monuments' past and related stories.

Today, the National Gallery Singapore is home to two permanent galleries—the DBS Singapore Gallery and the UOB Southeast Asia Gallery—with collections that represent the development of Singaporean and regional cultures selected from Singapore's National Collection, the world's largest public collection of modern and contemporary Southeast Asian art. In addition to this, there are special research galleries and rotating exhibition spaces that complement the permanent galleries. The National Gallery Singapore offers learning opportunities for all through a vibrant range of programs, such as artist talks, children's programs, exhibitions, and other related activities. It also houses an auditorium, function and seminar rooms, and the Keppel Centre for Art Education, specially established for families and schools.

**Figure 19.4:** Entrance area of the National Gallery Singapore showing the staircase to the basement level and the footbridges connecting the two historic buildings. (Source: studioMilou.)

## Value Creation

Cultural: National Gallery Singapore pins Singapore on the global map as a leader in Southeast Asian art and is a cultural landmark for locals and visitors alike. The restored buildings epitomize the growth of Singapore as a nation, evoking memories of the past for future generations and nurturing a sense of pride and identity for Singaporeans.

Economic: National Gallery Singapore has generated more business and job opportunities since the start of the revitalization project. Since its official opening and as of 2019, ten food and beverage outlets are now in operation in the buildings,[6]

---

6.  "Shopping and Dining," National Gallery Singapore, accessed November 25, 2019, https://www. nationalgallery.sg/see-do/shopping-and-dining.

and its various programs and events also help to provide employment opportunities for vendors and art educators. Moreover, in positioning this landmark as a cultural institution in the region, it has the potential to bring in more visitors, especially those interested in modern and contemporary visual arts.

Environmental: It retains and highlights the significance of the Civic District, both past and present. Together with the Cricket Club, Padang, and the Victoria Theatre Hall nearby, the monuments illustrate the strategic locations of key government buildings typical of the urban planning of British colonies.

Social: Both buildings were originally closed to the general public owing to their functions; however, now, a new social value has been created as the National Gallery Singapore is open to the general public. By day, the place offers education and learning opportunities through its exhibitions and other related programs. By night, it becomes a social venue with cafes, restaurants, and unique events, such as concerts, screenings, and private functions. Its children-centered Keppel Centre for Art Education, docent training, Family Weekends, Teachers' Club, and other free public programs establish it as an arts hub for a broad range of local audiences and help to foster a social network for like-minded people.

> Our goal was to offer an elegant and welcoming art gallery that deeply respects the historical importance of the existing buildings and creates new architectural layers, each placed upon the monuments with minimal intervention, to create exhibition and other spaces for sharing and nurturing Singaporean and Southeast Asian visual arts.[7]
>
> —Jean-Francois Milou of studioMilou

## Bibliography

Cornelius, Vernon, and Joanna H. S. Tan. "Former Supreme Court Building." *Singapore National Library Board.* Accessed June 20, 2017. http://eresources.nlb.gov.sg/infopedia/articles/SIP_774_2005-01-10.html.

Lalwani, Bharti. "The National Gallery Singapore—a Conversation with Jean-Francois Milou." *ASEF Culture 360 Online Magazine*, November 17, 2014. Accessed June 20, 2017. https://culture360.asef.org/magazine/national-gallery-singapore-conversation-jean-francois-milou/.

Ministry of Information, Communications and the Arts. "Speech by Dr Lee Boon Yang, Minister for Information, Communications and the Arts, at the Gala Reception of Singapore Biennale 2006, 2 September 2006, 8.00 PM at The National Museum of Singapore." Accessed June 20, 2018. https://web.archive.org/web/20070613012438/http://www.mica.gov.sg/pressroom/press_070320.htm.

Prime Minister's Office Singapore, "Prime Minister Lee Hsien Loong's National Day Rally 2005 Speech (English)." Last modified August 21, 2005. https://www.pmo.gov.sg/Newsroom/prime-minister-lee-hsien-loongs-national-day-rally-2005-speech-english.

---

7.  studioMilou Singapore, *National Gallery Singapore (studioMilou Architecture Book 3)* (Singapore: studioMilou documents, 2014), 37, https://www.studiomilou.sg/wp-content/uploads/2019/05/2014-studioMilou-Book-3_100dpi.pdf.

Seno, Alexandra A. "National Gallery Singapore." *Architectural Record*, February 1, 2016. Accessed June 20, 2017. http://www.architecturalrecord.com/articles/11491-national-gallery-singapore.

studioMilou Singapore. "National Gallery Singapore." Accessed June 20, 2017. https://www.studiomilou.sg/projects/the-national-gallery-singapore/.

studioMilou Singapore. *National Gallery Singapore (studioMilou Architecture Book 3)*. Singapore: studioMilou documents, 2014. https://www.studiomilou.sg/wp-content/uploads/2019/05/2014-studioMilou-Book-3_100dpi.pdf.

Wee, Jean, Min Li Foo, and studioMilou Singapore. *Connections: History and Architecture, City Hall and Supreme Court*. Singapore: Preservation of Sites and Monuments Division, National Heritage Board, Singapore, 2016.

# Military Case Studies

**Table 20.1:** Military case studies.

| Project Name | Location | Nature | New Use | Original Use | Timeframe |
|---|---|---|---|---|---|
| Crown Wine Cellars | Hong Kong | Government and private partnership project | Commercial/Recreation (wine cellars and private members' club) | Military (bunkers used to store arms and ammunition during World War II) | 2003–2004 |
| The Waterhouse at South Bund | Shanghai | Government and private partnership project | Commercial (boutique hotel) | Industrial/Military (Japanese army headquarters during World War II) | 2008–2010 |
| Gillman Barracks | Singapore | Government project | Cultural (art center) | Military (camp) | 2011–2012 |

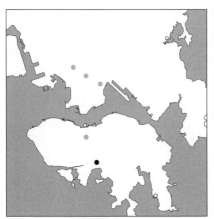

**Figure 20.1:** Location plan of Crown Wine Cellars, Hong Kong. (Drawn by Wai Shing Ng.)

**Figure 20.2:** Location plan of The Waterhouse at South Bund, Shanghai. (Drawn by Wai Shing Ng.)

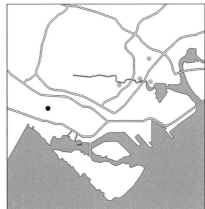

**Figure 20.3:** Location plan of Gillman Barracks, Singapore. (Drawn by Wai Shing Ng.)

# Crown Wine Cellars (Little Hong Kong), Hong Kong

Tiffany Tang

## Project Information

**Table 21.1:** Basic details of Crown Wine Cellars.

| | |
|---|---|
| Address | 18 Deep Water Bay Drive, Shouson Hill, Southern District |
| Old use | Military (bunkers used to store arms and ammunition during World War II) |
| New use | Commercial/Recreation (wine cellars and private members' club) |
| Heritage status | Not graded |
| Area | 998 square meters (including the newly constructed conservatory) |
| Project cost estimate | US$2.56 million (HK$20 million)[i] |
| Operator | Crown Wine Cellars |
| Developed/Funded by | Crown Worldwide Group—James Thompson (chairman/owner), Gregory De'Eb (project proponent/company principal) |
| Architect | Alice Lin (conservation architect); Hung Cheng (conservatory) |
| Contractor | Tony Lo |
| Start and completion date | August 2003–March 2004 |

i.   The Hong Kong dollar is pegged to the US dollar at about US$1=HK$7.8.

**Figure 21.1:** The conservatory of Crown Wine Cellars designed by Hung Cheng; a new addition to the Central Ordnance Depot (Little Hong Kong). (Source: Crown Wine Cellars.)

## Vision

To establish a viable, sustainable, and sympathetic public-private partnership to revitalize a significant but forgotten part of military heritage in Hong Kong.

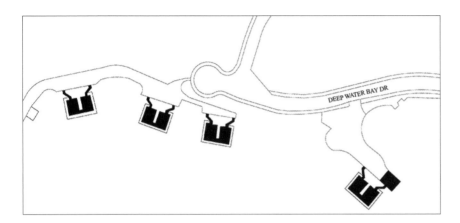

**Figure 21.2:** Site plan of the Crown Wine Cellars. (Drawn by Lavina Ahuja based on materials from Crown Wine Cellars.)

## Site History

The Central Ordnance (Munitions) Depot is one of two underground ammunition storage bunker facilities located on Hong Kong Island.[1] These facilities were constructed by the British around 1937, to store arms and ammunition for the defense of Hong Kong. To keep the location of the Central Ordnance (Munitions) Depot a secret, the British referred to the military site as Little Hong Kong (Heung Kong Tsai) after the nearby local fishing village of Aberdeen.[2] This secret military facility, originally composed of twenty-four concrete bunkers, was concealed in a valley within Shouson Hill. It has a unique history for being the last military position in the city to surrender to the invading Japanese army during World War II.

In 1941, as the last line of defense, the British commanding officer, Major Dewar, had wired and connected all twenty-four bunkers to a central detonator (located inside the depot headquarters) and had threatened to blow up all advancing Japanese troops along with the facility and the Allied forces present. Ironically, this impressed the Japanese advancing officer, Captain Suzuki, enough to enable the negotiation of an honorable surrender that saved all of the twenty-three Allied soldiers who were part of the final defense at Little Hong Kong.

After the war, the military continued to make use of the facility, which was made up of the bunkers, a depot headquarters building, guardhouse, sentry box, and a newly added security guard/troop bunker (suspected to have been constructed by the Japanese). This use continued until 1977, when the site was taken over by the Hong Kong Police Driving Academy.

Most of the bunkers were substantially altered in the mid-1980s because of two high-rise residential apartment buildings that were built in the vicinity of the site. This resulted in the loss of most of the original slopes, and sixteen bunkers were ultimately destroyed or badly damaged. The remaining eight bunkers were subsequently refitted and used by the Geotechnical Engineering Office (Hong Kong) from the mid-1990s until the early 2000s for rock core storage; under its tenancy the site gradually fell into disrepair.

---

1. The only underground bunkers that exist in Hong Kong are located at Shouson Hill and Lei Yue Mun.
2. Gregory De'Eb (General Manager of the Crown Wine Cellars), interviewed by author, Hong Kong, February 9, 2017.

In August 2003, Crown Wine Cellars Limited signed a lease with the Hong Kong SAR government to use the remaining eight bunkers as wine cellars and a clubhouse facility.

**Table 21.2:** Timeline of Crown Wine Cellars.

| | |
|---|---|
| 1937 | British Royal Engineers construct the Central Ordnance (Munitions) Depot, Little Hong Kong |
| 1941 (December 25) | Hong Kong officially surrenders to Japan |
| 1941 (December 27) | Little Hong Kong is the last allied position in Hong Kong to surrender to the invading Japanese Army |
| 1977 | Ownership of Little Hong Kong is transferred to the Hong Kong Police Driving Academy |
| Mid-1990s | Geotechnical Engineering Office (Hong Kong) takes over the site and uses it for rock core storage |
| 2003 | Crown Wine Cellars begins its tenancy at Little Hong Kong |
| 2007 | Little Hong Kong receives the Award of Merit at the UNESCO Asia-Pacific Awards for Cultural Heritage Conservation |

## Revitalization Concept

+ Optimizing the natural qualities of the military bunkers for professional wine storage by installing a sluice door and air-lock system, computerized climate control (to maintain the wine cellar at a constant temperature and humidity), and modern security systems.
+ Carefully restoring the historic site, with conversion of two of the original bunkers into a clubhouse and construction of a new glass conservatory.
+ Stabilizing the site by improving all aspects of the infrastructure, including reinforcement of the soil slopes above the bunkers, construction of surface drains and retaining walls, with replacement of the underground drainage, electrical, and water supply systems, and upgrading of the fire safety systems.

**Figure 21.3:** Main underground bunker adapted as a private member's club. (Source: Crown Wine Cellars.)

## Process and Partnership

The adaptive reuse of Little Hong Kong largely came about because of a conference talk delivered by the then–permanent secretary for commerce and economic development, Yvonne Choi, in 2000 that sought to enable Hong Kong to become a wine trading center in Asia and, as part of that process, to encourage private-sector parties to utilize selected abandoned military structures in Hong Kong for wine storage.[3] The government's plan was launched in the aftermath of the Asian financial crisis and was primarily intended to diversify Hong Kong's economy. However, the initiative was also part of the government's strategy to guarantee the survival of historically significant military sites in Hong Kong, which was not considered a priority by the colonial government.

Jim Thompson, the founder of the Crown Worldwide Group, and Gregory De'Eb, a career diplomat stationed in Hong Kong, learned about the underground military facilities and together investigated the feasibility of using these sites as wine cellars. They inspected many former military facilities throughout the city but selected Little Hong Kong because of its accessibility, dimensions, and overall suitability.

Following thirteen months of negotiation with various government departments, Crown Wine Cellars Limited signed a lease with the Hong Kong SAR government in 2003. Given that heritage conservation in Hong Kong was in its infancy, the Little Hong Kong lease was a pilot project utilizing a short-term tenancy (STT) of seven years, renewable upon open tender.

## Development Environment

Little Hong Kong was part of the first batch of former military sites offered for redevelopment in a largely unsuccessful attempt by the Hong Kong SAR government in 2000 to preserve aspects of the territory's military heritage. Other projects that were included were the Blue Pool Road Tunnels, Victoria Barracks, and numerous air-raid tunnels located in Aberdeen, underneath Pacific Place in Admiralty, and beneath Kowloon Park. A majority of these facilities could not be adapted for new uses because of a combination of site limitations and local legislation. The clubhouse operated by Crown Wine Cellars Limited had to be registered as a private members' club and comply with the Club Licensing Authority owing to zoning regulations.

Initially, Crown Wine Cellars Limited had to operate its wine cellar business as an inland bonded facility because of the relatively high tax on wine. However, the proposition for storing wine in the bunkers became more feasible upon an industry-led Hong Kong SAR government initiative to remove all taxes on the import of wine in 2008.

## Commercial Sustainability

The primary source of income for Crown Wine Cellars is a member-based wine storage subscription and venue rental. Despite a viable business model, the initial capital investment (combined with accrued interest, maintenance costs, and rents) has yet to be earned back after fifteen years of operation and two successive short-term

---

3. Yvonne Choi, then-permanent secretary for commerce and economic development, delivered a speech titled "Can Hong Kong Become a Trade Center for Alcoholic Drinks?" at a business conference in 2000. Various sites were identified for revitalization as wine cellars during the seminar. Interested attendees were invited to follow up. Back then there were no formal heritage bodies set up to manage and monitor such initiatives. Gregory De'Eb's first contact was with Sandra Lee and then Duncan Pescod, who was then the acting commissioner of tourism.

tenancy (STT) contracts, as revenue generation is limited by the restricted usable size of the facility and types of business operations permitted on the site.

The company has survived and remains viable through the expansion of storage operations to a second location,[4] which currently stores ten times the volume of wine as the Shouson Hill location. The second location does not face any of the STT-linked costs and limitations.

## Key Success Factors

+ Unique timing, political policy, and business circumstances that created a conducive environment for the project.
+ Entrepreneurial, passionate, and visionary developer team.
+ Genuine understanding of the commercial viability of the project and the importance of public accessibility.
+ Acceptance among all parties involved that the adaptive reuse process could only take place if the site's architectural integrity remained entirely intact.
+ Full support from the government in pursuing an unusual conservation project.

## Key Challenges

+ Lack of a formal heritage conservation framework (at that time) or previous examples from which to draw experience.
+ Time-consuming process of complying with rigid standard (and often contradictory) requirements from all government and quasi-government departments and institutions.[5]
+ Need to transfer all the government standard requirements (stated above) into a short-term tenancy (STT), which has become the basis of all future lease renewals.
+ Complex nature of the site and its multiple zoning regulations, including greenbelt and open space areas, required solutions that deviated from standard regulations adding another complicated factor to the regulatory procedures.[6]

## Keeping Heritage Alive

This once-forgotten bunker complex now celebrates an overlooked period in Hong Kong's history. The unique story of the site is kept alive through a wide range of activities, including regular guided tours for local schoolchildren and university students and a wide variety of charity, community, educational, and social institutions. A number of commemorative celebrations are also arranged annually, bringing together

---

4. Crown Data Centre I, 6 Kin Fung Circuit, Tuen Mun.
5. Such as (but not limited to) Agriculture, Fisheries and Conservation Department, Antiquities and Monuments Office, Buildings Department, Civil Engineering and Development Department, Club Licensing Authority, Drainage Services Department, Electrical and Mechanical Services Department, Geotechnical Engineering Office, Highways Department, Hong Kong Fire Services Department, Lands Department, Leisure and Cultural Services Department, Southern District Council, Town Planning Board, Transport Department, and even local residents.
6. Technical challenges included stabilizing the slope, as required by the Civil Engineering and Development Department (CEDD), to support the new uses, which involved removing the trees on site. The CEDD initially refused to consider any alternative slope stabilization method that would preserve the existing trees. The Agriculture, Fisheries and Conservation Department in turn refused the removal of any trees because of greenbelt zoning. Eventually, a new method, developed by an experienced slope stabilization company, was utilized that preserved all the trees and stabilized the slope according to the government specifications.

the few remaining veterans of the Battle of Hong Kong. Little Hong Kong was the first former military site in Hong Kong to receive a UNESCO Asia-Pacific Heritage Award for Cultural Heritage Conservation.

**Figure 21.4:** Underground wine cellar of the adapted Crown Wine Cellars. (Source: Crown Wine Cellars.)

## Value Creation

Cultural: Little Hong Kong is one of the few accessible military sites that is a physical reminder of the territory's role in World War II and the bitter circumstances of its fall and occupation by the Japanese. The conservation of the site has saved a valuable but almost forgotten relic from Hong Kong's military history.

Economic: The once-dilapidated former military site is now home to a world-class wine cellar as well as a unique clubhouse facility and event space. A successful and fast-growing business, Crown Wine Cellars contributes to the development of Hong Kong as Asia's undisputed rare and fine wine trading center.[7]

Social: Little Hong Kong operates as a private members' club, but the club's facilities are open for guest bookings with a specially created one-time "silver membership." Moreover, weekly networking events are held for both members and nonmembers, and a number of commemorative celebrations are also organized, in addition to other private events, such as art auctions and weddings, among others.

> Having played host to a number of historical, social, educational, cultural, and arts-related events, the restored Little Hong Kong has attracted people throughout the local community from all walks of life and across all age groups. Its conservation and current remembrance function demonstrate how military heritage is a powerful unifying factor to bring a community closer together.
>
> —*Project Team*

## Bibliography

Crown Worldwide Group. "Site History." Accessed December 3, 2018. https://www.crownwinecellars.com/.

---

7. In 2001, an estimated 15–17 percent of wine stored in the major overseas wine storage facilities belonged to Hong Kong owners (according to an interview with Gregory De 'Eb, general manager of the Crown Wine Cellars). By 2012, Hong Kong was the largest market for fine and rare wine auctions (See Philippe Espinasse, "Hong Kong Still Tops Wine Auction Sales," *South China Morning Post*, December 6, 2012, https://www.scmp.com/lifestyle/food-wine/article/1098142/hong-kong-still-tops-wine-auction-sales).

# The Waterhouse at South Bund, Shanghai

Hugo Chan

## Project Information

**Table 22.1:** Basic details of The Waterhouse at South Bund.

| | |
|---|---|
| Address | 1–3 Maojiayuan Road, Huangpu District, Shanghai |
| Old use | Industrial/Military (Japanese army headquarters during World War II) |
| New use | Commercial (boutique hotel) |
| Heritage status | Not graded |
| Area | 800 square meters (site area); 2,800 square meters (gross floor area) |
| Project cost estimate | Undisclosed |
| Operator | Unlisted Collection |
| Developed/Funded by | Unlisted Collection |
| Architect | Neri&Hu Design and Research Office (NHDRO) |
| Contractor | Shanghai Jinbo Shicai Architectural and Decoration Construction Co. Ltd. |
| Start and completion date | May 2008–May 2010 |

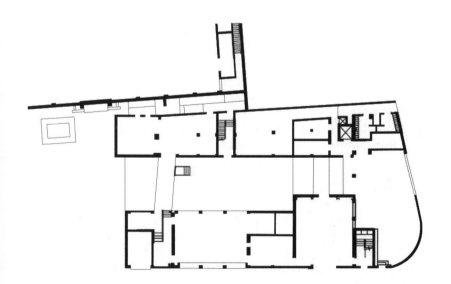

**Figure 22.1:** First-level plan of The Waterhouse at South Bund hotel. (Drawn by Wai Shing Ng based on materials from Neri&Hu.)

## Vision

To contrast the new and old and to blend the exterior and interior in order to convert
a historic warehouse building into a boutique hotel that offers spectacular views of
the Pudong skyline at a distance across Huangpu River.

## Site History

The original warehouse building was constructed in the 1930s. It served as the
Japanese army headquarters in Shanghai during World War II. After the Japanese
occupation and the founding of the People's Republic of China, the property was
requisitioned and allocated by the government as a grease factory. By the mid-2000s,
when a developer became interested in the site, the building was in dire condition and
served as temporary housing quarters for construction workers.

**Table 22.2:** Timeline of The Waterhouse at South Bund.

| | |
|---|---|
| 1930s | Warehouse building is constructed on Shiliupu dockyard |
| Late 1930s to 1945 | Building serves as the Japanese army's headquarters in Shanghai during World War II |
| 1949 | Building is requisitioned and used as a factory |
| Mid-2000s | Unlisted Collection leases the building for its adaptive reuse as an upmarket boutique hotel |
| 2010 | The Waterhouse at South Bund opens |

## Revitalization Concept

+ Contrasting old and new—restoring the original concrete building coupled with new steel additions over the existing structure to reflect and respect the site's industrial past, establishing a contextual connection with its history and the local culture.[1]
+ Creating a unique spatial experience by blurring the boundary between the exterior and interior and between the public and private realms.[2]
+ Visually connecting different spaces not only to bring an element of surprise but also to allow hotel guests to experience local street life and the unique spatial characteristics of the city.[3]

## Process and Partnership

The warehouse building was acquired by Unlisted Collection—an umbrella brand founded by the Singaporean hospitality specialist Loh Lik Peng.[4] The company's portfolio consists of unique, high-quality boutique hotels and restaurants in London, Shanghai, Singapore, and Sydney. All its hotels are set within heritage buildings that have been sensitively restored and adapted as modern lifestyle experiences for guests. In May 2008, the Shanghai-based Neri&Hu Design and Research Office (NHDRO) was commissioned to transform the derelict riverside warehouse building into a daring interpretation of modern Shanghai, where the new and old sit side by side.

1. Neri&Hu, "The Waterhouse at South Bund," accessed June 30, 2019, http://thepractice.neriandhu.com/en/works/the-waterhouse-at-south-bund.
2. Neri&Hu, "The Waterhouse at South Bund."
3. Neri&Hu, "The Waterhouse at South Bund."
4. Jordon Bishop, "The Waterhouse at South Bund: An Injection of Contemporary Design in Shanghai," *Forbes*, June 1, 2018, https://www.forbes.com/sites/bishopjordan/2018/06/01/waterhouse-south-bund-shanghai/#65b93bf36440.

## Development Environment

The warehouse building is located in the vicinity of the Expo 2010 Shanghai site
in the South Bund area. At the time of the project's development in the mid-2000s,
the neighborhood was a run-down residential area with only traces of trading and
shipping activities taking place in disused and underutilized dockyards and warehouses. In anticipation of the 2010 event, hotel facilities were in great demand, and
the local government was supportive of development that catered to tourists with
varied budgets. At the same time, the local government was looking to revitalize the
dilapidated neighborhood at the South Bund (including Dongjiadu fabric market
area, Shiliupu Wharf, and the residential quarter that is now known as The Cool
Docks), which would be visible to local and international visitors attending the Expo
2010 Shanghai.

The investor for this project, Unlisted Collection, saw a gap in the market for an upscale boutique hotel in a heritage setting that targeted tourists who sought and could afford a one-of-a-kind hospitality experience. The venture was (and remains) in line with the hospitality-specialist company's objectives: "All of our hotels are set within heritage listed buildings which have been sensitively restored and re-adapted into radical, cutting edge lifestyle concepts that culminate into an unforgettable experience for our guests."[5]

## Commercial Sustainability

The commercial sustainability of the project is dependent on the occupancy rates of the nineteen-room boutique hotel, where room prices range from RMB 1300 to 3200 (approximately US$190 to US$460) per night.[6] Income is also generated from food and beverage services and rental of the property's event space. The hotel is expected to be self-financing, which includes covering maintenance costs during the tenancy period.

## Key Success Factors

+ Unlisted Collection, which initiated this project, was experienced in creating viable hotel layouts and food and beverage venues in adaptive reuse projects.
+ The Waterhouse at South Bund project preserves historic elements of the building that evoke its industrial past and boldly reinterprets them as part of the hotel experience.
+ From the outset, the hotel investor and architects had a clear vision for the direction of the adaptive reuse project, and they fostered a strong partnership and working relationship from the design to marketing to operation stages, ensuring that the historic layers of the building and its contextual links to the surrounding urban fabric were properly conserved and represented.

## Key Challenges

+ On the verge of demolition for new development (serving as housing quarters for construction workers was only temporary), the building was in an extremely run-down state when negotiations for its renovation began.
+ Most historic elements of the site were not salvageable, which called into question the authenticity of its industrial heritage.
+ Because to the "sensitive nature" of its historic past (it was the headquarters of the Japanese army during the Japanese occupation of Shanghai), the historical and cultural significance of the heritage building was downplayed.

## Keeping Heritage Alive

Interventions to the industrial building's exterior were minimal, retaining its harmonious relationship with the surrounding streetscape in terms of human scale and visual linkage. An unobstructed view to Huangpu River and the Pudong skyline remained a key feature of the spatial layout, thereby reinforcing the physical and visual connections with the existing urban fabric.

---

5. Unlisted Collection, "About Us," accessed January 25, 2019, http://www.unlistedcollection.com/about.
6. "The Waterhouse at South Bund," Booking.com, accessed August 08, 2019, https://www.booking.com/hotel/cn/waterhouse-shanghai.html.

By preserving key original industrial features, such as the double-story vestibule space, exposed ceiling trusses, and stripped concrete and brick walls, the industrial past of the building's history was acknowledged and celebrated. To retain and represent the building's history, the design team intentionally mixed new gray bricks with old ones for the floor paving and recycled wood from the old building's rotting roof into tabletops for the restaurant and shutters facing the courtyard. Fading paint, holes in the walls of the decaying façades and interior surfaces, and water stains were preserved and presented for a better appreciation of the building's industrial past.

A clearly differentiable new steel structure was added above the existing building on the fourth floor to provide riverbank views and maintain a visual dialogue with the streets. Small openings were punctured through the interior of the double-story entrance to allow natural light and strengthen the internal visual connections. All new elements, including the concrete reception desk, flush windows, and steel columns and beams, were designed as distinctive new insertions.

**Figure 22.4:** Entrance and lobby of The Waterhouse at South Bund. (Source: Ho Yin Lee.)

## Value Creation

Cultural: The project speaks to the history of South Bund as a significant trading and shipping hub of colonial Shanghai. Although the boutique hotel reflects the more recent industrial past of the port, it is also a tangible reminder of the Japanese occupation during World War II.

Economic: The project has demonstrated to government officials and also to private developers the economic viability of adaptive reuse of heritage architecture for hospitality or other commercial uses. It is a model for saving other historic properties along the South Bund and throughout the city.

Environmental: The heritage property, alongside The Cool Docks, the renovated Shiliupu Wharf, and the Expo 2010 Shanghai venues, has significantly ameliorated the cityscape and public realm of the southern Huangpu River area. The revitalized waterfront promenade offers a continuous open space for the public to appreciate and enjoy the setting.

Social: The Waterhouse at South Bund helped revitalize a dying district with an aging population, deserted street life, and fading commercial activities by attracting hotel guests and visitors, reestablishing social bonds among new and old user groups.

> **We want to demonstrate a new way of preserving things. You don't have to clean it all up.**
>
> —*Founder of Neri&Hu Design and Research Office (NHDRO), Lyndon Neri*[7]

## Bibliography

Neri&Hu. "The Waterhouse at South Bund." Accessed June 30, 2019. http://thepractice.neriandhu.com/en/works/the-waterhouse-at-south-bund.

Pearson, Clifford. "The Waterhouse at South Bund." *Architectural Record*. Last modified September 16, 2010. https://www.architecturalrecord.com/articles/8259-the-waterhouse-at-south-bund?v=preview.

Unlisted Collection. "About Us." Accessed January 25, 2019. http://www.unlistedcollection.com/about.

---

7.  Clifford Pearson, "The Waterhouse at South Bund," *Architectural Record*, last modified September 16, 2010, https://www.architecturalrecord.com/articles/8259-the-waterhouse-at-south-bund?v=preview.

# Gillman Barracks, Singapore

Debbie Wong

## Project Information

**Table 23.1:** Basic details of Gillman Barracks.

| | |
|---|---|
| Address | 9 Lock Road, Singapore 108937 |
| Old use | Military (camp) |
| New use | Cultural (arts center) |
| Heritage status | Not graded |
| Area | 6.4 hectares |
| Project cost estimate | US$7.4 million (SG$10 million)[i] |
| Operator | Singapore Economic Development Board (EDB), the National Arts Council (NAC), and the Jurong Town Corporation (JTC) |
| Developed/Funded by | Singapore Economic Development Board (EDB), the National Arts Council (NAC), and the Jurong Town Corporation (JTC) |
| Architect | N/A |
| Contractor | Jurong Town Corporation (JTC) (renovation and construction) |
| Start and completion date | 2011–2012 |

i. The conversion rate is taken at US$1=SG$1.35.

**Figure 23.1:** External view of Block 9 at Gillman Barracks. (Source: Ho Yin Lee.)

## Vision

To establish Gillman Barracks as an iconic international destination for contemporary arts (both display and sale), while conserving the area's colonial history.

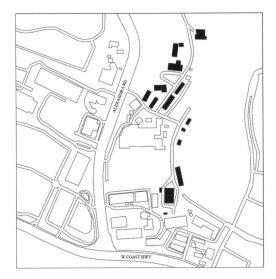

**Figure 23.2:** Site plan of Gillman Barracks. (Drawn by Lavina Ahuja based on materials from Gillman Barracks official website.)

## Site History

Named after General Sir Webb Gillman, a well-known officer of the British army, Gillman Barracks was set up to accommodate the expansion of the British infantry in Singapore. Completed in 1936, it sits on a site that was formerly a jungle and a swamp and included barrack buildings, married quarters, messes, regimental institutes, and sports facilities.[1] It was the site of a fierce battle with Japanese invaders in February 1942 and was one of the last British posts in Singapore to fall to the Japanese.[2]

In August 1971, Gillman Barracks was handed over to the Singapore government for a token sum of SG\$1 as part of the British military's withdrawal from Singapore.[3] The Singapore Armed Forces (SAF) moved into the camp, and the public gained access to the camp's sports facilities under the management of the National Sports Promotion Board. After the SAF vacated the camp in the 1990s, some blocks were demolished, and the government allowed the remaining buildings to be used for commercial purposes. The site was renamed Gillman Village in 1996.

In 2010, the government announced its plan to develop the area into a hub for arts-related activities and businesses, such as art galleries and art research centers. The site reverted to its original name, Gillman Barracks, and was developed for adaptive reuse as a contemporary arts enclave. The proposal was among the recommendations submitted by the Economic Strategies Committee, which specializes in evaluating the country's long-term economic development. The existing tenants of Gilman Barracks moved out in early 2011, and the government commenced the renovation and retrofit of the area and its fourteen colonial buildings.

1.  Valerie Chew, "Gillman Barracks," *Singapore Infopedia (Singapore National Library Board e-resources)*, July 2017. Accessed on June 17, 2019. http://eresources.nlb.gov.sg/infopedia/articles/SIP_1395_2008-12-06.html.

2.  Valerie Chew, "Gillman Barracks."

3.  "Barracks 'Sold' to S'pore Govt for a Dollar," *Straits Times*, August 21, 1971, http://eresources.nlb.gov.sg/newspapers/Digitised/Page/straitstimes19710821-1.1.32.

**Table 23.2:** Timeline of Gillman Barracks.

| | |
|---|---|
| 1936 | 1st Battalion, the Middlesex Regiment, moves into Gillman Barracks[i] |
| 1971 | Gillman Barracks is sold to the Singapore Government for SG\$1[ii] and the site is occupied by the Singapore Armed Forces (SAF) |
| 1984 | SAF start relocating to other areas[iii] |
| 1996 | Name of the camp is changed to Gillman Village[iv] |
| 2002 | Singapore Urban Redevelopment Authority (URA) launches its Identity Plan for Gillman Village and other areas of Singapore[v] |
| 2010 | Gillman Village reverts to its original name—Gillman Barracks[vi] |
| 2011 (February) | Existing tenants move out; Singapore Economic Development Board (EDB) proposes the adaptive reuse of the site as a creative arts cluster[vii] |
| 2011 | Jurong Town Corporation (JTC), the site's landlord, invites tenders for the refurbishment of existing buildings, improvement works, and development of the site[viii] |
| 2012 | Singapore's latest arts center is established in Gillman Barracks with thirteen galleries from ten countries[ix] |
| 2013 | Nanyang Technological University (NTU) Centre for Contemporary Art (CCA) Singapore opens at Gillman Barracks[x] |
| 2015 | Five art galleries close at Gillman Barracks[xi] |
| 2016 | Gillman Barracks Programme Office is set up to coordinate activities at the site and promote the arts center[xii] |

i.   "Second Infantry Regiment in Their New Home," *The Straits Times*, April 1, 1936, http://eresources.nlb.gov.sg/newspapers/Digitised/Article/straitstimes19360401.2.87.
ii.  Benny Ortega, "Colonel Who 'Sold' Gillman Barracks for Just One Dollar," *Singapore Monitor*, November 2, 1984, http://eresources.nlb.gov.sg/newspapers/Digitised/Article/singmonitor19841102-1.2.6.6.
iii. Benny Ortega, "Colonel Who 'Sold' Gillman Barracks."
iv.  Miranda Yeo, "New Life for Old Barracks," *The Straits Times*, May 16, 2015, http://news.asiaone.com/news/singapore/new-life-old-barracks.
v.   Valerie Chew, "Gilman Village," *Singapore Infopedia (Singapore National Library Board e-resources)*, accessed March 14, 2017, http://eresources.nlb.gov.sg/infopedia/articles/SIP_1395_2008-12-06.html.
vi.  "Our Favourite Place – Gillman Barracks," *Urban Redevelopment Authority*, accessed June 20, 2017, https://www.ura.gov.sg/ms/OurFavePlace/events/bench/locations/gillman-barracks.
vii. "Singapore Economic Development Board Calls for Expressions of Interests (EOI) for Galleries to Set Up in Gillman Barracks," *Singapore Government News*, June 14, 2011, http://eresources.nlb.gov.sg/.
viii. Valerie Chew, "Gillman Barracks."
ix.  Helmi Yusof, "Big Guns, Big Bang at Barracks," *The Business Times*, September 15, 2012, http://eresources.nlb.gov.sg/.
x.   Valerie Chew, "Gillman Barracks."
xi.  Valerie Chew, "Gillman Barracks."
xii. Lijie Huang, "Gillman Barracks Is Four," *The Straits Times*, September 20, 2016, http://eresources.nlb.gov.sg/.

## Revitalization Concept

+ Conserving and enhancing the distinctive character of Gillman Barracks, according to the Identity Plan unveiled by the Urban Redevelopment Authority (URA) in 2002.

+ Establishing an arts and research cluster through the adaptive reuse of the buildings in the barracks (changes reflected the requirements of individual gallery owners).

+ Introducing new commercial uses while retaining the area's colonial charm.

**Figure 23.3:** Overview of the site of Gillman Barracks post-revitalization. (Source: Ho Yin Lee.)

## Process and Partnership

Gillman Barracks is a government initiative that enhances Singapore's standing as an Asian art hub. The Urban Redevelopment Authority (URA) identified the Gillman Barracks site as an arts hub owing to its unique historic and spatial characteristics. The site was jointly developed by the Singapore Economic Development Board (EDB), JTC Corporation (JTC), and the National Arts Council (NAC).

EDB's role is to market and promote Gillman Barracks as a home for art businesses, including galleries, as well as to establish the Nanyang Technological University (NTU) Centre of Contemporary Art (CCA). JTC is Gillman Barracks' landlord and infrastructure developer, while NAC promotes the development of the Singaporean arts scene by supporting artists' participation in CCA programs and nurturing local arts literacy.

## Development Environment

The project was initiated by the Urban Redevelopment Authority's (URA) identification of the hillside barracks as an important site representing the city's colonial history that would benefit from preservation and enhancement of its distinctive character. This idea was further developed with the Economics Strategies Committee's proposal to establish an arts and creative industries cluster. Under this plan, new commercial uses were introduced, while retaining the area's colonial charm. The URA's public consultation on the new uses of the site and subsequent public support further reinforced and cemented the proposal, where 72 percent of the public interviewees were in favor of the new use, with arts and dining as the most preferred activities.[4]

## Commercial Sustainability

Rental for galleries range from SD$4,000 to SD$5,000 and it can require SD$20,000 a month or more to keep a gallery in operation.[5] Although no official statistics are available, it appears that five of the original seventeen galleries did not renew their leases in 2015, after almost three years in residence, citing low traffic, poor sales, and

---

4. Valerie Chew, "Gillman Barracks."
5. Deepika Shetty, "Nearly a Third of Gillman Barracks Galleries Have Decided Not to Renew Their Leases," *Straits Times*, April 11, 2015, https://www.straitstimes.com/lifestyle/arts/nearly-a-third-of-gillman-barracks-galleries-have-decided-not-to-renew-their-leases.

a slow start to the arts enclave.[6] Galerie Michael Janssen, which brought several major shows to Singapore, also left Gillman Barracks in February 2016 citing, "I felt the project has not taken off as envisioned by all of us who have left so far. It could be the best location for galleries in the entire region and in Asia, it has all the infrastructure, but challenges remain."[7] The vacated spaces were subsequently taken over by other arts and dining facilities.

## Key Success Factors

+ Despite low footfall in its early days, new initiatives were put in place to boost traffic and revitalize the area, such as more pop-up activities and partnerships with large-scale events—like the Art after Dark events, Singapore Art Week, and Singapore HeritageFest. These were met with support from the tenants and deemed successful, as they attracted more visitors to the center and helped the public gain a better understanding of the historic and cultural significance of Gillman Barracks.

## Key Challenges

+ Gillman Barracks is not a formally protected site.
+ Sustainability of the business model proved to be difficult because of the nature of the program (narrowly focused on contemporary arts).
+ The food and beverage options were also considered too limited, in terms of variety and pricing, to draw a wider range of visitors—unlike another former military barrack, Dempsey Hill, which was transformed into an "urban village."
+ Secluded and inaccessible location of the site poses the main challenge in drawing visitors.
+ Singapore's tropical climate and heat also make the visitor experience unpleasant, as there are only a few trees on site and no covered walkways.

## Keeping Heritage Alive

Gillman Barracks' landlord and infrastructure developer, Jurong Town Corporation (JTC), carried out extensive refurbishment works within the barracks, yielding about 4,200 square meters for art galleries, with the remaining 4,800 square meters of space dedicated to arts-related activities, such as research centers and studios, along with additional food and beverage outlets. Today (as of 2019), the site is home to eleven international art galleries as well as Art Outreach, Nanyang Technological University (NTU) Centre for Contemporary Art (CCA) Singapore, Playeum (a children-orientated art space), Singapore Design Label, SuperMama, and seven dining outlets, which are housed in the conserved colonial barracks.

Conservation of the main colonial building and former officers' married quarter (Block 9) has retained most of its architectural elements, such as the large windows, high arches, and wide corridors. It now serves as the main and largest block in the center. Similarly, Block 7, with its unique roof, was once the Army Kinema Corporation (AKC) and functioned as a cinema, and later a bar and bistro. Since its

---

6.   Deepika Shetty, "Nearly a Third of Gillman Barracks Galleries Have Decided Not to Renew Their Leases."
7.   Deepika Shetty, "Nearly a Third of Gillman Barracks Galleries Have Decided Not to Renew Their Leases."

latest revitalization, it has been transformed into commercial art galleries and exhibition spaces, and the AKC logo has been preserved on its exterior.

A nonprofit volunteer group, Friends of the Museums, conducts two types of guided tours for visitors—the weekly Art and History Tours and the monthly History and Heritage Tours.[8] The Art and History Tour provides insights into the contemporary works and the site's history, while the History and Heritage Tour shares more in-depth stories about the former occupants as well as the site's structures and landscape.

**Figure 23.4:** Interior view of one of the adapted art galleries of Gillman Barracks. (Source: Ho Yin Lee.)

## Value Creation

Cultural: The story of Gillman Barracks is shared with the public on a regular basis, generating greater public awareness of Singapore's colonial and military past. With the establishment of the Nanyang Technological University (NTU) Centre for Contemporary Art (CCA), the site presents itself as a creative hub for the creation, display, and exchange of contemporary art in Asia.

Economic: Gillman Barracks has attracted a dynamic mix of international and local galleries and helps reinforce Singapore as a marketplace for art sales and businesses. Educational organizations, galleries, and other retail and food outlets have brought about employment opportunities to local arts educators and vendors.

Environmental and Social: Gillman Barracks draws a larger, more diverse crowd of visitors with the introduction of free tours, the visual arts education organizations (Art Outreach and Playeum), and collaborations with other major arts and heritage events in town, infusing the place with vitality. While it is not a formally protected site, it would be a challenge to demolish Gillman Barracks owing to its adaptive reuse and the community's appreciation the venue.

---

8. "Gillman Barracks Outreach," Eventbrite, accessed June 17, 2019, https://www.eventbrite.sg/o/fom-gillman-barracks-outreach-5691212557.

> Gillman Barracks marks another example of Singapore's cluster development strategy at work. It will be an enclave of visual artists networking with curators, collectors, and art lovers from Asia and other parts of the world. This will encourage exchange and infusion of ideas which can further generate new ideas and collaborations.[9]
>
> —*Leow Thiam Seng, JTC's Director for New Business, Housing and Amenity Cluster*

## Bibliography

Chew, Valerie. "Gilman Barracks." *Singapore Infopedia (Singapore National Library Board e-resources)*, July 2017. Accessed on June 17, 2019. http://eresources.nlb.gov.sg/infopedia/articles/SIP_1395_2008-12-06.html.

Gillman Barracks. "About Gillman Barracks." Accessed on June 20, 2017. https://www.gillmanbarracks.com/about/vision.

Gillman Barracks. "Fact Sheet About Gillman Barracks." Last modified January 15, 2014. https://www.gillmanbarracks.com/files/press/Factsheet---Developments-at-Gillman-Barracks/file/FACTSHEET_Developments%20at%20GB%20(3Jan2014).pdf.

National Arts Council Singapore. "Singapore's Position as a Contemporary Art Destination Strengthens Gillman Barracks Art Galleries Line-Up." Last modified May 27, 2012. https://www.nac.gov.sg/media-resources/press-releases/Singapore-s-Position.html.

Samer, Bagaeen, and Celia Clark, eds. *Sustainable Regeneration of Former Military Sites*. London: Taylor & Francis, 2016.

Urban Redevelopment Authority. "Our Favourite Place—Gillman Barracks." Accessed June 20, 2017. https://www.ura.gov.sg/ms/OurFavePlace/events/bench/locations/gillman-barracks.

---

9.   National Arts Council Singapore, "Singapore's Position as a Contemporary Art Destination Strengthens Gillman Barracks Art Galleries Line-Up," last modified May 27, 2012, https://www.nac.gov.sg/media-resources/press-releases/Singapore-s-Position.html.

# Mixed Use Case Studies

**Table 24.1:** Mixed use case studies.

| Project Name | Location | Nature | New Use | Original Use | Timeframe |
|---|---|---|---|---|---|
| Prince Edward Road West Shophouses | Hong Kong | Quasi-government, private and public partnership project | Mixed commercial and cultural (shops, visual arts, and creative businesses related to the flower trade) | Mixed commercial and residential (shophouses) | 2008–2017 |
| Tianzifang | Shanghai | Private project supported by the government | Residential and commercial (creative industries, restaurants, and shops) | Mixed use (commercial, industrial [small factories], and residential) | 1998–ongoing |
| Clarke Quay | Singapore | Private project | Mixed use (dining, entertainment, and retail) | Commercial (godowns, shophouses, and trading port) | 2003–2006 |

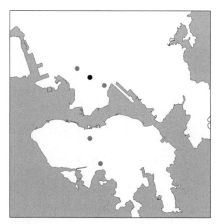

**Figure 24.1:** Location plan of Prince Edward Road West Shophouses, Hong Kong. (Drawn by Wai Shing Ng.)

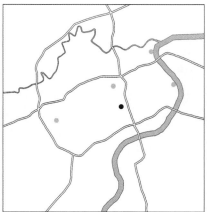

**Figure 24.2:** Location plan of Tianzifang, Shanghai. (Drawn by Wai Shing Ng.)

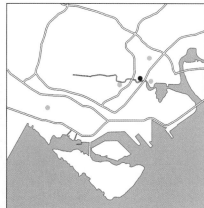

**Figure 24.3:** Location plan of Clarke Quay, Singapore. (Drawn by Wai Shing Ng.)

# Prince Edward Road West Shophouses, Hong Kong

Tiffany Tang

## Project Information

**Table 25.1:** Basic details of Prince Edward Road West Shophouses.

| | |
|---|---|
| Address | Nos. 190–204 and 210–212 Prince Edward Road West, Yau Tsim Mong District, Kowloon, Hong Kong |
| Old use | Mixed commercial and residential (shophouses) |
| New use | Mixed commercial and cultural (shops, visual arts, and creative businesses related to the flower trade) |
| Heritage status | Grade 2 Historic Buildings |
| Area | Ten shophouses with a total floor area of 1,440 square meters (gross floor area 4,334 square meters) |
| Project cost estimate | US$89.75 million (HK$700 million)[i] |
| Operator | No. 204—The Hong Kong Council of Social Service; Other units—various tenants |
| Developed/Funded by | Urban Renewal Authority (URA) |
| Architect | Urban Renewal Authority (URA) |
| Contractor | Various contractors |
| Start and completion date | 2008–2017 |

i.   The Hong Kong dollar is pegged to the US dollar at about US$1=HK$7.8.

**Figure 25.1:** Street view of the revitalized shophouses on Prince Edward Road West. (Source: Urban Renewal Authority.)

## Vision

To preserve the local streetscape and character, conserve the Grade 2 Historic Buildings, and revitalize ten shophouses on Prince Edward Road West for commercial and cultural use for the neighborhood community.

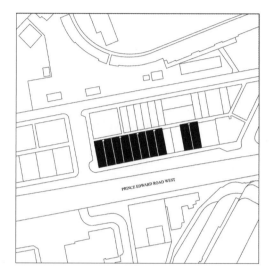

**Figure 25.2:** Site plan of the ten revitalized shophouses on Prince Edward Road West. (Drawn by Wai Shing Ng based on materials from the Urban Renewal Authority.)

## Site History

Nos. 190–204 and 210–212 of Prince Edward Road West is the largest surviving shophouse cluster in Hong Kong. The row of ten shophouses (originally there were sixteen), designed by a Franco-Belgian construction company in the early 1930s, stands out for its distinctive Art Deco style with its geometrically decorated balustrades and balconies with rounded corners.

The shophouses were originally designed for domestic use on the upper floors and retail use on the ground floors, but later the shophouses were largely occupied by a variety of commercial and institutional uses, such as dance schools, fitness centers, the flower trade, music studios, some religious institutions, and tutorial schools, with only some upper units utilized for residential purposes.[1] Taking advantage of the cluster's proximity to the popular Hong Kong flower market, the businesses flourished, but the prewar properties lacked modern services and fire safety facilities.

---

1.    For some years, the production studio of Mr. John Woo and Mr. Fruit Chan Kuo, world famous film directors, was located here.

**Table 25.2:** Timeline of Prince Edward Road West Shophouses.

| | |
|---|---|
| 1930s | Shophouses on Prince Edward Road West are built by G. Van Wylick from Credit Foncier D'Extreme Orient (a Franco-Belgian firm) as "modern flats" for middle-class families |
| 1940s | Site is occupied by the Japanese army during World War II, and used as a dormitory by the government |
| 1947 | Shophouses are used as private residential units with a variety of commercial uses on the lower floors |
| 2007 | Hong Kong SAR Chief Executive's 2007/08 Policy Address calls upon the Urban Renewal Authority (URA) to extend the scope of historic building protection[i] |
| 2007 | URA identifies a total of seventy-three pre-war shophouses with "outstanding heritage value" for a revitalization scheme. Among them are two rows along Prince Edward Road West and Shanghai Street (the only remaining rows among the group) |
| 2008 | URA commences the preservation-cum-revitalization project |
| 2010 (February) | Development Plan for the shophouses on Prince Edward Road West is approved by the Town Planning Board (TPB) |
| 2010 (March) | Antiquities Advisory Board (AAB) recognizes the properties on Prince Edward Road West as Grade 2 Historic Buildings |
| 2010 | URA starts property acquisition of the ten shophouses |
| 2011 | Renovation work starts |
| 2012 | Ground floor shops open |
| 2017 | Renovation work (of all phases) is complete |

i.   Office of the Chief Executive, *2007–08 Policy Address* (Hong Kong: Hong Kong SAR Government, October 10, 2007), http://www.policyaddress.gov.hk/07-08/eng/policy.html.

## Revitalization Concept

+ Restoring the original buildings by removing unauthorized building works and repairing decorative features as well as stabilizing structural components.
+ Retaining the original businesses and community network while encouraging new tenants with creative businesses related to the flower trade.

**Figure 25.3:** A florist shop on the ground floor of one of the revitalized shophouses. (Source: Urban Renewal Authority.)

## Process and Partnership

During the 1990s and 2000s, shophouses, once so typical of Hong Kong's streetscapes, were disappearing rapidly and were being replaced by modern high-rises. In 2007, in a bid to help preserve this part of the city's character, the Urban Renewal Authority (URA) commissioned a study to identify prewar shophouses with "outstanding heritage value" for a revitalization project. The study revealed seventy-three properties including two rows of shophouses, one along Prince Edward Road West and the other along Shanghai Street. The ten shophouses along Prince Edward Road West were seen as particularly important.

In 2010, the URA acquired the Prince Edward Road West shophouses as the first step in the project. The proposed reuse was determined in consultation with owners, tenants, and other stakeholders in the local flower market community. The URA decided to keep the use of the ground floors mainly related to the flower trade while the units on the upper floors were designated for arts and cultural uses (such as visual arts, as well as flower-related activities).

## Development Environment

The Prince Edward Road West shophouse project was the Urban Renewal Authority's (URA) first initiative in area- or cluster-based conservation. Over the years, the URA's urban renewal program involved demolition of shophouse clusters all across Hong Kong to be replaced by modern high-density developments.[2] A major enabling element to the shophouse revitalization project was the recognition of the shophouses on Nos. 190–204 and 210–212 Prince Edward Road West by the Antiquities Advisory Board (AAB) as Grade 2 Historic Buildings.

## Commercial Sustainability

The main purpose of the Prince Edward Road West project was to conserve one of the last two remaining rows of shophouses in this part of Hong Kong. The financial viability of such a project was not the prime concern, but rather its cultural and social impact for the neighborhood. The Urban Renewal Authority (URA), therefore, has accepted a below-market rental yield and has conservative expectations of the estimated payback period for the costs involved in the acquisition and renovation of the properties. Acquisition costs of these units were high because residential tenants were offered cash compensation or rehousing units by the Hong Kong Housing Authority. The compensation was based on the government's Home Purchase Allowance (HPA) policy, in which HPA is the difference between the market value of the resumed property and the value of a notional replacement (a seven-year-old flat in a similar location). Nondomestic properties were offered an ex gratia allowance on top of the market value.

## Key Success Factors

+ Urban Renewal Authority's (URA) policy to revitalize prewar shophouses.
+ Consensus during the public engagement exercise to retain the flower trade as an anchor business for the site.
+ Phased renovation work to allow normal operation of the existing businesses.

---

2.  URA has shophouse redevelopment projects in other parts of Hong Kong. A recent project in Sheung Wan stopped after prolonged opposition from local advocacy groups and residents.

+ Original businesses retained in the building to maintain its community network and keep the flower trade alive.

## Key Challenges

+ Compliance with modern safety regulations—for example, the regulations stipulated an enclosed staircase. To avoid destroying the original open staircases, the Urban Renewal Authority (URA) opted for a unit-by-unit renovation approach, which allowed the retention of the original staircases.
+ Upper floors of the buildings could not accommodate food and beverage use because of limited floor loading.
+ Poor building conditions were seen in some areas with a general lack of maintenance, unauthorized building works in common areas, and evidence of frequent leaks.
+ Acquisition of units took longer than expected, with some unit owners reluctant to sell. In 2018, the URA owned about 85 percent of the units.

## Keeping Heritage Alive

The Art Deco features on the columns, main entrances, and verandahs of the shophouses were repaired, and the internal staircases were restored. In one unit, the original floor tiles and wooden doors were retained. New materials that were added, such as doors and letter boxes, adopted a similar architectural style. Florists were selected as the ground-floor anchor tenants and other tenants were encouraged to creatively relate their businesses to the neighborhood's flower trade.

**Figure 25.4:** Nos. 202–204 Prince Edward Road West reopened as GoodPoint for use by social enterprises. (Source: Hong Kong Council of Social Service.)

## Value Creation

Cultural: The social enterprises in the shophouses organize art and cultural activities, a demand for which was seen in the local community. One of the tenants also organizes heritage tours to promote the sharing of history about the site and neighborhood.

Economic: The traditional flower business has been retained and even strengthened with higher patronage thanks to the striking renovation. The buildings no longer have a residential function; they are now a mixture of commercial, cultural, and social venues.

Social: Many of the previous florists returned to their shops in the revitalized buildings, keeping the community and the social network alive. The buildings are now also home to a social enterprise hub, which has an important social benefit for the neighborhood.

> Old buildings must be preserved when the community is still active and before its story disappears. There is no point keeping a building that doesn't have a soul anymore.
>
> —*Project Team*

## Bibliography

Office of the Chief Executive. *2007–08 Policy Address*. Hong Kong: Hong Kong SAR Government, October 10, 2007. http://www.policyaddress.gov.hk/07-08/eng/policy.html.

Urban Renewal Authority. "Prince Edward Road West/Yuen Ngai Street." Accessed December 3, 2018. https://www.ura.org.hk/en/project/heritage-preservation-and-revitalisation/prince-edward-road-west-yuen-ngai-street.

# Tianzifang, Shanghai

## Hugo Chan

## Project Information

**Table 26.1:** Basic details of Tianzifang.

| | |
|---|---|
| Address | Lanes 210, 248, and 274, Taikang Road, Huangpu District (formerly Luwan District),[i] Shanghai |
| Old use | Mixed use (commercial, industrial [small factories], and residential) |
| New use | Residential and commercial (creative industries, restaurants, and shops) |
| Heritage status | Not graded |
| Area | 29,000 square meters (site area); 35,000 square meters (gross floor area leased for new use)[ii] |
| Project cost estimate | Undetermined[iii] |
| Operator | Various operators |
| Developed/Funded by | Various developers[iv] |
| Architect | Various architects; Tongji Urban Planning and Design Institute (Shanghai City Taikang Road Historical Features Area Conservation and Adaptive Reuse Concept Plan, 2005) |
| Contractor | Various contractors |
| Start and completion date | 1998–ongoing |

i. The formerly separate jurisdictional districts of Luwan and Huangpu were merged on July 1, 2011 to form "Huangpu District."
ii. Xin-liang Zhou (resident representative/director, Tianzifang Management Committee), in discussion with the author, March 2017.
iii. Piecemeal investments and funding were provided by individual shop owners and tenants on renovation, and by local committee and management office on amelioration and utility works. Notable costs included: RMB 200,000 (2001)—rehabilitation of factory spaces and repaving of Lane 210, Taikang Lu by Zheng Rong-fa and Wu Mei-sen; RMB 18 million (2008)—a one-off fund allocated by local government for improvement of infrastructure and upgrade of existing residences.
iv. Notable partners include: Zheng Rong-fa, Wu Mei-sen, and Chen Yi-fei in the early stage; Tianzifang Shikumen Owners' Management Committee in 2004; Luwan District Office and Tianzifang Management Committee in 2008.

**Figure 26.1:** Entrance gate to Lane 210 of Taikang Road, Tianzifang. (Source: Hugo Chan.)

## Vision

To upgrade and transform a grid of historic lanes into a vibrant neighborhood for commercial, creative industry, and residential uses.

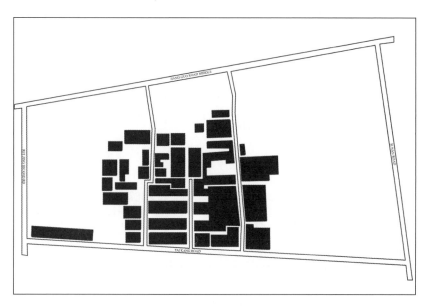

**Figure 26.2:** Site plan of Tianzifang. (Drawn by Hugo Chan based on materials from Shinohara, 2009: 750 and interviews with Eliza Wong and Mary Ye.)

## Site History

Bounded by Ruijin Second Road (formerly Route Père Robert during the French Concession era), Jianguo Middle Road (Rue Lafayette), Sinan Road (Rue Massenet), and Taikang Road (Rue Cassini), Tianzifang (as it is known today) entails a site area of 2.9 hectares. This includes *shikumen* housing developments of Zicheng Fang, Tiancheng Li, and Pingyuan Fang on Lanes 210, Lane 248, and Lane 274 of Taikang Road, respectively, constructed during 1912–1936.[1]

In 1998, a number of vacant factories and warehouses on Lane 210, Taikang Lu Road were first rented out for commercial use. The nonresidential uses gradually expanded and occupied spaces along Lanes 248 and 274 over the next few years. In 2008, the expansion slowed down owing to controls established by the Tianzifang Management Committee (田子坊管理委員會) and the local district office. By July 2009, over 55 percent of the housing units, accounting for roughly 25,000 square meters of floor area on Lanes 210, 248, and 274 of Taikang Road, were rented out for nonresidential use.[2] As of May 2017, roughly 60 out of the 671 original households have continued to reside in Tianzifang, while the majority of the residents have chosen to lease out their housing units for artistic, creative, and commercial uses.[3],[4]

**Table 26.2:** Timeline of Tianzifang.

| | |
|---|---|
| 1910s–1920s | As part of the French Concession area expansion (in 1914), roads are laid out and widened around the site, high-end residential and non-polluting service-oriented commercial uses are permitted under the newly enacted zoning plan for the area (which is now known as Tianzifang)[i] |
| 1920s–mid-1930s | Low-rise factories and *shikumen*-style housing units are built by developers with either a local or foreign background[ii] |
| Late 1930s–1940s | With the Sino-Japanese War and the Japanese Occupation, countless residences are damaged leading to deteriorating living conditions in the *shikumen* areas, including those in Tianzifang |
| 1950s–1960s | In response to Chairman Mao's call for the liberation of the female labor force, manufacturing teams are created and many *shikumen* houses and vacant spaces, such as those in the Tianzifang site, are converted into factories |
| 1990s | Due to economic restructuring, most factory operations are removed from neighborhoods within the urban core |
| 1998 | Zheng Rong-fa rents one of the factories on Lane 210, Taikang Road and intends to convert the 4,500-square-meter factory for commercial use |
| 1999 | Chen Yi-fei moves into a studio at Nos. 2–3, Lane 210, Taikang Road and renovates the space based on his experience of working in a factory-converted-studio in New York City in the 1980s |
| 2001 | Zheng Rong-fa and Wu Mei-sen rehabilitate a number of old factories on Lane 210, Taikang Road and invest in repaving the lane and ameliorating the public space |

1. Qinggong Jiang and Wenlei Xi, *Shanghai Shikumen* (Shanghai: Tongji University Press, 2012), 146.
2. Hiroyuki Shinohara, "Mutation of Tianzifang, Taikang Road, Shanghai," *The 4th International Conference of the International Forum on Urbanism (IFoU)*, 2009, 751.
3. Xin-liang Zhou (resident representative/director, Tianzifang Management Committee), in discussion with the author, March 2017.
4. Hai Yu (professor, Department of Social Science at Fudan University), in phone discussion with the author, May 2017.

| | |
|---|---|
| 2004 | For the first time, a residential space (adjacent to Lane 210, Taikang Road) is rented out for non-residential use, to a fashion designer as a studio and boutique shop |
| 2005 | Tianzifang Shikumen Owners' Management Committee appoints the Tongji Urban Planning and Design Institute to carry out the Shanghai City Taikang Road Historical Features Area Conservation and Adaptive Reuse Concept Plan (上海市泰康路歷史風貌區保護與利用概念規劃) |
| 2005 | Tianzifang is named one of the first creative industry clusters of Shanghai |
| 2008 | Shanghai government relaxes the regulations against the conversion of residential properties to non-residential uses (popularly known as *ju gai fei*, loosely translated as "residence changed to non-residence"), specifically to enable the adaptive reuse of Tianzifang's residential properties for commercial use |
| 2008 | Luwan District Government allocates RMB 18 million for improvement of the area's infrastructure and upgrade of existing residences (Luwan District Office and Tianzifang Management Committee are set up under the directive of the local district government to oversee the management and regulation of Tianzifang) |

i.  Commission Des Établissements Classés (Commission of Classified Establishments) was founded in September 1924, and Règlements Sur Les Établissements Classés (or loosely translated as "Regulations on the Classified Establishments" in English) was enacted in 1928 (with subsequent amendments in 1934 and 1941). See: Sun Qian, *Shang Hai Jin Dai Cheng Shi Gong Gong Guan Li Zhi Du Yu Kong Jian Jiang She (Urban Public Administrative System and Spatial Construction in Modern Shanghai)* (Nanjing: Southeast University Press, 2009), 320.

ii. *Shikumen* (stone-framed gate) residences were predominately built by Western and Chinese landlords for local tenants in the concession areas back in the colonial period, with the peak during the 1890s to 1930s.


## Revitalization Concept

+ Gradually establishing a place for artists and creative industries in the former French Concession area by renovating and upgrading traditional vernacular buildings and converting them into artists' studios, boutique shops, and restaurants, while allowing local residents to remain in their own homes and retain their everyday lifestyle.

+ Adopting a different approach to large-scale redevelopment projects, which frequently eradicate historic neighborhoods, as commonly seen in major cities in China and throughout Asia.

+ Conserving by means of adaptive reuse to demonstrate a "functionally mixed, socially inclusive and economically uplifting . . . model of self-organized urban regeneration that leads to more inclusive urban community."[5]

5.  Shinohara, "Mutation of Tianzifang," 749.

**Figure 26.3:** Bird's-eye view of
Tianzifang. (Source: Hugo Chan.)

## Process and Partnership

In the late 1990s, as the market economy gradually drove out most factory operations
in the downtown neighborhoods of Shanghai, six factories on Lane 210, Taikang
Road closed down, leaving a total of more than 20,000 square meters of vacant space.
Toward the end of the decade, Zheng Rong-fa (then director of the subdistrict office
of Dapuqiao Precinct) rented one of the factories on Lane 210, Taikang Road, and
intended to convert it to commercial use. The 4,500–square meter factory, built in
the 1920s, had been left vacant since the late 1990s and had since been occupied by
small businesses, including a barber shop, a bathhouse, a noodle shop, and a scissors
shop, causing some discomfort to nearby residents. Zheng saw the economic potential of the property and partnered with Wu Mei-sen, a veteran in the arts and cultural
field, to promote and attract investments to develop the site into an arts and culture–
oriented community. As a first step, Wu Mei-sen invited his American friends for a
tour of Lane 210, Taikang Road. Subsequently, a huge party was held at the premises
with hundreds of artists from around the world, and by the end of the evening all the
workspaces in the factory venue were rented.[6]

In 1999, Chen Yi-fei, a renowned overseas (and returning) Shanghainese painter,
moved into Nos. 2–3, Lane 210, Taikang Road, and set up his studio there. Before
long, such famed Chinese artists as photographer Deke Erh and musician Wang Jie
also moved into Taikang Road and set up their studios, galleries, and music schools.
In the same year, the Administrative Committee of Taikang Road Art Street (泰康路
藝術街管理委員會) was established with the help of Wu Mei-sen, Zheng Rong-fa,
and other pioneering tenant artists to manage the leasing of the factory units and
assess the suitability of incoming tenants and the nature of their businesses.

In 2001, Zheng Rong-fa and Wu Mei-sen undertook the rehabilitation of an
additional number of old factories in the vicinity with an amount of RMB 200,000
(mostly generated by prepayment from future tenants). Two years later, the esteemed
Chinese painter Wang Yong-yu named the site Tian-zi-fang, after the first ever
painter in Chinese history as documented in *Shi Ji* (Historical Records, 史記), Tian

---

6.   Jieqiong Wang, Zigang Yao, and Alan Peter March, "Preservation and Regeneration via Hai Pai
     Cultural Renaissance—a Case Study of Tianzifang Creative Quarter in Shanghai," *The 4th International
     Conference of the International Forum on Urbanism (IFoU)*, 2009, 289–99.

Zi-fang (田子方). Next to the last character, *fang* (方), soil ("土") was added to form 坊—meaning a public gathering place in Chinese—instilling hope that Tianzifang would serve as a nourishing ground for the cultivation of artists and creative industries and would grow into a seedbed for artists as well as a platform for intellectual and cultural exchange.

In 2004, Zhou Xin-liang, a resident on Er Jing Xiang (an auxiliary lane linked to Lane 210), became the first tenant to rent out his room for nonresidential use, to a fashion designer. In the same year, Tianzifang Shikumen Owners' Management Committee (田子坊石庫門業主管理委員會), a nongovernmental organization, was formed by local residents and tenants to orchestrate and regulate the renovation of shops and residences.[7] In 2007, within a span of six months, nonresidential tenants (including creative industry and commercial uses) increased from 69 to 157, accounting for a total floor area of more than 5,000 square meters on Lanes 210 and 248, Taikang Road. Nonresidential uses in Tianzifang continued to expand and encroach on the residential neighborhood, covering most of Lanes 248 and 274, with a wide array of commercial uses, such as bars, restaurants, and retail boutique shops.

Fearing overcommercialization and intensification of conflicts between residents and shop owners, the Tianzifang Management Committee was established under the directive of the local government in lieu of the Shikumen Owners' Management Committee. This newly founded committee, together with the Residents' Committee (居民委員會) and the Street Office (街道辦事處), came to a consensus to "freeze" the business nature in the Tianzifang area. In particular, the number of food and beverage–related uses were controlled at fifty-eight, and no more such uses would be approved, given an increasing concern over fire safety, noise level, and sewage issues on the part of both residents and government officials.[8]

## Development Environment

Tianzifang and its environs were predominately populated by neatly laid-out and well-designed New-Style[9] and Garden-Style[10] *shikumen* housing developments built between the 1910s and 1930s. Even though the streetscape and architectural design for the *shikumen* residences in Tianzifang are historically of high quality (the few exceptions being the former site of Xinhua Art College, established in 1937, along with ten small firms and seventeen *dan wei* [work units] factories built in the 1930s), there was no national- or municipal-level protected built heritage within the precinct. Its prime location within the city center made it an enticing target for property developers, and it was seen as "ripe" for development.

According to interviews with shop operators in Tianzifang, there was an unconfirmed rumor of demolition circulating in the community in early 2005, when the government started to impose increasingly rigid regulations on fire safety and drainage requirements, especially for the food and beverage trade in the residential area.

---

7.  Xin-liang Zhou (resident representative/director, Tianzifang Management Committee), in discussion with the author, March 2012 and August 2013.

8.  Xin-liang Zhou (resident representative/director, Tianzifang Management Committee), in discussion with the author, March 2012 and August 2013.

9.  Popular during the period between 1924 and 1938, the New-Style *shikumen* houses evolved from the earlier residence design, with improvement in layout, orientation, soundproofing, and ventilation to appeal to a market of increasingly affluent and sophisticated buyers as World War I came to an end.

10. Garden-Style *shikumen* housing developments peaked at the 1930s with the upsurge of foreign and diversified populations in the concession areas. These types of properties were arranged in semidetached or detached layouts instead of the typical row arrangement and were three stories or taller, constructed of reinforced concrete components and load-bearing brick walls, thus generally more spacious, in terms of public space, unit area, and ceiling height.

Artists, residents, shop operators, and tenants were all skeptical of Tianzifang's future; prospective investments and businesses were put on hold, and the once-fevered revitalization effort slowed. Around the same time, an entire residential block south of Taikang Road was acquired by a Taiwanese developer and was being demolished. The Tianzifang area was also being considered for redevelopment by the same developer.

Hoping to resist the development pressure and alter the government's decision to demolish Tianzifang, the Tianzifang Shikumen Owners' Management Committee appointed the Tongji Urban Planning and Design Institute to conduct the Shanghai City Taikang Road Historical Features Area Conservation and Adaptive Reuse Concept Plan. The historical significance and financial viability were confirmed by the concept plan, and the strong opposition to the redevelopment plan led to the local government's reconsideration of the future of the area. In December 2005, Tianzifang was recognized by the Shanghai Municipal Economic and Information Technology Committee (SHEITC) and Shanghai Creative Industry Center as one of Shanghai's top ten most influential creative industry clusters for the year 2005.

On March 13, 2008, the Shanghai government relaxed the regulations against the conversion of residential properties to nonresidential uses (popularly known as *ju gai fei*, loosely translated as "residence changed to nonresidence"), specifically to enable the adaptive reuse of Tianzifang's residential properties for commercial use. On April 12, 2008, two years before the Expo 2010 Shanghai opened, the Luwan district government allocated a one-off funding of RMB 18 million for improving infrastructure and upgrading residences in the Tianzifang neighborhood, further acknowledging the cultural and economic values of the place and its importance as a creative industry hub and sightseeing attraction to be showcased to visitors from around the world.

## Commercial Sustainability

With concerted efforts by artists, commercial tenants, government officials, local residents, and private investors, Tianzifang (originally comprising a traditional community of *shikumen* houses and *dan wei* factories) has been gradually transformed into an artist commune with boutique shops, cafes, galleries, and studios in 1998. In the span of less than a decade, the place expanded from a singular residential lane with a communal courtyard to an entire neighborhood with more than ten streets and alleys of varying sizes and characters, receiving as many as 60,000 and 90,000 visitors daily during weekends and Golden Weeks, respectively,[11] and on average 20,000 visitors on a daily basis, far exceeding the capacity of 7,000–8,000 visitors as originally expected.[12]

The increasing popularity poses threats to the safety and commercial viability of the site. To mitigate safety concerns, visitor-flow control measures have been enforced since May 2016. On Golden Week holidays, more than one hundred police officers and thirty security guards monitor the various entry points to Tianzifang to ensure that no more than 5,000 visitors are on the premise at any given time.

According to a research study conducted by the Department of Social Science at Fudan University in late 2015, tenants were paying as high as RMB 80,000 per month for rent, which is on par with a similar space in Xintiandi.[13] More than half of

---

11. The weeklong public holidays in China during Chinese New Year in January/February, Labor Day in May, and National Day in October.
12. Xin-liang Zhou (resident representative/director, Tianzifang Management Committee), in discussion with the author, March 2017.
13. Xintiandi is arguably one of the most successful commercially driven conservation-led redevelopment projects in Shanghai, if not China, with upmarket shops and restaurants converted from historic *shikumen* houses and alleyways.

the leases were under one year and more than 20 percent of the commercial tenants were in operation for less than one year. Overall, only 27 percent of the tenants were making profits while close to 21 percent were losing money. Forty percent of the tenants were reported to have a balanced budget. The turnover rate remains high, and an increasing number of artists and shop operators are considering moving out of Tianzifang because of increasing rents. [14] Only 2 percent of the noncommercial use is culture related, while boutique shops account for 23 percent and arts and crafts shops and restaurants each account for roughly 15 percent of the overall business composition.[15]

In an interview conducted in 2015, Wu Mei-sen, then-chairperson of Tianzifang Chamber of Commerce, revealed that the commercial tenants of Tianzifang came from more than twenty countries and together contributed more than RMB 30 million in tax revenue annually, providing more than 8,000 job opportunities. In spite of concerns of overcommercialization, he contended that Tianzifang had set a great example for a financially viable cultural conservation effort.[16]

## Key Success Factors

+ Close-knit social network and self-initiated committees and organizations that monitor and manage the place and its activities.
+ Unique architectural typology of *shikumen* houses and maze-like alleys provide visitors and shoppers with a unique spatial experience.
+ Prime location within the historic center, complemented by its "old Shanghai" setting and easy accessibility by public transportation.

## Key Challenges

+ Though the former factory and warehouse spaces were easily adapted as artists' studios and office spaces for creative industries, it was challenging to convert the tightly spaced residential housing units for retail and food and beverage uses.
+ The width of the alleys and lanes, as well as the scale of the courtyards and public spaces, were not designed for heavy traffic, causing congestion, especially on holidays, and severe maintenance issues for some properties.
+ The increasing number of nonresidential uses were not entirely compatible with the original residential use, and given the relatively compact spatial layout, conflicts and quarrels between residents and commercial tenants were inevitable.
+ Self-initiated committees and quasi-governmental organizations had to be set up to closely regulate and monitor existing and new businesses, as well as to manage the needs and aspirations of different user groups.
+ Exorbitant rent is driving out most of the tenants who moved to Tianzifang around the early 2000s, particularly the artists and creative industry companies, leaving behind more commercially inclined businesses, such as high-end restaurants and tourist souvenir shops.

---

14. Hai Yu (professor, Department of Social Science at Fudan University), in phone discussion with the author, May 2017.
15. Zhang Yan, "Shanghai Tianzifang," *China Economic*, last modified August 30, 2016, http://www.ce.cn/culture/gd/201608/30/t20160830_15387242.shtml.
16. "Numbers of Visitors and Businesses of Tianzifang Getting Close to Xintiandi, but Soon Turning into 'City God Temple,'" *Winshang*, last modified June 10, 2015, http://sh.winshang.com/news-488720.html.

## Keeping Heritage Alive

The objective of the project is to preserve the "hard" shell of Tianzifang—the architectural features, scale, and spatial experience of a unique vernacular typology. It strives to conserve the human scale provided by *shikumen* houses and mazelike alleys, which provide visitors with a unique spatial experience. The architectural features and decorative elements of the houses have been largely conserved and sometimes reinvented to offer an interpretation of the historical significance and layering of the site.

The project also retains the "soft" core of its cultural significance—the people, networks, and social interactions. It manages to preserve a portion of the existing residential population and provides residents with the option of staying in the neighborhood or renting out their homes (as opposed to being evicted or forcibly relocated as is the case with many redevelopment projects). Adaptive reuse helps maintain the cultural identity, social capital, and social cohesiveness of the place.

The project has revitalized a place in decline. Vacant and obsolete factory and warehouse spaces have been infused with compatible new uses. Derelict housing units have been upgraded to allow for amenities of modern-day comfort and to introduce flexibility for nonresidential uses. Public spaces and utilities have been improved with revenue generated from tenants' contributions and government funding.

**Figure 26.4:** The historic lanes of Tianzifang supporting a vibrant neighborhood for commercial, creative industry, and residential uses. (Source: Hugo Chan.)

## Value Creation

Cultural: The popularity of Tianzifang has helped to promote the cultural significance of *shikumen* as an architectural typology. A number of interest groups and nongovernmental organizations (NGOs) have since been founded to advocate for the conservation of the typology as well as Shanghai's other architectural heritage. The diverse cultural backgrounds and nature of incoming tenants and businesses helps create a unique and dynamic place.

Economic: Increasing rents and visitor numbers attest to the economic success of Tianzifang, which in turn demonstrates the monetary value of the *shikumen* and gives government officials and private developers an example of a financially robust alternative to demolition.

Environmental: The popularity of Tianzifang serves as a model for other *shikumen* residential blocks across Shanghai facing demolition.

Social: Self-initiated, nonprofit committees and organizations have been formed to manage the site, thereby helping to retain social cohesiveness and reinforce the strong social network built up by different users throughout different phases of project development.

> **The soul of Tianzifang lies in its cultural significance and is built upon a solid business model.**
> 〔田子坊的存在當以文化為靈魂、以商業為基礎〕
>
> —*Wu Mei-sen, Chairperson of Tianzifang Chamber of Commerce*[17]

## Bibliography

Jiang, Qinggong, and Wenlei Xi. *Shanghai Shikumen*. Shanghai: Tongji University Press, 2012.

"Numbers of Visitors and Businesses of Tianzifang Getting Close to Xintiandi, but Soon Turning into 'City God Temple.'" *Winshang*. Last modified June 10, 2015. http://sh.winshang.com/news-488720.html.

Shinohara, Hiroyuki. "Mutation of Tianzifang, Taikang Road, Shanghai." *The 4th International Conference of the International Forum on Urbanism (IFoU)*, 2009.

Sun, Qian. *Shang Hai jin dai cheng shi gong gong guan li zhi du yu kong jian jiang she* [*Urban public administrative system and spatial construction in modern Shanghai*]. Nanjing: Southeast University Press, 2009.

Wang, Jieqiong, Zigang Yao, and Alan Peter March. "Preservation and Regeneration via Hai Pai Cultural Renaissance—a Case Study of Tianzifang Creative Quarter in Shanghai." *The 4th International Conference of the International Forum on Urbanism (IFoU)*, 2009.

Zhang, Yan. "Shanghai Tianzifang." *China Economic*. Last modified August 30, 2016. http://www.ce.cn/culture/gd/201608/30/t20160830_15387242.shtml.

Zhu, Ronglin. *Jie du Tian Zi Fang* [*Deconstruct Tianzifang*]. Shanghai: Wen Hui Chu Ban She, 2009.

---

17. "Numbers of Visitors and Businesses of Tianzifang Getting Close to Xintiandi."

# Clarke Quay, Singapore

Debbie Wong

## Project Information

**Table 27.1:** Basic details of Clarke Quay.

| | |
|---|---|
| Address | 3 River Valley Road, Singapore 179024 |
| Old use | Commercial (godowns, shophouses, and trading port) |
| New use | Mixed use (dining, entertainment, and retail) |
| Heritage status | Conservation area |
| Area | 34,000 square meters |
| Project cost estimate | US$137.5 million (SG$186 million)[i] |
| Operator | Various operators |
| Developed/Funded by | CapitaLand Retail |
| Architect | Alsop Architects (design consultant); RSP Architects Planners & Engineers (local partner) |
| Contractor | Kajima Overseas Asia Pte. Ltd. |
| Start and completion date | 2003–2006 |

i.   The conversion rate is taken at US$1=SG$1.35.

**Figure 27.1:** A view of Clarke Quay showing the newly installed silent fans and large ETFE canopy structures along the main walkways. (Source: Ho Yin Lee.)

## Vision

To design a mixed-use scheme that increases commercial and leisure activities and gives the riverfront area a new identity, repositioning Clarke Quay as a vibrant and attractive destination.[1]

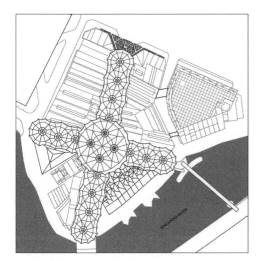

**Figure 27.2:** Site plan of Clarke Quay. (Source: Drawn by Wai Shing Ng based on materials from SMC Alsop.)

## Site History

Clarke Quay is an area on the north bank of the Singapore River, a vital trade route and port for Singapore since Raffles's arrival in 1819. Clarke Quay was named after Lieutenant General Sir Andrew Clarke, second governor of the Straits Settlements.[2] The area used to contain the colonial government's gunpowder magazine and later became a godown (warehouse) center.[3]

Clarke Quay's history is intertwined with that of the Singapore River. It is characterized by riverside warehouses and two/three-story shophouses. By the 1840s, it was bustling with shipping activities, which continued well into the twentieth century. With Singapore's independence in 1965 and the subsequent relocation of cargo services to a modern facility in Pasir Panjang, the area became derelict. The river had also become extremely polluted as it served as a sewer for the city's increasing population. A ten-year Singapore River cleanup program was launched in 1977.[4]

Because of the historical and architectural significance of the site and buildings, the Urban Redevelopment Authority (URA) recognized Clarke Quay with conservation status in 1989. Plans were made to revitalize the area and turn it into a commercial, entertainment, and residential precinct. The first phase of revitalization began in the 1990s, after being leased to DBS Land (later CapitaLand) under the URA Sale of Sites Programme.[5] A family-oriented Clarke Quay Festival Village was developed and officially opened in 1993. A decline in gross revenue led to the area being rezoned as a "night zone" with bars and pubs, gradually turning Clarke Quay into a tourist-oriented entertainment area.

1.  All Design, "Clarke Quay," accessed January 25, 2019, https://all.design/posts/clarke-quay.
2.  Urban Redevelopment Authority, "Clarke Quay," accessed June 17, 2019, https://www.ura.gov.sg/Conservation-Portal/Explore/History?bldgid=CKQY.
3.  Jing Yao Wang and Chye Kiang Heng, "Conservation in Singapore—the Experience of Clarke Quay," in the *Asian Cities—Legacies of Modernity, 7th mAAN International Conference* (New Delhi: India International Centre, 2009), accessed June 20, 2017, https://www.academia.edu/293106/Conservation_in_Singapore_the_Experience_of_Clarke_Quay.
4.  Felicia Choo, "5 Interesting Facts about the Singapore River Clean-Up," *Straits Times*, July 5, 2014, https://www.straitstimes.com/singapore/5-interesting-facts-about-the-singapore-river-clean-up.
5.  Chwee Lye Low, "Singapore River: Six Strategies for Sustainability," in *Spatial Planning for a Sustainable Singapore*, ed. T. C. Wong, B. Yuen and C. Goldblum (Dordrecht: Springer, 2008), 87.

The Singapore River Master Plan identified Clarke Quay as an area that required a sensitive combination of conservation and adaptive reuse for its shophouses and warehouses. The project involved the restoration of five blocks of sixty godowns and shophouses (with a specific requirement that façades and roof designs be maintained), construction of new buildings, and the creation of a promenade to make the site more pedestrian friendly. It reopened as a family-friendly attraction with more than 170 retail shops, seventeen food and beverage outlets, and a S$25 million adventure ride that included heritage elements from Singapore's past.[6] This first attempt was not successful for a combination of reasons, including, possibly, the lack of a heritage tourism market at the time and the absence of transportation links to the rest of the city via the Mass Rapid Transit (MRT) or riverboat services.

Table 27.2: Timeline of Clarke Quay.

| | |
|---|---|
| 1819 | Site is used as a port for maritime trade |
| 1850s–1950s | Godowns and shophouses are built; the area continues to flourish as a busy dining, entertainment, and shipping destination |
| 1965 | Singapore gains independence; shipping activities relocate to Keppel Harbour (and other areas) resulting in neglect of Clarke Quay[i] |
| 1970s | Site is acquired for redevelopment and the residents gradually resettle in new public housing facilities |
| 1977 | Start of the ten-year Singapore River cleanup program[ii] |
| 1986 | Tourism Product Development Plan is set in place to revitalize the Singapore River District |
| 1989 | Clarke Quay is recognized as a conservation area |
| 1990s | DBS Land (later CapitaLand) leases the entire area of Clarke Quay under the Urban Redevelopment Authority (URA) Sale of Site Programme[iii] |
| 1992 | Site opens as a family-oriented Festival Village |
| 1995–1996 | Clarke Quay faces a decline in gross revenue |
| 1996 | Site transforms into a "night zone" with a number of bars and pubs |
| 2001 | Clarke Quay becomes a tourist destination with dining and entertainment facilities |
| 2003 | CapitaLand revitalizes the area targeting local people; Alsop Architects is commissioned for the project |
| 2006 | Clarke Quay officially opens after renovation with a twenty-four-hour entertainment license and a 100 percent occupancy rate[iv] |
| 2012 | CapitaLand announces a new S$15.6 million extension to Clarke Quay[v] |
| 2013 | New extension is completed with a new frontage on River Valley Road and more than fifteen new dining and entertainment options |

i.   Alex Chow, "Clarke Quay," *Singapore Infopedia (Singapore National Library Board e-resources)*, last modified September 8, 2014, http://eresources.nlb.gov.sg/infopedia/articles/SIP_863_2004-12-16.html.
ii.  Felicia Choo, "5 Interesting Facts about the Singapore River Clean-Up," *The Strait Times*, July 5, 2014, https://www.straitstimes.com/singapore/5-interesting-facts-about-the-singapore-river-clean-up.
iii. Chwee Lye Low, "Singapore River: Six Strategies for Sustainability," in *Spatial planning for a sustainable Singapore*, ed. T. C. Wong, B. Yuen, and C. Goldblum (Dordrecht: Springer, 2008), 87.
iv.  Jing Yao Wang and Chye Kiang Heng, "Conservation in Singapore – The Experience of Clarke Quay," in the *Asian Cities – Legacies of Modernity*, 7th mAAN International Conference (India: India International Centre, New Delhi, 2009), accessed June 20, 2017, https://www.academia.edu/293106/Conservation_in_Singapore_the_Experience_of_Clarke_Quay.
v.   K. L. Ng, "Clarke Quay: Revamp Draws Visitors, Revenue," *The Straits Times*, August 21, 2012.

---

6.   Chye Kiang Heng and Vivienne Chan, "The 'Night Zone' Storyline: Boat Quay, Clarke Quay and Robertson Quay," *Traditional Dwellings and Settlements Review* 11, no. 2 (2000): 46.

## Revitalization Concept

+ Revitalizing a historic area, while upgrading its infrastructure, to refresh Clarke Quay's image.
+ Eliminating poor quality restaurants, street stalls, and walkways to revive the waterfront as a spacious pedestrian-friendly zone.
+ Improving Clarke Quay's infrastructure and quality of nightlife by changing the mix of tenants to cater to the taste of local urban professionals.
+ Constructing a series of podlike dining platforms (known as lily pads) by the riverside and installing silent fans and large willowy umbrellalike structures consisting of ethylene tetrafluroethylene (ETFE) cushioned canopies (known as angels) along the main walkways, to improve the environment for visitors.[7]

**Figure 27.3:** A view of Clarke Quay from the Singapore River showing the pod-like dining platforms known as lily pads. (Source: Ho Yin Lee.)

## Process and Partnership

The Urban Redevelopment Authority (URA) gazetted Clarke Quay as a heritage conservation area and launched a Sale of Sites Programme in 1989 to open the area for private development. Only three bids were placed during the sales period, and the URA decided to tender the area as a single site to ensure coherence in site development and better coordination. This was in contrast to the approach taken with the neighboring Boat Quay, where redevelopment was under the control of individual landlords. The tender was awarded to DBS Land (now CapitaLand) for the initial revitalization of the site.

After the unsuccessful outcome of the area's first revitalization, another plan was put in place in 2003 to improve Clarke Quay's economic and social sustainability. The scheme ensured a better tenant mix by targeting larger local audiences of professionals. The plan focused on the riverfront, which is a traditional linear arrangement of shophouses facing the river. Alsop Architects was commissioned to redesign the shophouse façades, interior streetscapes, and waterfront dining areas in two development phases with emphasis on addressing the environmental issue associated with Singapore's tropical climate. By this period, cultural heritage tourism was more common, and the opening of the new Clarke Quay Mass Rapid Transit

---

7.   Arcspace, "Clarke Quay," last modified July 12, 2012, https://arcspace.com/feature/clarke-quay/.

(MRT) station, along with the introduction of a riverboat service, helped to increase the public accessibility of the site. Consumption patterns had also changed domestically, with a higher demand for niche experiences in heritage areas. In 2006, the renovated Clarke Quay reopened with a twenty-four-hour entertainment license and a 100 percent occupancy rate. Today, it remains one of the most expensive and economically important places in Singapore.

## Development Environment

Clarke Quay was redeveloped twice over the span of more than twenty years (1980s–2008). During this time, the Urban Redevelopment Authority (URA) released two plans, the Singapore Tourism Board released three plans, and DBS Land (the owner) initiated two renovations of the site. The redevelopment of the site was controlled by these plans, which shared an objective of creating a tourism landmark with commercial and recreational functions. The development and subsequent challenges and issues illustrated the need for integrated planning between all stakeholders. There was also a shift in tourism and lifestyle demands in the 2000s.

## Commercial Sustainability

The first revitalization of the site increased visitor traffic to Clarke Quay, which was further aided by the completion of the Mass Rapid Transit (MRT) Station in 2003. In 2012, after completion of the second revitalization, it was recorded that Clarke Quay received about one million visitors per month.[8] Sixty percent of the tenants were restaurants and eateries while 30 percent were entertainment outlets and 10 percent were offices.[9]

## Key Success Factors

+ Creating a comfortable microclimate through the design of cooling systems and sophisticated shading in interesting installations, thereby aesthetically enhancing the riverfront and streets while reducing the ambient temperature of the site by four degrees Celsius.
+ Timely reconsideration of the tenant mix to rebrand the area for local urban professionals, nurturing the domestic clientele.
+ Completing the Mass Rapid Transit (MRT) infrastructure and the building of the new mixed-use complex (One Central) across the river from Clarke Quay.

## Key Challenges

+ Misjudgment of the readiness of the public to accept the Festival Village proposal of the first revitalization effort.
+ Focus of key decision makers from the Singapore Economic Development Board and the Singapore Tourism Board on tourism, rather than cultural heritage, regarding their relative potential in facilitating economic development of the site.

---

8.  Spark Architects, "Clarke Quay," accessed June 20, 2017, http://sparkarchitects.com/portfolio_page/clarke-quay-redevelopment/.
9.  Alex Chow, "Clarke Quay," *Singapore Infopedia (Singapore National Library Board e-resource)*. September 8, 2014. Accessed June 20, 2017. http://eresources.nlb.gov.sg/infopedia/articles/SIP_863_2004-12-16.html.

+ Revitalization of the site by sensitive conservation and adaptive reuse of the heritage buildings catering to both the occupants and the users/visitors.
+ Design of the streets and waterfront that ameliorates Singapore's warm temperature and heavy rainfall in a sensitive manner without simply creating enclosed, air-conditioned spaces.

## Keeping Heritage Alive

The project not only adapted the heritage buildings but also conserved the site's existing fabric and character-defining elements where possible—for example, the two-story River House, a southern Chinese Teochew-style mansion built in the 1880s and today the oldest building in Clarke Quay, was faithfully restored. The historic Read Bridge (1886–1887) and Ord Bridge (1886) were conserved, linking Clarke Quay to the south bank of the river.

In the latest revitalization scheme, the creation of an elevated dining area that projects over the river has added to the waterfront experience and highlighted the significance of the river. This is reinforced by the installation of a series of elevated lily pads covered by sun/rain umbrellas, known as Bluebells, that animate the water's edge, reflecting the Singapore River, and are reminiscent of traditional Chinese lanterns during Mid-autumn Festival. Despite this, the postmodern design of the canopies and dining platforms in the latest revitalization were criticized as deviating from the original ambience and history of Clarke Quay.[10]

**Figure 27.4:** The adaptive reuse of Clarke Quay as a mixed-use scheme, repositioning it as a vibrant and attractive destination. (Source: Ho Yin Lee.)

## Value Creation

Cultural: Together with the nearby Boat Quay and Robertson Quay, the adaptive reuse of Clarke Quay has revived the Singapore River. It now bustles with people and activities, as it did in the past. Although the retention of its sociocultural past as a trading and residential district has not been possible, it has been given a new lease of life with a fresh cultural connection.

Economic: The project has created business opportunities (in particular, for dining and entertainment ventures) and job opportunities, welcoming around one million visitors a month. Its vibrant atmosphere has also contributed to the Singapore brand as a tourist destination, and it was voted as Singapore's Best Nightspot at the AsiaOne People's Choice Awards in 2014, awarded the 2015 Certificate of Excellence

---

10.  Chow, "Clarke Quay."

by TripAdvisor, and identified as one of the fifty iconic places to visit in Singapore.[11] A dramatic fourfold increase in foot traffic and a major hike in rental value was reported since its latest revitalization.[12]

Environmental: The addition of the ethylene tetrafluroethylene (ETFE) cushioned canopies, providing shade from the sun and protection from the rain, has made the area more attractive to visitors. It also serves as a model for other projects that need to address similar challenges.

Social: Clarke Quay was, and continues to be, one of the busiest entertainment and food and beverage areas in Singapore, attracting locals and tourists alike.

> **What is interesting is the addition of a single roof acting as a visual icon that has succeeded in attracting people back to Clarke Quay as an essential leisure and pleasure area of Singapore.[13]**
>
> —*Will Alsop of Alsop Architects*

## Bibliography

All Design. "Clarke Quay." Accessed January 25, 2019. https://all.design/posts/clarke-quay.

Arcspace. "Clarke Quay." Last modified July 12, 2012. http://www.arcspace.com/features/alsop-architects/clarke-quay/.

CapitaLand. "Transforming Singapore." Last modified August 2015. http://inside.capitaland.com/spaces/city/201508-transforming-singapore.

Choo Felicia. "5 Interesting Facts about the Singapore River Clean-Up." *Straits Times*, July 5, 2014. https://www.straitstimes.com/singapore/5-interesting-facts-about-the-singapore-river-clean-up.

Chow, Alex. "Clarke Quay." *Singapore Infopedia (Singapore National Library Board e-resource)*. September 8, 2014. Accessed June 20, 2017. http://eresources.nlb.gov.sg/infopedia/articles/SIP_863_2004-12-16.html.

Heng, Chye Kiang, and Vivienne Chan. "The 'Night Zone' Storyline: Boat Quay, Clarke Quay and Robertson Quay." *Traditional Dwellings and Settlements Review* 11, no. 2 (2000): 46.

Lin, Eunice M. "Adaptive Re-use of the Historic Boat Quay Singapore River, Singapore." *Aga Khan Program for Islamic Architecture, Harvard University*. Accessed June 20, 2017. http://web.mit.edu/akpia/www/AKPsite/4.239/singa/singa.html.

Low, Chwee Lye. "Singapore River: Six Strategies for Sustainability." In *Spatial Planning for a Sustainable Singapore*, edited by T. C. Wong, B. Yuen and C. Goldblum, 87. Dordrecht: Springer, 2008.

RSP Architects Planners & Engineers. "Clarke Quay: Entertainment Hub in Historic District." Accessed June 20, 2017. http://119.81.49.10/project/show?id=344.

Spark Architects. "Clarke Quay." Accessed June 20, 2017. http://www.sparkarchitects.com/portfolio_page/clarke-quay-redevelopment/.

---

11. CapitaLand, "Transforming Singapore," last modified August 2015, https://www.capitaland.com/international/en/about-capitaland/newsroom/inside/2015/aug/inside-201508-transforming-singapore.html.
12. Spark Architects, "Clarke Quay."
13. "Alsop's Asian Success," *World Architecture News*, last modified August 10, 2006, accessed August 8, 2019, https://www.worldarchitecturenews.com/article/1499572/alsops-asian-success.

Urban Renewal Authority. "Clarke Quay." Accessed June 20, 2017. https://www.ura.gov.sg/Conservation-Portal/Explore/History?bldgid=CKQY.

Wang, Jing Yao, and Heng, Chye Kiang. "Conservation in Singapore—the Experience of Clarke Quay." In the *Asian Cities—Legacies of Modernity, 7th mAAN International Conference*. New Delhi: India International Centre, 2009. Accessed June 20, 2017. https://www.academia.edu/293106/Conservation_in_Singapore_the_Experience_of_Clarke_Quay.

# Residential Case Studies

**Table 28.1:** Residential case studies.

| Project Name | Location | Nature | New Use | Original Use | Timeframe |
| --- | --- | --- | --- | --- | --- |
| Blue House Cluster | Hong Kong | Government and private partnership project | Residential and multifunctional service complex (housing, shops, and food and beverage outlets) | Residential and commercial (shophouses) | 2012–2017 |
| Huai Hai Lu 796 | Shanghai | Government and private partnership project | Commercial and cultural (art gallery, offices, luxury retail, and private club) | Residential | 2007–2008 |
| Space Asia Hub | Singapore | Private project | Commercial (furniture showroom, office, and store) | Residential and commercial (villa and shophouse) | 2009–2011 |

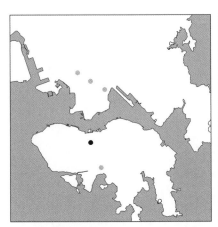

**Figure 28.1:** Location plan of the Blue House Cluster, Hong Kong. (Drawn by Wai Shing Ng.)

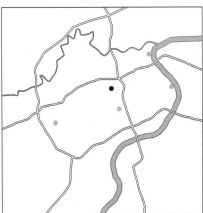

**Figure 28.2:** Location plan of Huai Hai Lu 796, Shanghai. (Drawn by Wai Shing Ng.)

**Figure 28.3:** Location plan of Space Asia Hub, Singapore. (Drawn by Wai Shing Ng.)

# Blue House Cluster, Hong Kong

Tiffany Tang

## Project Information

**Table 29.1:** Basic details of the Blue House Cluster.

| | |
|---|---|
| Address | Stone Nullah Lane, Wan Chai, Hong Kong |
| Old use | Residential and commercial (shophouses) |
| New use | Residential and multifunctional service complex (housing, shops, and food and beverage outlets) |
| Heritage status | Blue House (72–74A Stone Nullah Lane): Grade 1 Historic Building; Yellow House (2–8 Hing Wan Street): Grade 3 Historic Building; Orange House (8 King Sing Street): Not graded |
| Area | 2,369 square meters |
| Project cost estimate | US$10.7 million (HK$83.6 million)[i] |
| Operator | St. James' Settlement (SJS) |
| Developed/Funded by | Community Cultural Concern, Heritage Hong Kong Foundation, Development Bureau (DevB), Hong Kong SAR government |
| Architect | LWK & Partners (HK) Ltd. |
| Contractor | Milestone Builder Engineering Limited |
| Start and completion date | 2012–2016 (Yellow House and Orange House); 2012–2017 (Blue House) |

i.  The Hong Kong dollar is pegged to the US dollar at about US$1=HK$7.8.

**Figure 29.1:** External view of Blue House from Stone Nullah Lane. (Source: Ho Yin Lee.)

## Vision

To conserve and revitalize the historic buildings, local community network, and other associated intangible cultural traditions of the Blue House Cluster for their continued contributions to the Wan Chai neighborhood.

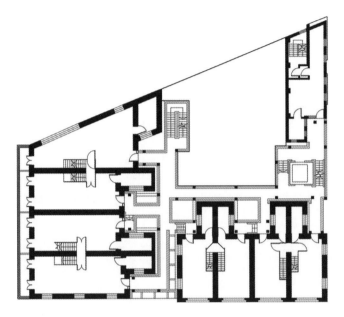

**Figure 29.2:** First-floor plan of the Blue House Cluster. (Drawn by Wai Shing Ng based on Urban Renewal Authority materials.)

## Site History

The Blue House Cluster (collectively, the Blue House, Yellow House, and Orange House) showcases the typical configuration of early twentieth-century Chinese tenement buildings (*tong lau*), with shops on the ground floor and residential units on the upper floors. Built in the 1920s (with the exception of the Orange House), these shophouses accommodated Chinese residents as well as a variety of commercial venues ranging from a pre–World War II English school to a bonesetter's clinic established in the 1960s and existing to date. The site is a key landmark in the neighborhood and reflects deep-rooted connections with the local community.

Prior to revitalization, most of the residents were community elders who had been living in the Blue House Cluster for many years. However, the condition of the buildings was poor, and extensive repairs and conservation were required. This informed the revitalization concept for the project, as outlined below.

**Table 29.2:** Timeline of the Blue House Cluster.

| | |
|---|---|
| 1922 | Yellow House (2–8 Hing Wan Street) is built |
| 1923 | Blue House (72–74A Stone Nullah Lane) is built (accommodating the shrine of Wah To,[i] Kang Ham Free School, Yat Chong College, and the Trade Association for Fishmongers) |
| 1956 | Orange House (8 King Sing Street) is built |
| 1950s–1960s | Ground floor of 72 Stone Nullah Lane (Blue House) operates as a bonesetter's clinic and a martial arts school |
| 1978 | Ownership of Blue House is transferred to the government |
| 2006 | Urban Renewal Authority (URA) and the Hong Kong Housing Society (HKHS) announce a revitalization-cum-preservation project for the Blue House Cluster |
| 2009 | Development Bureau (DevB) includes the Blue House Cluster in Batch II of the Revitalisation Scheme |
| 2010 | St. James' Settlement's (SJS) project, "Viva Blue House," is chosen to revitalize the Blue House Cluster as a multifunctional service complex |
| 2017 | Conservation of the Blue House Cluster is completed and the project receives the Award of Excellence at the UNESCO Asia-Pacific Awards for Cultural Heritage Conservation |

i.   Prior to the construction of the Blue House, a building stood on the site of 72–74A Stone Nullah Lane and functioned as the Wah To Hospital. In 1886, the hospital ceased operation, however, the building retained a shrine serving the Deity of Chinese medicine, Wah To. (See: LWK & Partners (HK) Ltd., *Conservation Management Plan for Viva Blue House, Blue House Cluster Revitalization Scheme* [Hong Kong: Antiquities and Monuments Office Hong Kong SAR Government, October 2011], https://www.amo. gov.hk/form/Blue%20House%20Cluster-HIA.pdf.)

## Revitalization Concept

+ Revitalization based on a "community-led, bottom-up and participatory heritage conservation model [which] integrates culture and heritage into development and pioneers community revitalisation"[1] allowing original residents to remain in the complex while their living conditions are improved.
+ Upgrading of housing conditions and improvement of structural safety through appropriate conservation and installation of new services and facilities.
+ Establishing educational services (the Livelihood Museum and a Confucian school), "mom-and-pop" stores to promote local cultural knowledge, and social enterprises (a dessert house and vegetarian restaurant serving traditional treats).

1.   Batch II of Revitalisation Scheme, Hong Kong SAR Government, "Viva Blue House: The Blue House Cluster," last modified May 21, 2018, accessed August 8, 2019, https://www.heritage.gov.hk/en/rhbtp/ ProgressResult2_Blue_House_Cluster.htm.

Figure 29.3: View of the courtyard of the Blue House Cluster. (Source: Ho Yin Lee.)

## Process and Partnership

St. James' Settlement (SJS), Hong Kong's premier nongovernmental organization providing social services to the needy since 1849, collaborated with the local community, conservation experts, and the Wan Chai District Council in 2006 to initiate community-led revitalization of the Blue House Cluster. This process pushed back the Urban Renewal Authority's (URA) and Hong Kong Housing Society's (HKHS) intent to redevelop the property.

The SJS, along with the Community Cultural Concern group and Heritage Hong Kong Foundation, developed the Viva Blue House project, which was submitted to and selected under Batch II of the Development Bureau's (DevB) Revitalisation Scheme.

## Development Environment

The Urban Renewal Authority (URA) and Hong Kong Housing Society's (HKHS) original proposal was to redevelop the Blue House Cluster and relocate its residents. When the site was included in Batch II of the Revitalisation Scheme, it presented an opportunity for St. James' Settlement (SJS) to provide a more suitable alternative, ensuring the buildings' retention. As part of this scheme, the Hong Kong SAR government provided funding (HK$79.4 million) over 2012–2017 for essential structural and building works, as well as a one-off grant (HK$4.2 million) to meet operating deficits for the initial two years.[2]

## Commercial Sustainability

St. James' Settlement (SJS) self-financed the maintenance costs of the Blue House Cluster and its facilities during a tenancy period of six years. Income streams include

---

2. Council Business Division 1, Legislative Council Secretariat, "Panel on Development, Meeting on 22 January 2019, Updated Background Brief on Heritage Conservation Initiatives," Legislative Council Paper No. CB(1)456/18-19(06) (January 16, 2019), accessed August 8, 2019, https://www.legco.gov.hk/yr18-19/english/panels/dev/papers/dev20190122cb1-456-6-e.pdf.

rent from tenants (both commercial and residential) as well as contributions from the Friends of Blue House Association, in addition to funds raised from special events, guided tours, and museum visits.

Although the rental yield is at a below-market rate for this location, it is expected that the project will break even by its third year of operation (2020). Out of a total of twenty residential units, eight accommodate preexisting tenants, and twelve are rented out through the Good Neighbour Scheme[3] at rents ranging from HK$11,500 to HK$31,000 for unit areas of 361 square feet to 880 square feet. Ground-floor spaces are rented out as exhibition and recreational areas, offices, restaurants, and shops.

## Key Success Factors

+ Participatory bottom-up approach to revitalization championed by a non-governmental organization (NGO) trusted by the local community.
+ Unique collaboration of the district council, an NGO, and passionate academics to work closely with local residents and the neighborhood throughout the revitalization project.
+ Delicate balance in design—minimum intervention to the architectural features of the building, while allowing for modifications to introduce modern services and fixtures.
+ Commitment to upgrade and revive a dilapidated building, while maintaining its architecture, original functions, and residents.
+ Promotion of sustainable rental policy and careful tenant selection process to identify "good neighbors" who can contribute to the human capital of the cluster.
+ Personalized renovation works for preexisting tenants according to their needs.

## Key Challenges

+ To avoid temporary relocation of residents, a phased work approach was adopted.
+ Rents were waived as compensation for tenants who had to relocate to other units during work.[4]
+ With the objective of changing as little as possible, meeting building ordinance requirements and complying with other standard requirements and regulations was demanding and time consuming.
+ Adherence to best practice in conservation was demonstrated by retaining original floor tiles and windows wherever possible.
+ The tenant-selection process—according to the Good Neighbour Scheme"—was experimental.

## Keeping Heritage Alive

The residents and people in the immediate neighborhood have embraced the Blue House Cluster as a center for community activities. All events are self-initiated and community driven, such as the art jamming, celebrations for the Mid-autumn Festival, kid's classes, movie screenings, music nights, and an open market. The dessert house

---

3.  The Good Neighbour Scheme is an initiative to retain the Blue House Cluster's traditional *tong lau* lifestyle (emphasizing community living), where only eleven flats of the entire cluster are made available for rent. Tenants are selected based on unusual criteria: experienced in organizing community activities, outgoing, and willing to contribute to the neighborhood.
4.  Suki Chau (team leader of Cultural Preservation and Community Engagement, St. James' Settlement), in discussion with Dr. Ho Yin Lee (one of the authors), August 22, 2019.

and vegetarian restaurant have kept the food tradition alive, while the Wan Chai Livelihood Museum contributes to an understanding of the neighborhood's past by showcasing more than 400 objects donated by local residents. Stone Nullah Lane is now an increasingly popular destination among locals and visitors looking for a diverse, engaging, and vibrant leisure destination.

**Figure 29.4:** Inside the Blue House Cluster's Livelihood Museum. (Source: St. James' Settlement.)

## Value Creation

Cultural: Not only have the buildings of the Blue House Cluster been conserved but the cultural connections and local stories have also been kept alive. Wan Chai culture is preserved and strengthened as the heritage site establishes itself as a cultural landmark for locals and tourists.

Economic: During the conservation of the cluster, several employment opportunities were created, and upon completion several full- and part-time permanent positions were generated for underprivileged groups in the local community. Visitors are attracted to the area, bringing vitality to the local economy. The project sets an example by showing that authentic mixed-use low-rise tenement buildings can have an economically viable future.

Environmental: The living conditions of the original residents of the cluster have improved while units have remained affordable.

Social: New community and social services in the cluster have encouraged and strengthened social networks and skills exchange at the neighborhood level as well as throughout the wider community, such as the community-initiated festival celebrations and the Community Oriented Mutual Economy Hall, among others.

> Keeping the people, keeping the place.
>
> —*Project Team*

## Bibliography

Batch II of Revitalisation Scheme, Hong Kong SAR Government. "Viva Blue House: The Blue House Cluster." Last modified May 21, 2018. Accessed August 8, 2019. https://www.heritage.gov.hk/en/rhbtp/ProgressResult2_Blue_House_Cluster.htm.

Council Business Division 1, Legislative Council Secretariat. "Panel on Development, Meeting on 22 January 2019, Updated Background Brief on Heritage Conservation Initiatives." Legislative Council Paper No. CB(1)456/18-19(06), January 16, 2019. Accessed August 8, 2019. https://www.legco.gov.hk/yr18-19/english/panels/dev/papers/dev20190122cb1-456-6-e.pdf.

Development Bureau Hong Kong SAR Government. "Viva Blue House: The Blue House Cluster." Last modified May 21, 2018. https://www.heritage.gov.hk/en/rhbtp/ProgressResult2_Blue_House_Cluster.htm.

LWK & Partners (HK) Ltd. *Conservation Management Plan for Viva Blue House, Blue House Cluster Revitalization Scheme*. Hong Kong: Antiquities and Monuments Office Hong Kong SAR Government, October 2011. https://www.amo.gov.hk/form/Blue%20House%20Cluster-HIA.pdf.

Viva Blue House. "Good Neighbour Scheme." Accessed December 3, 2018. http://www.vivabluehouse.hk/en/menu/60.

# Huai Hai Lu 796, Shanghai

Hugo Chan

## Project Information

**Table 30.1:** Basic details of Huai Hai Lu 796.

| | |
|---|---|
| Address | No. 796, Huai Hai Road, Huangpu District (formerly Luwan District),[i] Shanghai |
| Old use | Residential |
| New use | Commercial and cultural (art gallery, offices, luxury retail, and private club) |
| Heritage status | Excellent Historical Building, Shanghai City |
| Area | 4,200 square meters (site area); 4,500 square meters (gross floor area) |
| Project cost estimate | US$15 million (RMB 101 million)[ii] |
| Operator | Various operators |
| Developed by/Funded by | Richemont Group |
| Architect | Kokaistudios |
| Contractor | Shanghai Construction Decoration Group |
| Start and completion date | 2007–2008 |

i. The formerly separate jurisdictional districts of Luwan and Huangpu were merged on July 1, 2011 to form "Huangpu District."
ii. The conversion rate is taken at US$1=RMB6.74; UNESCO, "Huai Hai Lu 796," in *Asia Conserved Volume II: Lessons Learned from the UNESCO Asia-Pacific Awards for Cultural Heritage Conservation (2005–2009)*, ed. Montira Horayangura Unakul (Bangkok: iGroup Press, 2013), 354.

**Figure 30.1:** External view of the Twin Villas. (Source: Ian Babbitt.)

## Vision

To juxtapose two historic villas and the modern addition of a gallery space from the 1990s to provide an interesting commentary on the relationship between old and new, and conservation and development.[1]

**Figure 30.2:** Ground-floor plan of Huai Hai Lu 796. (Drawn by Wai Shing Ng, based on materials from Asia Conserved Volume II.)

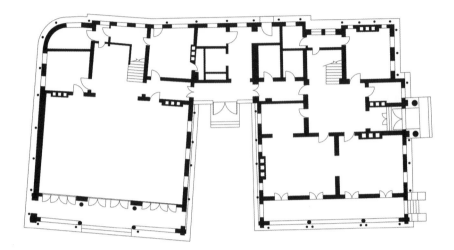

## Site History

Huai Hai Lu 796 consists of two adjoining villas that were originally the residence of a well-known Shanghainese comprador, Jiang Bing-sheng. The east and west buildings were constructed in 1921 and 1927, respectively. They represent the pinnacle of design and construction of private villas and mansions during Shanghai's concession era. Built six years apart and connected by a corridor at the back, the design of the second villa was intended to replicate the original one in almost all of its details. The symmetry of the two buildings led to the nickname "Twin Villas."[2]

After the founding of the People's Republic of China in 1949, the buildings were requisitioned as the Beijing Cinema and subsequently housed an aviation agency and film agency. Gradually, the site fell into disuse and dereliction. With changing ownership over the years, substantial alterations and ad hoc repair works were made to the architectural details, façades, and structures, jeopardizing the authenticity and integrity of the place.[3]

1.    UNESCO, "Huai Hai Lu 796," in *Asia Conserved Volume II: Lessons Learned from the UNESCO Asia-Pacific Awards for Cultural Heritage Conservation (2005–2009)*, ed. Montira Horayangura Unakul (Bangkok: iGroup Press, 2013), 354.
2.    UNESCO, "Huai Hai Lu 796," in *Asia Conserved Volume II*, 354.
3.    Brenda Wang, "Huaihai Lu 796—Rebirth of the Classic," *Vantage Shanghai*, May 30, 2012.

**Table 30.2:** Timeline of Huai Hai Lu 796.

| | |
|---|---|
| 1921 | East villa is constructed |
| 1927 | West villa is constructed |
| 1949 | Property is requisitioned and used as a cinema (and subsequently as an office space) |
| 1990s | Service building on the northern edge is demolished. Construction of a new concrete structure on the northeastern corner commences (but was never completed) |
| 2002 | Richemont Group decides to renovate the twin villas into a fashion and luxury destination |
| 2007 | Kokaistudios is commissioned as the project architect and the adaptive reuse project commences |
| 2008 | Huai Hai Lu 796 complex opens to the public after 15 months of design and construction work |
| 2009 | Huai Hai Lu 796 receives the Award of Merit at the UNESCO Asia-Pacific Awards for Cultural Heritage Conservation |

## Revitalization Concept

+ Restoring the villas to their original 1920s appearance and configuration, in accordance with the highest possible standards.[4]
+ Conservation based on exhaustive research not only of the original character and materials of the place but also the different stages in the buildings' history.
+ Prioritizing reclamation and reinsertion of the original architectural features and carefully retrieving the surviving architectural features as much as possible.

**Figure 30.3:** Luxury boutique inside the adapted Huai Hai Lu 796. (Source: Kokaistudios.)

## Process and Partnership

The adaptive reuse of Huai Hai Lu 796 was undertaken as a collaborative project between the public and private sectors. The building is owned by the government and was leased to a private company, the Richemont Group (one of the world's leading luxury-goods companies), for its restoration and a commercially viable new use. In 2002, the Richemont Group wanted to set up a retail outlet in Shanghai and

---

4.    UNESCO, "Huai Hai Lu 796," in *Asia Conserved Volume II*, 354.

discovered the villas in the heart of the former French Concession area. Attracted by the historic ambience and heritage of the place, the Richemont Group decided to restore and repurpose the ensemble as a luxury fashion destination.

In 2007, in a highly competitive international competition, the renovation project was awarded to Kokaistudios, which had recently opened a permanent office in Shanghai upon completion of the Bund 18 project (elaborated in the "Institutional Case Studies" section). After fifteen months of intensive design and construction work by local and foreign professionals and artisans, the Huai Hai Lu 796 complex opened to the public in September 2008.[5]

## Development Environment

Huai Hai Lu, known as Avenue Joffre in the concession era, was historically the cosmopolitan and commercial hub of the former French Concession area, lined with exclusive residences, restaurants, and high-end shops. Following the founding of the People's Republic of China, all commercial establishments, including those on Huai Hai Lu, were nationalized and assigned to government agencies and state-owned companies. Even so, Huai Hai Lu retained its importance as the shopping hub of Shanghai.

Since the early 1990s, as China's market reform was in full operation and foreign investment was particularly welcomed, Huai Hai Lu has drawn the attention of foreign developers with its strategic location and commercial potential. Overseas-funded redevelopment and renovation projects started to take place in the vicinity, including the opening of Shanghai's first McDonald's outlet in 1994 at No. 588, Huai Hai Lu[6] and Parkson Department Store (by a Malaysian developer) in 1996 at No. 918, Huai Hai Lu.[7] Therefore, when the Richemont Group expanded its market in China and looked for a "home" in Shanghai, this property, situated on a vibrant commercial street yet tucked inside a secluded, quiet compound, was an attractive option.

## Commercial Sustainability

Since its opening in 2008, the newly transformed Huai Hai Lu 796 has enjoyed commercial success.[8] Despite some turnover (for example—the pioneer tenant ShangArt gallery has moved out and been replaced by Richemont Retail Academy), the occupancy rate remains high. Its list of tenants includes luxury brands Vacheron Constantin and Dunhill as well as Kee Club, a Hong Kong–based private club. The project won the Award of Merit at the UNESCO Asia-Pacific Awards for Cultural Heritage Conservation in 2009, which helped attract media attention from around the world to tap into its target customer base. It has since been the designated venue for numerous high-profile commercial and cultural events.[9]

5.  Andrea Destefanis (founder/principal architect, Kokaistudios), in discussion with the author, December 2016.

6.  Mac Mac Alumni Association, "First MacDonald's in These Chinese Cities," *Sina* (blog), accessed January 25, 2019, http://blog.sina.com.cn/s/blog_697fdebb0100k6tu.html?tj=1.

7.  Parkson, "Milestones," accessed January 2019, http://www.parksongroup.com.cn/html_en/about_parkson/Milestones.php.

8.  Andrew Yang, "Road to Smarter Shopping in Shanghai," *New York Times*, February 26, 2009, https://www.nytimes.com/2009/03/01/travel/01surfacingcol.html.

9.  Huai Hai Lu 796, "Twin Villas," accessed January 25, 2019, http://www.796huaihailu.com/en/TwinVillas.htm.

## Key Success Factors

+ Right timing—the project was made possible at a time when the local government increasingly relied on revenue from liquidating its assets while realizing the importance of preserving and reusing its architectural legacies. It was also at a time with a formidable market environment, conducive to foreign investment, that was rewarded not only in monetary but also in cultural terms.
+ After completion of the Bund 18 project, the architects were more experienced in collaborating with local artisans, contractors, and construction workers, as well as in dealing with local governmental departments and the local working culture. Similar to Bund 18, this project also demonstrated dedication by the project team and investors, who strove to make this landmark adaptive reuse project something they could be proud of and showcase to the world.

## Key Challenges

+ Prior to the restoration, the building suffered severe structural damage from decades of negligence and insensitive additions and repairs by a succession of owners.
+ Building façades were in poor shape, and many decorative features needed to be replicated to restore the buildings' original appearance and at the same time, show its evolution.
+ Modern fittings were required, and various services, such as electrical and plumbing, were in need of upgrading to suit the building's proposed new use. These new services needed to respect and complement the building's heritage character.
+ Most of the original exterior surfaces were covered by layers of concrete render. The conservation team found a traditional technique to remove the added layers without damaging the original Shanghai plaster. Local artisans skilled in this traditional technique were tasked with patching missing parts of the terrazzo-like appearance of the surfaces.[10]

## Keeping Heritage Alive

With the experience gained from the Bund 18 project, the architectural design team adhered to the principle of authenticity, placed strong importance on architectural details, and sought a high degree of care and craftsmanship throughout the restoration process. One remarkable example was the conservation of the carved woodwork of the main staircase balustrades, which were hand-cleaned and meticulously restored by age-old techniques. Also, all of the original metal and wood doors, brass handles, and steel windows were reengineered, repaired, and reinstalled by local artisans and workers. The architects insisted on replicating the original screws and nails, thereby retaining a detailed sense of authenticity in the completed work.[11]

The patina of the place was also conserved in this adaptive reuse effort. Instead of demolishing the partially completed concrete structure built in the 1990s, the architects decided to rehabilitate this later addition as an art gallery space. In using design features and materials that complemented (without mimicking) the original structures, the modern addition was clearly distinguishable from the old while respecting and reflecting the compound's multiplicity of historical layers.[12]

---

10. Andrea Destefanis (founder/principal architect, Kokaistudios), email message to author, December 30, 2019.
11. UNESCO, "Huai Hai Lu 796," in *Asia Conserved Volume II*, 354.
12. UNESCO, "Huai Hai Lu 796," in *Asia Conserved Volume II*, 354.

The project provided authorities with a robust business model as well as a technical benchmark for restoration work. Collaborative efforts between international experts and local artisans throughout the restoration facilitated knowledge exchange across countries and professions.[13] During different phases of the project and after its completion, it has continued to attract interest from local and overseas university students, allowing for ongoing exchange of knowledge in heritage conservation.

**Figure 30.4:** Ground-floor verandah of the east villa after its adaptive reuse, with university students visiting to learn about the site's conservation. (Source: Ho Yin Lee.)

## Value Creation

Cultural: The street and public realm amelioration notably contributed by Huai Hai Lu 796 has helped reclaim Huai Hai Lu's former reputation as the cultural, entertainment, and shopping destination of Shanghai. Huai Hai Lu 796 won the Award of Merit at the UNESCO Asia-Pacific Awards for Cultural Heritage Conservation in 2009, cited for being "an outstanding example of restoration at its highest level . . . that . . . will continue to be enjoyed for many generations to come."[14]

Economic: Huai Hai Lu 796 has set an impressive example of reusing an aging heritage site in an economically viable manner. Subsequent to the success of Bund 18, the architectural design team applied its experience to this adaptive reuse project. The economic success of Huai Hai Lu 796 helped trigger other nearby projects of a similar nature, contributing to an increase in land value and rent for properties in the vicinity. The expertise and skills of local artisans and construction workers using traditional techniques for conservation were increasingly valued. A notable example is the conservation of Rong Zhai by Fondazione Prada (completed in 2017), where the restoration works of the historic mansion were executed by the team trained through the Huai Hai Lu 796 project.[15]

Environmental: Similar to that of Bund 18, the healthy cost-benefit balance sheet of Huai Hai Lu 796 has considerably changed the development mentality of fellow private developers, government officials as well as the general public, thereby

13. UNESCO, "Huai Hai Lu 796," in *Asia Conserved Volume II*, 355.

14. UNESCO Bangkok, "2009 UNESCO Asia-Pacific Heritage Awards," accessed January 25, 2019, https://bangkok.unesco.org/sites/default/files/assets/article/Asia-Pacific%20Heritage%20Awards/files/2009-winners.pdf.

15. Andrea Destefanis, email message to author, December 30, 2019.

saving not only this historic compound but many of its neighbors in the heart of the former French Concession area.

Social: Despite its upmarket commercial use and security control, much of the site is open to the public and visible from bustling Huai Hai Lu. Together with a newly created garden, the complex contributes to the improvement and continuity of the streetscape and community network.

> To restore and renovate historic buildings is an architectural practice that is not codified by fixed rules or methodologies but is based on one simple open principle, namely that each building has been designed with different intentions, built with different methodologies and materials, and has passed through a unique history of events and damages.[16]
>
> —*Project Team*

## Bibliography

Huai Hai Lu 796. "Twin Villas." Accessed January 25, 2019. http://www.796huaihailu.com/en/TwinVillas.htm.

Mac Mac Alumni Association. "First MacDonald's in These Chinese Cities." *Sina* (blog). Accessed January 25, 2019. http://blog.sina.com.cn/s/blog_697fdebb0100k6tu.html?tj=1.

Parkson. "Milestones." Accessed January 25, 2019. http://www.parksongroup.com.cn/html_en/about_parkson/Milestones.php.

Unakul, Montira Horayangura, ed. *Asia Conserved Volume II: Lessons Learned from the UNESCO Asia-Pacific Awards for Cultural Heritage Conservation (2005–2009)*. Bangkok: iGroup Press, 2013.

UNESCO Bangkok. "2006 UNESCO Asia-Pacific Heritage Awards." Accessed January 25, 2019. https://bangkok.unesco.org/sites/default/files/assets/article/Asia-Pacific%20Heritage%20Awards/files/2006-winners.pdf.

UNESCO Bangkok. "2009 UNESCO Asia-Pacific Heritage Awards." Accessed January 25, 2019. https://bangkok.unesco.org/sites/default/files/assets/article/Asia-Pacific%20Heritage%20Awards/files/2009-winners.pdf.

*Vacheron Constantin: Manufacture Horlogere; Geneve, depuis 1755*. Shanghai, 2008.

Wang, Brenda. "Huaihai Lu 796—Rebirth of the Classic." *Vantage Shanghai*, May 30, 2012.

---

16.  UNESCO, "Huai Hai Lu 796," in *Asia Conserved Volume II*, 355.

# Space Asia Hub, Singapore

Debbie Wong

## Project Information

**Table 31.1:** Basic details of Space Asia Hub.

| | |
|---|---|
| Address | 77 Bencoolen Street, Singapore 189653 |
| Old use | Residential and commercial (villa and shophouse) |
| New use | Commercial (furniture showroom, office, and store) |
| Heritage status | Conserved building |
| Area | 4,000 square meters |
| Project cost estimate | US$37 million (SG$50 million)[i] |
| Operator | Space Furniture Singapore |
| Developed/Funded by | Space Furniture |
| Architect | WOHA Architects Pte. Ltd. |
| Contractor | Shanghai Chong Kee Furniture & Construction Pte. Ltd. |
| Start and completion date | 2009–2011 |

i.  The conversion rate is taken at US$1=SG$1.35.

**Figure 31.1:** External view of Space Asia Hub from Bencoolen Street. (Source: WOHA.)

## Vision

To create a contemporary retail showroom for premium furniture while retaining the charm of a historic villa and shophouse.[1]

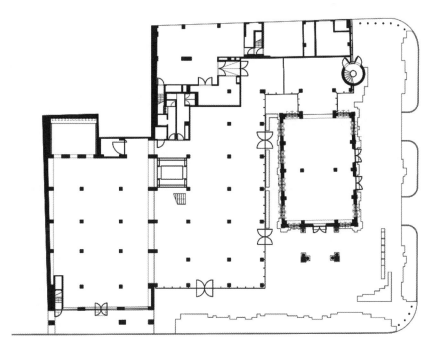

**Figure 31.2:** Ground floor plan of Space Asia Hub. (Drawn by Wai Shing Ng, based on materials from WOHA.)

## Site History

Space Asia Hub is housed within a cluster of heritage buildings in one of Singapore's conservation areas. The showroom is composed of two conserved buildings and a connecting glass infill structure. The two conserved buildings are The Villa (a villa at No. 81, formerly a hotel) and The Heritage House (a combined shophouse at Nos. 71 and 73, formerly a bakery). The newly inserted structure, the Glass House, is built on the plot of No. 77 using the structural framework of the preexisting building (a bungalow that was demolished in the early 1990s and redeveloped as a four-story commercial building).[2] During the 1996 redevelopment, Nos. 71, 77, and 81 were grouped together, where No. 71 and its sister shophouse, No. 73, were amalgamated by removal of their internal structures and party walls.[3] The Villa and The Heritage House were extravagant in form, with an eclectic combination of colonial, Chinese, and Malay elements.[4] Originally part of a large collection of prewar shophouses and bungalows lining busy Bencoolen Street, today, they are rare surviving examples of such typologies.

1. WOHA, "Space Asia Hub—Singapore," accessed June 24, 2019, https://www.woha.net/images/project_images/136301760430/pdf/SpaceAsiaHub.pdf.
2. Urban Redevelopment Authority, "Architectural Heritage Awards 2012—77 Bencoolen Street," accessed June 20, 2017, https://www.ura.gov.sg/Corporate/Get-Involved/Conserve-Built-Heritage/Architectural-Heritage-Season/-/media/2292EB568648453EA1E11D7294C06820.ashx.
3. Urban Redevelopment Authority, "77 Bencoolen Street."
4. Urban Redevelopment Authority, "77 Bencoolen Street."

**Table 31.2:** Timeline of Space Asia Hub.

| | |
|---|---|
| Late 1800s | Three buildings, Nos. 71, 77, and 81, are built on (present-day) Bencoolen Street |
| 1950s | No. 81, originally a bungalow, is converted into a hotel |
| 1996 | Redevelopment results in the grouping of Nos. 71, 77, and 81 as a single development |
| Mid-2000s | Site is used as a karaoke bar |
| 2009 | WOHA is commissioned by Space Furniture for the adaptive reuse of the site |
| 2011 | Space Asia Hub officially opens |

## Revitalization Concept

+ Contrasting old and new as a design strategy with an emphasis on the spatial clarity of the historic forms.
+ In-depth historical research and documentation to better understand the original structures and the different alterations carried out over the years.
+ Sensitive restoration of the façades of The Villa and The Heritage House, while enhancing the showroom interior with new timber trusses to provide free spans revealing a high-volume column-free space—reminiscent of the industrial layout of the former bakery.
+ Connecting the two heritage buildings by inserting a contrasting infill glass building on the plot of No.77, hinged on the structural framework of the earlier building.

**Figure 31.3:** View of Space Asia Hub showing the heritage buildings and the glass infill building. (Source: WOHA.)

## Process and Partnership

Space Asia Hub is a private initiative launched by Space, a premier retailer in the luxury lifestyle and contemporary furniture industry in the Asia-Pacific region. Originally with showrooms in Australia, Space recognized the potential in the luxury segment of retail design and decided to launch a flagship store in Singapore. WOHA, a Singapore-based architectural practice, was commissioned to take on this initiative.

## Development Environment

The Urban Redevelopment Authority (URA) paid particular attention to the aesthetic and urban design impact of the Glass House (the glass infill) between the two heritage buildings, to ensure a quality outcome that would enhance and showcase the historical significance of the two heritage buildings and establish an appropriate public space. URA also facilitated and supported research regarding the specific details of certain architectural features during the restoration process—for example, determining the historic façade and window treatment of No. 73, which had substantially eroded over the years.

## Commercial Sustainability

Since its launch on Bencoolen Street, Space Asia Hub has become Southeast Asia's largest and most progressive retailer of contemporary design furniture.[5]

## Key Success Factors

+ Urban Redevelopment Authority (URA) was actively involved in the design process along with WOHA, where the teams worked closely together. URA was prescriptive in describing the conservation approach for this project—all new extensions had to be complementary but different in form, material, and finish from the old.
+ The project received a URA Architectural Heritage Award in 2012. It was also short-listed in the New and Old category of the 2012 World Architecture Festival and was awarded the 2013 Green Good Design Award (awarded by the Chicago Athenaeum: Museum of Architecture and Design and The European Centre for Architecture Art Design and Urban Studies). More recently, it received an Honourable Mention in the 16th Singapore Institute of Architects Architectural Design Awards 2016.

## Key Challenges

+ Working in a gazetted conservation area and connecting separate heritage buildings into one seamless functional space for a premier furniture retailer.
+ Needing to make a statement with a contemporary urban corner without compromising the character of the existing structures.
+ Requiring a sealed and air-conditioned building complex, as it was to be a showroom (because of the restoration and renovation approach, returning to natural ventilation was not an option; unfortunately, this may affect the "health" of the building fabric in the long run).

## Keeping Heritage Alive

The main building elements of The Villa and The Heritage House were restored, such as the exposed brickwork façades of the heritage structures and the white interior surfaces of the villa. A public space was created at the fringe of the historic buildings by introducing street furniture to allow the conserved site to be appreciated within the eclectic neighborhood. The plaza has become a woven tapestry of terracotta and

5.   Space Furniture Singapore, "About Us," accessed July 24, 2019, https://www.spacefurniture.com.sg/about-us.html.

pebble wash strips in color tones with reference to traditional materials and regional "sarong" textiles. These finishes flow into the interior, giving the impression of a continuous and inviting urban space that integrates the buildings and provides generous spaces for events and activities.[6]

**Figure 31.4:** The furniture showroom of Space Asia Hub. (Source: WOHA.)

## Value Creation

Cultural: Retaining the last few prewar buildings on Bencoolen Street symbolizes the importance of this once-busy thoroughfare, densely packed with shophouses and villas. The project is accessible by the public even though it is privately owned and operated.

Economic: It is a flagship showroom for Space Furniture in the Asia-Pacific and has contributed to the growth of this premier furniture retailer in the region.

Environmental: Located in the dynamic arts and cultural district of Singapore, Space Asia Hub sets a benchmark for how adaptive reuse can be an appropriate conservation approach for protecting heritage in an urban context.

Social: Space Asia Hub broadens the design experience for the local public through various public activities and events (for example, it provided an exhibition space for the 2011 President's Design Award). Design competitions and workshops, in collaboration with designers, have been launched for local design students. It also plays a role in cultivating an appreciation for good design among consumers in Singapore.

---

6. "Space Asia Hub/WOHA," *Archdaily*, last modified December 12, 2011, https://www.archdaily.com/190691/space-asia-hub-woha.

WOHA sensitively restored the facades through archival research, opening up the interior spaces and introducing a new 21st Century glass house infill. The contrast between "old" and "new" enhances the stature of the conserved buildings and the overall development. We updated the old buildings respectfully to meet their modern purpose as a singularly stunning and commercially attractive upmarket gallery for premium furniture.[7]

—*Wong Mun Summ, Founding Director, WOHA*

## Bibliography

Australian Institute of Architects. "2012 Finalist: Space Asia Hub—WOHA." Accessed on June 20, 2017. http://wp.architecture.com.au/international/spaceasiahub/.

Lim, Jerome. "Lost in Space." *The Long and Winding Road* (blog). October 16, 2012. https://thelongnwindingroad.wordpress.com/tag/space-asia-hub/.

Sanchez, Valeria. "Space Hub Asia." *Rave the C.R.A.V.E.* (blog), January 13, 2016. https://ravethecraveblog.wordpress.com/2016/01/13/space-hub-asia/.

Space Furniture Singapore. "About Us." Accessed June 20, 2017. https://www.spacefurniture.com.sg/about-us.html.

Urban Redevelopment Authority. "Architectural Heritage Awards 2012—77 Bencoolen Street." Accessed June 20, 2017. https://www.ura.gov.sg/Corporate/Get-Involved/Conserve-Built-Heritage/Architectural-Heritage-Season/-/media/2292EB568648453EA1E11D7294C06820.ashx.

WOHA. "Space Asia Hub—Singapore." http://woha.net/images/project_images/136301760430/pdf/SpaceAsiaHub.pdf.

Walsh, Adrian. "Space Asia Hub Singapore." *e-architect*. December 15, 2011. http://www.e-architect.co.uk/singapore/space-asia-hub.

Zimmer, Lori. "Singapore's Space Hub Asia Unifies a Historic Villa and a Shophouse with a Modern Glass Block." *Inhabitat*. January 13, 2016. http://inhabitat.com/singapores-space-hub-asia-unifies-a-historic-villa-and-a-shophouse-with-a-modern-glass-block/.

---

7.   Serena Khor (Public Relations, WOHA), e-mail message to author, July 17, 2019.

# Concluding Discussion on Adaptive Reuse in the Asian Context

Katie Cummer

## Introduction

This concluding chapter briefly summarizes the tradition of adapting old buildings for new uses and the increasing modern trend toward adaptive reuse projects in the spirit of sustainable development. Notes and key takeaways from the experience of the Asian urban centers of Hong Kong, Shanghai, and Singapore are addressed as a means to articulate adaptive reuse as a conservation practice particularly suitable for rapidly developing Asian cities. Areas for further research are discussed, with brief concluding remarks on the future direction of adaptive reuse in Asia and other areas of the globe.

## Adaptive Reuse Trends

As noted throughout this book, adaptive reuse is not a new approach. For centuries societies have been repurposing old buildings for new uses.[1] As mentioned previously, the Pantheon in Rome is the perfect case in point. Originally a pagan temple (believed to have been constructed in 27 BC), it was converted to a church in the seventh century AD. The Hagia Sophia in Istanbul is a similar such example and another equally famous one. Originally built as a Christian basilica (in the sixth century AD), it was converted into an Ottoman mosque in the fifteenth century and ultimately became a museum in the mid-twentieth century, with debates being held today in the twenty-first century about converting it back to a mosque.[2] There are numerous other examples throughout the world of historical adaptive reuse projects; they are simply not referred to in such terms.

The practice and approach in Asia dates back many years as well, even if it was not categorized or referred to as adaptive reuse. Whether repurposing institutional buildings in Hong Kong, industrial buildings in Shanghai, or military sites in Singapore,

---

1. Candace Richards, "Reinventing Heritage Buildings Isn't New at All—the Ancients Did It Too," *Conversation.* January 2, 2017, https://theconversation.com/reinventing-heritage-buildings-isnt-new-at-all-the-ancients-did-it-too-70053.
2. Umar Farooq, "Voices Grow Louder in Turkey to Convert Hagia Sophia from a Museum Back to Mosque," *Los Angeles Times,* June 24, 2017, https://www.latimes.com/world/middleeast/la-fg-turkey-hagia-sophia-20170615-story.html. In fact, in July 2020, it was converted back into a mosque when Turkey's President "announced the decision after a court annulled the site's museum status." Orla Guerin, "Hagia Sophia: Turkey Turns Iconic Istanbul Museum into Mosque," *BBC News,* July 10, 2020, https://www.bbc.com/news/world-europe-53366307.

the tradition of taking old buildings and giving them a new lease of life has a long history in Asia, well before the modern discussion of sustainability emerged. Today, however, this approach is intricately intertwined with nations and cities grappling with the challenges of sustainable development and citizens' desires to recognize, protect, and promote their heritage places, typically in relation to identity formation.[3]

## Sustainable Development and the New Urban Agenda

As the world comes to accept and better understand the impacts of climate change and the growing need for sustainable development, the United Nations' New Urban Agenda (NUA) is an important guide for communities and nations going forward. It is ambitious and encourages "transformative commitments through an urban paradigm shift grounded in the integrated and indivisible dimensions of sustainable development: social, economic and environmental."[4] As has been repeated throughout this book, it is ultimately in cities' and countries' best interest to have heritage assets used rather than left derelict or demolished. Avoiding demolition, in particular, to make use of the embodied energy inherent in an already constructed building, is an important push with regards to sustainable development.

As stated in relation to Australia, "The protection and ongoing use of heritage places is an important strategy for sustainability in our cities, towns, and places. This retains embodied energy, reduces waste, and minimizes consumption of natural resources. Adapting heritage places uses and extends their inherent durability and integrates these buildings into contemporary life."[5] There is a need in Asia specifically, but in the world generally, to address our waste issues; and recycling buildings, much like the worldwide push for recycling all that we can, is a logical and economic choice. However, it is a conscious choice and one that governments and people need to deliberately and intentionally work on. As revealed through the various case studies in this book, adaptive reuse is not necessarily a cheap or easy endeavor, however, the myriad dividends make it worthwhile, extending both the physical and economic life of these buildings.

## Adaptive Reuse as a Key Sustainable Conservation Practice

Although the focus of this book has been on the history and experience of three Asian centers, there are similar results from around the world highlighting the benefits and challenges of adaptive reuse as a conservation approach.[6] "Adaptive reuse can empower cities to make more effective use of space for people and businesses, while still preserving the historic character of the built environment."[7] "Design for

---

3.  See Tracey L.-D. Lu, "Heritage Conservation in Post-colonial Hong Kong," *International Journal of Heritage Studies* 15, nos. 2–3 (March–May 2009): 258–72, in relation to Hong Kong; Esther H. K. Yung, Edwin H. W. Chan, and Ying Xu, "Community-Initiated Adaptive Reuse of Historic Buildings and Sustainable Development in the Inner City of Shanghai," *Journal of Urban Planning and Development* 140, no. 3 (September 2014 Building and Heritage Tourism in a Multiracial City," *Localities* 2 (2012): 117–59, in relation to Singapore.

4.  United Nations Habitat, *New Urban Agenda*, A/RES/71/256 (October, 2016), http://habitat3.org/the-new-urban-agenda/.

5.  Heritage Council of NSW, "Better Placed: Design Guide for Heritage," working draft for comment published 2018, 28, https://www.environment.nsw.gov.au/-/media/OEH/Corporate-Site/Documents/Heritage/better-placed-heritage-design-guide.pdf?la=en&hash=6433F53174451AF9D6483B8D69 36D9C10B31FC45.

6.  Rayman Mohamed, Robin Boyle, Allan Yilun Yang and Joseph Tangari, "Adaptive Reuse: A Review and Analysis of Its Relationship to the 3 Es of Sustainability," *Facilities* 35, nos. 3–4 (2017): 138–54.

7.  Urban Hub, "Sustainability: Urban Landmarks Find a New Purpose with Adaptive Reuse Architecture," *Urban Hub*, October 10, 2018, http://www.urban-hub.com/sustainability/urban-landmarks-find-a-new-purpose-with-adaptive-reuse-architecture/.

the re-use of a heritage site can play an important role in bringing it back into public favor, negotiating multiple agendas, and providing amenity for neighbors and visitors as well as the owners."[8]

However, as revealed through the various essays in this book and the experience of these different Asian centers, it takes time to build momentum and faith in the adaptive reuse process. A common thread for these three cities is the interconnection between government-led and privately led projects. Although each jurisdiction has its own timing and sequencing, there is an interesting interplay between government-led projects influencing private projects and vice versa. In Hong Kong, the boom in adaptive reuse projects has largely been encouraged by the government, in particular through its Revitalising Historic Buildings through Partnership Scheme.[9] After more than a decade of government-owned buildings being revitalized, more and more private developers are embarking on such initiatives as well. Meanwhile, in Shanghai, it was a series of privately owned projects that encouraged the government and other private developers to pursue such conservation projects. Lastly, in Singapore, there was a parallel path of the government exploring adaptive reuse, particularly in relation to area conservation, while smaller-scale private projects were also embarked upon. As also mentioned throughout this book (the individual city essays and the broader Heritage Awards chapter as well), the increasing recognition and appreciation of adaptive reuse projects in the region has also further galvanized additional revitalization projects, a trend that will hopefully continue.

As illustrated in the essays and the case studies of this book, the results of these adaptive reuse projects are varied and complex, with a range of benefits for a range of stakeholders. There are economic, environmental, and social impacts, often both positive and negative, on the surrounding community. As addressed above, to have adaptive reuse as a viable and successful conservation approach for a city or nation, there is a need for government buy-in paired with community interest and grassroots initiatives. It seems that for this to be a sustainable and sustained conservation approach, these two factors are needed. It is also important to remember that in comparing these various projects from various jurisdictions, every project is different. There is no formula of "one size fits all" when it comes to adaptive reuse, as each individual building given a new lease of life is its own unique place, with its own unique history and its own unique story to tell. However, in examining these projects, and comparing and contrasting the experience of these different jurisdictions, it can help to inform, guide, and inspire subsequent projects, encouraging innovation and continued renewal throughout the region.

## Areas for Further Research

The intent of this publication is to highlight some of the challenges and triumphs of adaptive reuse. As is the case with any publication, there are always additional areas to explore. As outlined in the Introduction's literature review, although scholars have examined adaptive reuse generally and specifically for certain parts of the globe, there is a need for additional research, particularly in the Asian context. Adaptive reuse projects are increasing in most Asian cities and nations; however, there has not been as much scholarly study or documentation of these initiatives. It would be of particular interest to carry out more in-depth studies on the longer-term results of adaptive reuse projects, looking at the specific metrics outlined in the third essay of this book.

8.   Heritage Council, "Better Placed," 36.
9.   Please note the British spelling of "Revitalisation" is intentional, as this is its proper name as used by the Hong Kong SAR government.

As more projects are completed and with multiple years of operation, there is greater insight to be garnered and analysis to be done. Beyond this more detailed analysis, other areas of additional possible research include examination of other jurisdictions in Asia. Rapidly developing regions, such as Myanmar and other places in China, would be worthwhile areas of possible further study. It is hoped that this publication, and perhaps others like it, can help to inform and encourage others to embark on adaptive reuse projects, hopefully learning from some of the challenges and pitfalls others have encountered.

## Concluding Remarks: The Future of Adaptive Reuse in Asia

Although there are growing numbers of completed adaptive reuse projects in Asia, generally, and in Hong Kong, Shanghai, and Singapore, specifically, there are many more opportunities for additional projects and innovative approaches to revitalization in the future. As mentioned above, a major benefit at this juncture is that there are more completed projects with statistics three, five, and in some cases, more than ten years postcompletion, which can help to show and support the benefits and opportunities that adaptive reuse projects can hold. As mentioned throughout this book, it is in the best interest of communities around the globe to explore and encourage adaptive reuse as part of their sustainable development. For, as eloquently outlined in the Australian *Design Guide for Heritage*, "Heritage places create the setting for contemporary life connecting communities to the past, and helping to shape futures."[10]

## Bibliography

Farooq, Umar. "Voices Grow Louder in Turkey to Convert Hagia Sophia from a Museum Back to Mosque." *Los Angeles Times*, June 24, 2017. https://www.latimes.com/world/middleeast/la-fg-turkey-hagia-sophia-20170615-story.html.

Heritage Council of NSW. "Better Placed: Design Guide for Heritage." Working draft for comment published 2018. https://www.environment.nsw.gov.au/-/media/OEH/Corporate-Site/Documents/Heritage/better-placed-heritage-design-guide.pdf?la=en&hash=6433F53174451AF9D6483B8D6936D9C10B31FC45.

Lu, Tracey L.-D. "Heritage Conservation in Post-colonial Hong Kong." *International Journal of Heritage Studies* 15, nos. 2–3 (March–May 2009). 258–72.

Mohamed, Rayman, Robin Boyle, Allan Yilun Yang, and Joseph Tangari. "Adaptive Reuse: A Review and Analysis of Its Relationship to the 3 Es of Sustainability." *Facilities* 35, nos. 3–4 (2017). 138–54.

Richards, Candace. "Reinventing Heritage Buildings Isn't New at All—the Ancients Did It Too." *Conversation*, January 2, 2017. https://theconversation.com/reinventing-heritage-buildings-isnt-new-at-all-the-ancients-did-it-too-70053.

United Nations Habitat. *New Urban Agenda*. A/RES/71/256. October, 2016. http://habitat3.org/the-new-urban-agenda/.

Urban Hub. "Sustainability: Urban Landmarks Find a New Purpose with Adaptive Reuse Architecture." *Urban Hub*. October 10, 2018. http://www.urban-hub.com/sustainability/urban-landmarks-find-a-new-purpose-with-adaptive-reuse-architecture/.

Yeoh, Brenda. "Singapore's Chinatown: Nation Building and Heritage Tourism in a Multiracial City." *Localities* 2 (2012). 117–59.

Yung, Esther H. K., Edwin H. W. Chan, and Ying Xu. "Community-Initiated Adaptive Reuse of Historic Buildings and Sustainable Development in the Inner City of Shanghai." *Journal of Urban Planning and Development* 140, no. 3 (September 2014). 117–59.

---

10.  Heritage Council, "Better Placed," 24.

# Index